The Intelligent School

Second edition

Barbara MacGilchrist, Kate Myers
and Jane Reed

SAGE Publications
Los Angeles • London • New Delhi • Singapore

ISBN 987-0-7619-4774-5
ISBN 987-1-7619-4775-2 (pbk)

First published 1997 by Paul Chapman Publishing Ltd
Second edition 2004
Reprinted 2004, 2006, 2008

SAGE Publications Ltd
1 Oliver's Yard
55 City Road
London EC1Y 1SP

SAGE Publications Inc
2455 Teller Road
Thousand Oaks
California 91320

SAGE Publications India Pvt Ltd
B–42 Panchsheel Enclave
PO Box 4109
New Delhi 110 017

SAGE Publications Asia-Pacific Pte Ltd
33 Pekin Street #02-01
Far East Square
Singapore 048763

British Library Cataloguing in Publication data
A catalogue record for this book is available from the British Library

Library of Congress Control Number: 2003112196

Typeset by Dorwyn Ltd., Rowlands Castle, Hampshire
Printed and bound in Great Britain by
Cromwell Press Limited, Trowbridge, Wiltshire

*Dedicated to our teachers' teachers and
our friend and colleague James Learmonth (1939–2003)*

Contents

Contents

Foreword

When the first edition of *The Intelligent School* was published in 1997, I was asked to provide a brief foreword. In this, I expressed a view that the book was particularly relevant in that year. I welcomed the way the authors had drawn together key findings from four related areas of research (school effectiveness, school improvement, learning and teaching). I hoped that this synthesis would prove useful for the many class teachers who were expected to achieve improvements in the performance of their pupils. I also noted that MacGilchrist, Myers and Reed – researchers with solid backgrounds in senior positions in schools and local education authorities – were asserting that teachers, by learning from the good practice identified in the synthesis, would be likely to become active promoters of change.

The notion that heads and teachers can be active promoters of change may surprise some. As I commented at the time, we have grown too accustomed to seeing them oppressed by external changes, subject to unfair criticism and learning to rely on outside experts or on the Office for Standards in Education (OFSTED) for evaluation. MacGilchrist, Myers and Reed show that there is an alternative and that it is much healthier for everyone: pupils, parents and teachers, as well as society in general.

Traditionally, books based on research findings have not proved very popular with teachers. People forget, however, that the teaching profession is relatively new. In the nineteenth century the first entrants to it were either untrained graduates working in public (private) schools or pupil monitors regurgitating the lessons they had recently learned in their elementary schools. Only in recent years have the entry qualifications approached those commonly accepted in other professions. Not surprisingly, therefore, the tradition – so strong in fields such as medicine or law – of keeping up with research reports is undeveloped among teachers. Thankfully, this negative attitude is declining as the number of teachers enrolling in universities for part-time higher degrees and contributing to the literature of good practice illustrates.

In the first edition of *The Intelligent School* the authors suggested that the synthesis they had produced was 'much more than the sum of its parts'. They identified nine intelligences that a school needed to develop. Underpinning their view was the notion that schools are organic and dynamic institutions and that those working in them must develop the power and responsibility to take charge of their own destiny. In 1997 this was fighting talk. Such talk represented a new spirit emerging from the profession. After years of being cowed, it was standing up and fighting for what it believed was important.

This first edition of *The Intelligent School* encouraged teachers and all those associated with learning in schools to look to research for ideas and inspiration. The success of the book demonstrates that many practitioners agreed. This second edition pushes the stakes still higher. In doing so, the authors have continued to write clearly and directly. They have again found good ways to relate academic findings to practical experience.

I congratulate MacGilchrist, Myers and Reed on the success of the first edition. I applaud the inclusion of new material in the second. The addition of two new intelligences to do with operational and systemic intelligence and the use of the nine intelligences to offer a new framework for school improvement extends and develops their argument. The restructuring of the chapters improves the overall coherence of the book. The inclusion of pupils' ideas and comments enrich the practical examples threaded throughout the book.

In 1997, many in the profession believed that the days of diktat were drawing to an end. What a shock to discover that this was not the case. As someone who has retired, and is no longer involved in the education system, I want to recommend – even more vehemently than when I was working – the close study of this book and I do not mean just by teachers and local education authority officers. Education policy-makers and ministers, especially, might learn a great deal from it.

Peter Mortimore
Richmond
September 2003

Acknowledgements

This book is dedicated to the teachers and pupils with whom we have had the privilege of working. It is the lessons they have taught us that have inspired us to write. Thanks go especially to all those who provided us with practical examples of their work, some of which we have incorporated into the book. Thanks go to the children whose thoughts and ideas we have included. We are also indebted to the many researchers on whose work we have drawn and to Tim Brighouse, Brian Caldwell, Tony Purcell and Lesley Saunders who found the time to read and comment on early drafts, and to Peter Mortimore for writing the foreword to the book. Special thanks and gratitude go to Nikki Carter and in particular Jackie Lee for their commitment, enthusiasm and support in ensuring that the book came to fruition.

Barbara MacGilchrist
Kate Myers
Jane Reed
2004

In times of change, learners inherit the earth, while the learned find themselves beautifully equipped to deal with a world that no longer exists. (Hoffer)

Continuous learning – for everyone – is central to the notion of the *intelligent school*.

Introduction

- The purpose of the book
- The structure of the book
- How the book can be used

The purpose of the book

This book has been written for those who have the major responsibility for making schools work, namely classroom teachers and members of staff who have leadership and management responsibilities at whatever level and in whatever type of school. It is a book that may also be of interest to policy-makers and to those who work in a support role with schools. Our purpose in writing *The Intelligent School* is to offer a practical resource to schools to enable them to maximize their improvement efforts. Our aim is to help schools to be *intelligent* organizations; in other words, the type of school that can synthesize different kinds of knowledge, experience and ideas in order to be confident about current achievements and to have the ability to decide what to do next.

Three of us have written the book together. Between us we have more than 100 years' experience of working in and with primary, secondary and special schools, local education authorities and academic institutions. The book grew out of a number of concerns that we found we shared:

- the need to recognize that there is no blueprint for improving schools, rather schools can be enabled to make intelligent, informed decisions about what is likely to work best for them;
- the need to focus school improvement efforts on the classroom;
- the need to make research findings more accessible and usable for teachers;
- the need to support practitioners in making better shared sense of what they are implicitly doing;
- the need to celebrate and disseminate some of the good practice already going on in schools across the country;
- the need to make a language of learning and teaching our own.

We have tried to distil and share some of the knowledge, experience and ideas we have gained from working with both academics and practitioners. We want to enable schools to become more familiar with relevant research and to ask the sorts of questions we often ask ourselves: 'What do these findings mean for us, particularly on a wet Friday afternoon. In what ways can we use them to help us to become more effective?' Our review of the research literature is by no means exhaustive. We have chosen research findings that we think are interesting and of considerable importance for practitioners. We have used practical examples provided by schools, local education authorities and education consultants to illustrate some of the different ways in which schools, often intuitively, have put some of the research theory into practice.

The three of us share a further concern. 'School improvement' has become the 'flavour of the month'. Unfortunately, the media interpretation of this trend, often encouraged by political pronouncements, has been that many state schools are failing and that drastic measures are needed to 'pull them up by their bootstraps'. This scenario does not match with our experience. We are agreed that, regrettably, there definitely are some schools that for a variety of reasons are seriously failing their pupils, and that in such cases drastic measures are needed. However, as far as the majority of schools are concerned, our experience is that headteachers and their staff are endeavouring to seek ways of continuously improving their effectiveness. As Hopkins, Ainscow and West (1994) have put it: 'You don't have to be ill to get better.'

Our experience also tells us that whilst some schools, because of their particular circumstances, are successful at improving themselves with limited external support, many schools are seeking help with their improvement efforts. Such an attitude has pluses and minuses. On the plus side, for example, it means that these schools are receptive to change and want to improve, both of which are important prerequisites for moving forward. On the negative side, however, this can encourage a dependency culture whereby schools seek blueprints or formulae that they can apply in a mechanistic way regardless of their own particular context and culture. This, in turn, encourages external consultants and agencies to offer simplistic solutions to what are often very complex issues.

Through our work as Associate Directors of the Institute of Education's International School Effectiveness and Improvement Centre, and through Kate's work with the Leadership *for* Learning Network at the University of Cambridge, we are also only too well aware of the academic debates about the relationship between school effectiveness and school improvement research, and about the dangers of simplistic interpretations of complex research findings. We share these concerns. We also consider that the findings of these two areas of research are not enough in themselves. We believe that *learning and teaching* are at the heart of school improvement. They are the core business of schools. Therefore, knowledge about the findings of research into both effective learning and effective teaching is also essential. We feel that for a school to work successfully it needs to be able to *put the pieces together* from these four areas of research in an *intelligent* way so as to see the connections between them and then to consider, in relation to its own context, the practical implications for the classroom and for the school as a whole.

This book attempts to address these shared concerns. It aims to inform practitioners of some of the key messages from these four interrelated areas of research and to illustrate, through the use of real examples, a variety of ways in which these findings can be pieced together in a practical way to improve learning and teaching. It also includes real examples of children and teachers at work because we believe that a major way of improving schools is to enable them to share and learn from one another's practice.

We take a fresh look at schools as organizations and, building on our collective experience, we argue that 'putting the pieces together' of school effectiveness and school improvement with learning and teaching is not as simple as it sounds, nor as some people would have us believe. It is certainly not a mechanistic or linear activity. All important is the capacity a school has to use this knowledge. We draw on Gardner's (1983; 1999) notion of multiple intelligence and on recent thinking about the nature of organizations to offer a new way of looking at schools and their capacity to improve. We identify nine intelligences that when used in combination enable a school to have the capacity to achieve its goals successfully. We argue that: *'the intelligent school is greater than the sum of its parts'*. Through the use of its 'corporate intelligence' it is in a powerful position to improve its effectiveness. We offer a new framework for school improvement that combines the intelligences in a systemic way.

The structure of the book

In Chapter 1 we consider the *intelligent school* in times of change to provide a context for the book. In Chapters 2 and 3 we identify some of the important findings being disseminated from the school effectiveness and the school improvement literature. We emphasize the strengths and the limitations of these findings and argue that they must not be seen as an end in themselves or as sufficient to make schools work effectively. In Chapter 4 we reflect on the nature of learning. We begin with a consideration of some of the different theories about how we learn and about the purpose of learning. We then reflect on what it means to be a learner, the different ways in which learning can take place and on what learners themselves expect from those who teach and work with them. In Chapter 5 we turn our attention to sources of evidence concerned with the characteristics of effective teaching and consider the nature of teaching in relationship with learning. We examine the features of teaching for learning and how teachers manage the process of teaching for learning. We conclude with an exploration of the notion of a learning and teaching PACT to maximize children's learning in the classroom.

The focus of Chapter 6 is the professional development of teachers, in other words, teachers' own learning. We concentrate on some of the practical ways in which schools provide teachers with opportunities to learn with and from one another 'on the job' and from best practice elsewhere. We argue that teachers' learning and pupils' learning are inextricably linked.

Chapter 7 concerns the school as a whole. The focus is on the title of the book – *The Intelligent School*. We draw together the themes developed in the previous chapters and translate these into nine different but interdependent intelligences. We describe the characteristics of these intelligences and argue that, when they are used in combination, they enable a school to apply the knowledge and skills it has to maximum effect in classrooms and across the school as a whole. We use the intelligences to offer a new framework for improvement that enables a school to have the capacity to improve. We reflect on the implications of this *corporate intelligence* for school leaders.

The final chapter is a postscript in which we consider the notion of *intelligent schooling* of the future. We raise questions that we believe need to be asked about schooling and suggest possible alternatives for the future.

How the book can be used

Our intention is that *The Intelligent School* can be used by individual teachers, groups of teachers and whole-school staffs. The first chapter provides the context for the book. In the chapters that follow, each ends with some questions for consideration to offer an agenda for discussion and reflection. The questions can be used by individual or groups of teachers or as a catalyst for school-based professional development sessions. The chapter on the nine intelligences provides a framework for the staff as a group to examine their capacity for improvement. We have tried to formulate ideas and questions in such a way as to offer both a challenge and a support to schools in their efforts to make a real difference in terms of the quality of education they provide for their pupils.

1

The *intelligent school* in times of change – setting the scene

- Political change – the educational reform agenda in England and Wales
- The information and communication technologies revolution
- Socio-economic changes and inequalities

We have entered a new millennium with sophisticated science and spectacular technology but still without the knowledge of how to educate *all* our children. (MacBeath and Mortimore, 2001, p. 1)

At the beginning of the twenty-first century 'school' still remains the 'place' where the vast majority of our young people are formally educated. Although, even at this point in time, access to school cannot be taken for granted. This was evidenced by the plight of girls in Afghanistan at the turn of the century and remains the reality for several million young people in Africa for whom there is still no formal schooling. Time therefore in school is precious and for pupils it cannot be repeated. Yet, as the quote from MacBeath and Mortimore reminds us, all is not well. They are making the point that in the context of an agenda that promotes education for all, the learning needs of all children are still not being met. This concern was highlighted in a report by Her Majesty's Chief Inspector (OFSTED, 2002, p. 20) in which he stated that: 'Inclusion will be truly successful only if we recognise the achievements and progress of all pupils'.

Schools serve the needs of the present and the future. They have a crucial role to play in the lives and learning of their pupils now and as they inherit the daunting and exciting tasks that face them as citizens in the twenty-first century. Schools also have a responsibility for their future students. Roland Barth (1988) summed this up when he described schools as 'four walls surrounding the future'.

The key lesson from research about effective schools is that schools can make a difference for the better (Edmonds, 1979; Rutter et al., 1979; Mortimore et al., 1988) or even for the worse (Myers, 1995). This is a very powerful message, probably the most powerful that has come from this area of literature. It both empowers and challenges practitioners, bestowing the

1

possibility of making a difference to the life chances of children alongside giving them responsibility for doing so. It heightens the imperative to ensure that our education system meets the needs of *all* pupils.

In the school effectiveness and school improvement (SESI) literature there has been general acceptance that an effective school can be described as: 'one in which pupils progress further than might be expected from consideration of its intake' (Mortimore, 1991, p. 9), and one which 'adds extra value to its students' outcomes in comparison with schools serving similar intakes' (Sammons, Hillman and Mortimore, 1995, p. 3). However, the assumptions about the purpose of education underlying these definitions of effectiveness are rarely challenged and explored. Schools serving very similar intakes can give their pupils very different experiences and achieve different outcomes for their pupils, and there is growing evidence that this is the case (Gray et al, 1999; MacBeath and Mortimore, 2001). But we would argue that there is now an urgent need to reconsider these definitions of effectiveness in the context of reconsidering what it means to be an educated person. Significant changes have taken and are taking place in the UK and on a global scale that have a direct bearing on the future of education. These changes raise serious questions about the appropriateness of the ways in which schools and schooling are currently conceived, organized and judged.

In particular, there are three significant changes to which we want to draw attention:

- unprecedented large-scale educational reform being undertaken in the UK and in many other parts of the world;
- the revolution occurring in information and communication technologies (ICT);
- fundamental social and economic global changes.

In the sections that follow, we take a look at some of these significant changes because they provide a crucial context for considering the whole concept of the *intelligent school* now and in the future.

Political change – the educational reform agenda in England and Wales

New Labour came to power in 1997 after 18 years of Conservative rule. 'Education, education, education' was placed at the top of the agenda. They embarked on what they called a 'crusade' to modernize schools and the profession as a whole. It soon became clear that central control over education was to be significantly increased. A succession of Green and White Papers, along with the creation of a Standards and Effectiveness Unit within the Department for Education and Employment, heralded the changes to come. An unprecedented system-wide education reform agenda was initiated. There was a sense of urgency to demonstrate that schools must be and can be made more effective and held publicly accountable for what they do. The message to schools and to local education authorities (LEAs) was one of 'zero tolerance of failure'. The culture of 'naming and shaming' underperforming schools and LEAs, begun by the previous government, became the order of the day along with getting tough on teachers.

Despite warnings from school effectiveness researchers and from those critical of school effectiveness research, New Labour cherry-picked some of the findings of school effectiveness research and interpreted the basic message that 'schools can make a difference' in a simplistic way. Similarly, warnings from the school improvement literature that 'change takes time', is 'complex' and that a 'one-size-fits-all model' is inappropriate were ignored.

Improving the quality of school leadership and the teaching of the basic skills of literacy and numeracy in primary schools were seen as key levers to combating underachievement and putting the performance of English schools on a par with their international counterparts. Of particular significance was the rapid introduction of the National Literacy and Numeracy Strategies. The content of literacy and numeracy lessons throughout the primary years and how that content was to be taught were prescribed. For the first time, ambitious literacy and numeracy targets were set for pupils leaving primary schools and the then Secretary of State put his own job on the line by promising to resign if these targets were not met.

The assessment of pupil performance through a significantly enhanced testing regime, particularly in the early years and throughout the primary years of schooling, was put in place. Schools became much more publicly accountable for the performance of their pupils and this accountability was ensured through the publication of inspection reports on individual schools by OFSTED. At the same time, the publication of LEA inspection reports heightened their accountability too.

These changes were accompanied by a range of initiatives to target, in particular, inner-city underachievement and encourage the private sector, especially the business community, to become much more heavily involved in education. The initiatives included Education Action Zones, Excellence in Cities programmes, summer schools and encouraging the establishment of an increasingly diverse range of schools, for example, specialist schools, City Academies and faith schools. Between 1997 and 2001, £120 million of business sponsorship had been made available for the government's education agenda. The involvement of the private sector has resulted in some schools and some LEAs being run entirely by private companies.

The government also looked to the private sector to conduct educational research. For example, HayMcBer secured an unprecedented grant to develop a new Leadership Programme for Serving Headteachers and to conduct research into the characteristics of teacher effectiveness. The latter research was used as the basis for the introduction of a national performance-related pay scheme for practising teachers in 2000.

These substantial changes in the education system in England were achieved in a very short space of time. They were accompanied by a change in morale within the profession. The euphoria within the education world at the removal of the long-ruling Conservative Party with memories of the introduction of the National Curriculum and the related Standard Assessment Tasks (SATs) was short-lived. Many teachers and LEA personnel were taken by surprise at New Labour's determination to crack down on low standards and weed out underperforming schools and teachers by diktat rather than consultation. For example, the Literacy and Numeracy strategies and the accompanying compulsory in-service training was an unprecedented challenge to primary practice. Whilst some schools welcomed the initiative, others felt undervalued and that their professionalism was being undermined.

A related increase in bureaucracy took its toll particularly in relation to target-setting and inspection. The naming and shaming of schools continued to attract relentless press coverage, which was fuelled by the high profile of Her Majesty's Chief Inspector at the time. The government's continuous focus on poor schools and poor teachers overshadowed their efforts to recognize and celebrate good practice. The use of slick phrases such as the need to eradicate 'bog-standard comprehensive education' used by Alastair Campbell, the Prime Minister's Director of Communications and Strategy in 2001, were seen within the profession as yet further attacks on teachers trying to do their best in often very challenging circumstances, particularly for those working in schools serving very disadvantaged communities. There was concern that policy-makers and practitioners appeared to be growing further and further apart. MacBeath and Mortimore (2001) reminded us that: 'Politicians and policy makers have a specific interest in the here and now and are constrained to work within the boundaries of what their constituents expect of an educational system' (ibid., p. 1).

While all of this was happening, many would argue that a not unrelated change was gathering momentum. By the turn of the century, teacher shortage in England was a serious issue although at first it was concealed by the use of supply and temporary teachers increasingly recruited from overseas. There was a plethora of government initiatives to stem a haemorrhaging of teachers from the profession and to encourage new recruits. Training salaries were introduced, as were financial incentives to encourage teachers of shortage secondary subjects, such as science and mathematics, to enter and stay in teaching. Quick routes into teaching along with fast-track promotion were also opened up. At the time of writing recruitment has improved but retaining high-quality teachers remains an urgent challenge.

Reflecting on large-scale educational reform, Elmore (2000, p. 4) argues that:

Standards-based reform has a deceptively simple logic: schools and school systems should be held accountable for their contributions to student learning.
Society should communicate its expectations for what students should know and
be able to do in the form of standards, both for what should be taught and for
what students should be able to demonstrate about their learning. School administrators and policy makers, at the state, district and school level, should regularly evaluate whether teachers are teaching what they are expected to teach and
whether students can demonstrate what they are expected to learn. The fundamental unit of accountability should be the school, because that is the organisational unit where teaching and learning actually occurs. Evidence from
evaluations of teaching and student performance should be used to improve
teaching and learning and, ultimately to allocate rewards and sanctions.

He describes how this logical approach to reform has become a fundamental
part of American education. He argues that this type of reform is essential to
counteract the 'loose-coupling' model of school that has been endemic in the
school system in the UK and in the USA. By loose-coupling he means the
autonomy that class teachers have traditionally had to decide what and how
to teach. He suggests that this autonomy has been directly or indirectly supported by headteachers who have acted as a buffer to protect teachers from
external control. He describes how 'standards-based' reform is often greeted
with dismay and disbelief by experienced educators, who are battle-worn vet-
erans of past educational reform campaigns.

Elmore reminds us that: 'The logic of standards-based reform is fundamentally at odds with the logic of loose-coupling' (ibid., p. 8). He identifies three
reasons for this. The former reform touches directly on teachers in classrooms
by determining the content of what is to be taught and how it is to be taught
and by setting performance standards. It introduces a cause-and-effect relationship between teaching and pupil outcomes. As a result it explicitly localizes
accountability for student learning. In other words, it places responsibility firmly
at the door of schools and those who work in them. In principle, this is perfectly
reasonable. In practice, however, the complex issues underlying this principle
are rarely taken into account as we discuss in detail in Chapters 2 and 3.

Elmore goes on to comment that:

It carries the increasingly explicit message that students learn largely as a consequence of what goes on inside schools. Hence, schools are being asked to account
for what students are actually taught and what they learn as a consequence of that
teaching. And whatever one may think about this theory – that students generally
learn what they are taught, if they are taught with skill and understanding – it has
a strong political, economic and social appeal. (Ibid., p. 9)

As Myers and Goldstein (1998) have argued, it neatly shifts the blame for failure from central and local government to the individual school. Also, what

'standards-based' reform tends to ignore is the complexity of schools and schooling and the complex relationship between learning and teaching. It looks for quick fixes and creates a culture of blame in which teachers and schools are held responsible for a narrow set of prescribed pupil outcomes. It focuses on performance rather than the development of pupils as learners. It sets teacher autonomy on a collision course with reform that is externally initiated and controlled, and creates the impression that the latter is superior and more effective than the former. It is perceived as ignoring the professionalism of teachers and assuming that teachers will 'de facto' take ownership of someone else's change agenda. Bringing about change brings with it tensions and possible contradictions. These need to be addressed to ensure that those responsible for learning and teaching at the 'chalk face' can exercise their professional judgement, albeit in the context of a local or national education policy framework.

Caldwell and Spinks (1998) have identified three different stages, or tracks, as they call them, in educational reform.

- *Track 1*: Building systems of Self-Managing Schools
- *Track 2*: Unrelenting Focus on Learning Outcomes
- *Track 3*: Creating Schools for the Knowledge Society

Track 1 involves putting in place a dual strategy for reform. The first concerns establishing a centrally controlled curriculum, a common system of assessment and a means of holding schools accountable for student outcomes. The second involves devolving responsibility to schools particularly in respect of the local management of resources. In England and Wales this was the strategy adopted by the Conservative government through the Education Reform Act in 1988. This put in place a National Curriculum and a national testing system to assess standards at ages 7, 11, 14, 16 and 18. The Act also introduced Local Management of Schools (LMS) whereby schools found themselves for the first time responsible for the management and use of a range of resources including staffing, staff development and premises. A few years later in 1993 a framework for the national inspection of schools was introduced by transforming Her Majesty's Inspectorate into the Office for Standards in Education (OFSTED).

Underlying LMS was a different kind of loose-coupling from that described by Elmore. MacBeath and Mortimore (2001, p. 23) describe the premise upon which this aspect of the reform was based:

The vision is of a loosely coupled, or entirely uncoupled, system of self-managing schools, founded on three essential premises:

1) that governors and headteachers are better placed to determine priorities than their education authorities;

2)   that schools should be the unit of improvement and accountability;
3)   that good schools will survive and the best schools will thrive in a market opened to parental choice.

Caldwell and Spinks's second track concerns improving teaching and an unrelenting commitment to improving the learning outcomes of all students. It includes advances in technology to support learning. New Labour adopted this strategy through its emphasis on the high stakes literacy and numeracy targets for all schools and all pupils, by encouraging an annual testing regime for pupils aged 5 and onwards and by the publication of league tables. Embedded within their reform policy was the establishment of a performance culture throughout the system controlled from the centre. At the same time, New Labour pursued the use of market forces to encourage competition and the rapid expansion of new types of schools, in particular, specialist schools which were planned to represent 50 per cent of all secondary schools by the year 2003.

Track 3 looks to the future. It offers a 'gestalt' for schooling in the third millennium. 'A perceived organised whole that is more than the sum of the parts ... . It is schooling for the knowledge society, because those who manage information to solve problems, provide service or create new products form the largest group in the workforce' (Caldwell and Spinks, 1998, p. 12). Caldwell and Spinks, argue that this approach to education renders the current fabric of schooling obsolete and requires a transformation of schools as we know them. We will return to this 'track' in the last chapter as it contributes to our concept of *intelligent schooling* in the future.

Track 3 relates to the rapid changes we describe later in this chapter that are taking place in information and communications technology. It concerns the need for schools to ensure that young people are able to access, interpret, critique, create and use new knowledge for themselves and others, and that they develop the capacity for lifelong learning. We will be arguing in the last chapter that *intelligent schooling* must accommodate these changes within the context of a reconsideration of what it means to be an educated person in the twenty-first century. We will be proposing a different education reform agenda with a view to ensuring that all young people have the capacity to meet the uncertainties and challenges to come, especially against the backdrop of the significant socio-economic changes that we identify in this chapter.

Proponents of New Labour's educational reform agenda would argue that it embodies at least the first two strategies outlined by Caldwell and Spinks and is moving towards the third. Evidence of the third strategy would be in the form of, for example, the establishment of the National Grid for Learning, rethinking the role and status of vocational training within the 14 to 19 curriculum and encouraging learning mentors from within the community. However, at the time of writing a mixed picture is beginning to emerge about the impact of New Labour's education policy.

The 2000 primary SATs results indicated that standards in literacy and numeracy in primary schools were continuing to improve. By 2002, however, the picture was less clear. The national targets were not achieved and performance outcomes had plateaued, something that practitioners and educational researchers had been predicting for some time. There can be no doubt, however, that something pretty drastic needed to be done to reduce and endeavour to remove the previous lottery for primary children in the teaching of English and mathematics. The huge variation, for example, in reading standards between schools, and in particular, between schools serving similar intakes, was a cause for serious concern. There are few people who would disagree that it is essential to ensure that all young people have the necessary literacy and numeracy skills that form part of the building blocks needed for lifelong learning, but this should not be at the expense of other essential building blocks.

By 2002 Her Majesty's Chief Inspector (OFSTED) was warning that the National Literacy and Numeracy Strategies were having a negative impact on the breadth and balance of the primary curriculum. They were leading to too much curriculum time being spent on the drive to raise attainment levels in English and mathematics. The report pointed out that in the majority of schools: 'it is aspects of subjects that bring them (English and mathematics) to life – enquiry, problem-solving and practical work – that have suffered most. This represents a serious narrowing of the curriculum' (OFSTED, 2002, p. 18). In their evaluation of the Strategies, Earl et al. (2003) also found evidence that using the achievement of Key Stage 2 level 4 or above as the measure of a school's success was having a negative effect on the primary curriculum. Subjects such as the arts were being squeezed out and there was evidence of teachers spending too much time teaching to the test.

The negative impact on the primary curriculum of the reform agenda has been confirmed by Pollard et al. (2000) in their Primary Assessment, Curriculum and Experience (PACE) project. The purpose of the project was to examine the impact of the focus on performance outcomes, particularly SATs, on primary pupils and their teachers. As a result of their study, they concluded that: 'It is doubtful that they (recent reforms) have overcome the seemingly endemic problem of pupil motivation and engagement in learning within schools' (Ibid., p. 290) and an overemphasis on the basics in modern education policy could

> unwittingly lead to a *reduction* in pupil motivation … a significant proportion of pupils seem to have become instrumentally concerned with 'playing the system', with superficial learning and trying to avoid boredom … . Whilst many children may 'perform' despite their lack of intrinsic engagement, our research suggests that we should be particularly concerned about the attitudes and lifelong learning skills of pupils. (Ibid., p. 297)

The growing concerns about the setting of unrealistic targets for primary schools and the impact that this has had on the curriculum led the government to rethink its strategy for primary education. A new strategy was launched in May 2003 (DfES, 2003). It included a welcome emphasis on the importance of a broad curriculum, the use of assessment for learning, raising the status of teacher assessment and enabling schools to set their own targets rather than having them imposed locally or centrally. This significant shift in government policy provides an opportunity for primary schools to take much more control of their improvement agenda.

The picture in secondary schools at the turn of the century portrayed a worrying scene. In 2001 more than a quarter (26 per cent) of all pupils finished compulsory schooling without a 'good' GCSE, i.e. less than grade C. Although this was a slight improvement on 1996/97 when it was 29 per cent, the gap between the best and worst GCSE results widened. Although the system is designed in a way that not all pupils are able to get a 'good' GCSE, the gap is a cause for concern. The number of students who left school with nothing to show for 11 years of full-time education rose for the first time since 1998; 5.5 per cent did not get a single G grade.

By 2002 less than 75 per cent of 17-year-olds in the UK were in education compared with approximately 95 per cent in Germany and Japan. The 2002 Government Green Paper (DfES, 2002) 14–19: *Extending Opportunities, Raising Standards*, aims to persuade all young people to stay in education or training until the age of 19 by introducing a wider variety of academic and vocational courses from age 14. Critics argue that this is no incentive for low achievers and there are concerns that the proposals could cut across the inclusive agenda. Addressing these concerns David Hargreaves (2002, p. 19) argued that: 'We must not botch the job. Performance measures that give adequate recognition to a wider range of vocational qualifications will be essential to successful change.'

Hargreaves (2001a) a year earlier, when he was head of the Qualifications and Curriculum Authority (QCA), joined the critics of the English education system who claim that children in our state schools are over-tested and as a result are being turned off education.

> Pupils are massively over-tested and over-examined … . Exams such as GCSEs have become ends in themselves rather than a device to meet specific educational purposes … . Something has gone wrong if the drive for more qualifications is beginning to overwhelm the purpose of supporting the progression of the individual's learning. (Ibid., p. 14)

Richard Garner in an article in the *Independent* in January 2002 reminded us that:

9

We are currently producing the most tested and examined generation of children ever to leave UK schools ... . The pressure on all schools – both primary and secondary – to outperform their neighbours in national performance tables is compelling too many teachers to make damned sure they do teach to the test! (Ibid., p. 4)

He warned that we are in danger of young people suffering 'burn-out or qualification fatigue' before they even start university.

Perhaps it is not surprising that an increasing number of school children in England are 'voting with their feet' and not attending school. In his Annual Report (OFSTED, 2002), Her Majesty's Chief Inspector reported that attendance is unsatisfactory or poor in nearly a quarter of schools with 10,000 pupils (mostly aged between 14 and 16) completely missing from the state school system, and that the problem could be getting worse. He warned that the gap between the best and the worst schools is widening, that there was significant underachievement in seven schools in every 100, and that the gap between the attainment of boys and girls was still wide.

Writers such as Bentley (1998) and Senge (2000a) argue that much more fundamental changes are needed in the education system, and the vision underpinning it, if we are going to enable young people to develop into confident, self-fulfilled lifelong learners capable of contributing to the development of society in the future. We argue in the next three chapters, that the concentration on the performance of both pupils and schools is likely to have a detrimental effect on the quality of pupils' learning and their learning outcomes. Other writers share our concern.

In commenting on the Literacy and Numeracy Strategies, Davies (2001, p. 4) is of the view that:

Whether the 'shallow' learning which is replicated by tests is accompanied by 'deep' learning and understanding remains to be seen. However, there is little doubt that a 'floor' has been put under standards. How the changes develop is critical. Will schools be given the freedom to explore the 'ceiling' of achievement or will they keep responding to increased targets (the floor) in the basic skills to the neglect of broader educational outcomes and achievement? The direction of this change will be a crucial decision for a second 'New Labour' administration: can it provide a framework for schools or will it be seduced by over-prescription to control the system?

Watkins (2002, p. 11) warns that: 'Pupil performance, teacher performance and school performance are unquestioned expressions today ... . Measures which are only partial indicators of performance become adopted as goals in themselves; getting good GCSEs becomes conflated with getting a "good education".' He reminds us that:

Factory schools (at the onset of the 21st Century) focusing on compliance out-comes do not sit well alongside knowledge-generating companies dealing with unknowns … . It is becoming clearer that those schools which do best on all measures currently are those which are fiercely independent and prepared to work against the grain of the present (performance) culture. (Ibid., p. 12)

He goes on to argue that policy-makers need: 'To develop and broadcast a dis-course which *values learning*, and is prepared to do this independently of the sort of performance outcomes with which we are currently saddled, which are reflections of a 20th Century machine view of schools' (ibid.). Watkins argues for the need to build strong communities of learners. Such views resonate with those of Senge (2000a, p. 51) who argues that: 'By continuing to prop up the industrial-age concept of schools through teacher-centred instruction, learn-ing as memorizing, and extrinsic control, we are preparing students for a world that is ceasing to exist.'

Claxton (2000b) asks the question: what would schools be like if they were truly dedicated to helping all young people become confident, competent, life-long learners? He reminds us that: 'you can be good at school without learn-ing to be good at life – and vice versa' (ibid., p. 7). He is of the view that schools can raise exam results without raising their students' 'learnacy'. He argues that core life skills are essential for all young people in the twenty-first century so that young people can learn 'to get smarter … and become better "real-life learners"' (ibid., p. 6).

We now examine these concerns about the development of lifelong learning skills and attitudes in the context of the revolution taking place in information and communication technologies.

The information and communication technologies revolution

The globalization and expansion of information availability and storage is almost beyond our comprehension. By 1996 the knowledge base was doubling every four years (Watkins et al., 1996). At the time of writing, seven years later, this is probably a modest figure given the significant technological changes that have taken place in the UK alone, since then. For example, the growth in edu-cational software packages has burgeoned and Internet access in schools for chil-dren of all ages is becoming the norm. This was confirmed in 2001, when the Department for Education and Skills released information about the number of computers in maintained schools in England. The findings were based on a rep-resentative sample of primary, secondary and special schools. Ninety-six per cent of primary schools reported that they were connected to the Internet com-pared with 17 per cent in 1998. Over 99 per cent of secondary schools were connected compared with 83 per cent in 1998 and 97 per cent of special schools were connected to the Internet compared with 31 per cent in 1998.

Access to home computers and ownership of mobile phones are also becoming increasingly the norm. In 2001 the largest Internet-based survey by the Office for National Statistics was conducted in Britain. It involved 53,000 7- to 16-year-olds in 360 schools. It showed that 85 per cent of secondary pupils and 78 per cent of primary pupils had access to a home computer. For those without such access, libraries, Internet cafés and other outlets are now becoming readily available in the high street, although there remains a concern that children from low-income homes who do not have easy access to computers will be further disadvantaged. The survey also revealed that nearly 60 per cent of secondary-aged pupils and one in six 7- to 11-year-olds owned their own mobile phone. In 2002 the first 'third-generation' mobile phones were introduced into the UK from Japan. In the same year, the telecommunications company Orange began to showcase Europe's first 'intelligent house', which, using third-generation telephony, is harnessing and 'humanizing' technology to provide everyday services in the home.

Back in 1996 Dalin and Rust argued that global revolutions in 'knowledge creation' would have a profound influence on pupils' lives. We have put 'knowledge creation' in inverted commas here because there are a number of writers who use the term when discussing the ICT revolution. We want to make the point that whilst knowledge is all powerful it is dependent not just on access to information, but on how individuals interpret and use that information to create new knowledge for themselves and others. Noss and Pachler (1999, p. 201) warn that 'access to information and its active cognitive processing are essential'. They argue that 'we need to address – as an urgent policy issue – what kinds of new *knowledge* is made accessible by technology, and how these fit with the needs of the citizen of the 21st century' (ibid., p. 195).

Kress (2001), has argued that the effects of information and communication technologies will have global significance for education, irrespective of who has access to them. Knowledge-as-information has become available 24 hours a day. This cuts right across the traditional time frames of schools. Knowledge-as-information is no longer vested in the authority of the teacher and is a challenge to the traditional school curriculum. It assumes usefulness for the individual depending on the particular task in hand. The gap between ' school knowledge' and 'out of school knowledge' has become wider, with many young people viewing the latter as potentially more relevant to their needs and aspirations. Kress argues that:

> It is reasonable to say that the school and those responsible in various ways for schooling have neither fully understood, acknowledged, or been able to deal with these transformations, let alone bring about changes in the school's purposes, forms and structures and relations which would begin to address them. The school increasingly operates in an environment in which the structures and

the frameworks which supported it have disappeared, have been dismantled, and no new frames have as yet become clear or accepted. (Ibid., p. 8)

Hill (2001) agrees with Kress that schooling is becoming increasingly out of step with changes in society. He states that the new knowledge society must lead to a reconceptualization of educational goals and the nature of public schooling. In a similar vein, Claxton (2000a, p. 5) argues that 'young people know that schools are not equipping them to face the complex demands and uncertainties of the future, or even of the present'. We will return to these issues in the final chapter when we explore the concept of *intelligent schooling*. In the meantime, the changes taking place in information communication technologies are closely interlinked with socio-economic changes, which in turn pose enormous challenges for the education system in the twenty-first century.

Socio-economic changes and inequalities

In 1994 Aronowitz and De Fazio cautioned that as knowledge becomes more widely accessible and more complex, the information gap between the 'haves' and the 'have nots' will widen. Similarly, Davies (2001) questions whether the impact of technologies on knowledge creation and learning will unite or divide society. Davies argues that 'it is knowledge that is the prime resource in the modern economy and society. Training for today's jobs will not be as important as educating young people with "thinking skills" and the ability to work together collaboratively to create the new assets of the modern society' (ibid., p. 3). Davies draws attention to the impact of global, interconnected markets on jobs. He reminds us that in the UK the need for traditional assembly-line semi-skilled and skilled jobs, particularly in the manufacturing sector, is declining as assembly work becomes relocated elsewhere in the world at a lower cost. He argues that it is critical that schools enable young people to develop skills particularly in relation to the expanding global sector of work linked more often than not with information and communication technologies. Only then will young people be able to take advantage of these new employment opportunities.

In 2000 the European Council launched an ambitious agenda to turn the European Union into the most competitive and dynamic knowledge-based economy in the world by 2010. In 2002 the European Commission claimed that progress in achieving this aim was being held back due to lack of appropriate skills. In an article in the *Financial Times*, Betts (2002, p. 8) warned that: 'Business now wants governments to increase the emphasis on teaching basic skills at all levels of education including developing a culture and attitude to promote life-long learning, innovation and entrepreneurship.'

Davies (2001) comments on the impact of a range of changes taking place in society. He describes how:

> The change in employment patterns, the breakdown of traditional family group-
> ings, the decline in religious practice and the growth of consumerism have all
> impacted on the social capital supporting the child ... The change affects many
> schools so that they now need to provide the social, as well as the intellectual,
> capital for children. (Ibid., p. 3)

Social capital is about what we gain via relationships and connections with
other people. The Office of National Statistics defines it as 'networks together
with shared norms, values and understandings that facilitate co-operation
within and among groups'. Hargreaves (2001b, p. 498) draws on the work of
Putnam (2000) and describes how his work 'documents the power of social
capital to make people "healthy, wealthy and wise" and demonstrates ... that
social capital has a powerful positive impact, second only to poverty, on education and children's welfare'. Putnam's argument is that high social capital
leads to better educational outcomes.

Bentley (1998) draws attention to the potential negative impact of the
knowledge economy in the context of the present education system. He
argues that:

> The growth of the knowledge economy has the potential to create social divi-
> sions just as deep as those in the 19th and 20th centuries ... many schools can
> do no more than contain and control their pupils, lacking the support, the wider
> resources and the vision to connect young people with any capacity for self-
> directed learning or any meaningful long-term opportunity. (Ibid., p. 181)

Bentley also comments on the growing number of young people who are on
the margins and who are not in formal education and training. He argues that
their life chances have been drastically reduced by the failure of public
services to motivate and educate them and the failure of their communities
to establish connections with anything that offers hope or meaningful
opportunity. Some of his concerns were confirmed, as we described earlier,
in the *Annual Report from Her Majesty's Chief Inspector* (OFSTED, 2002,
p. 19):

> We are becoming increasingly aware from data that there is a significant group
> of 'missing' pupils who should be in school, but are not, and about whom,
> almost by definition, we know very little. In total, these groups represent a sig-
> nificant number of pupils who are still being failed by the system. It is important
> to be aware of this when welcoming the improvements in the system at large and
> the marked success of some schools in meeting the needs of these groups of
> pupils.

Leadbeater (1999) joins those who are becoming increasingly concerned
about socio-economic inequalities. He argues that:

14

A trend towards inequality is deeply ingrained in modern society. Poorer people are less able than rich people to cope with the risks inherent in the global economy. To reverse this trend we need to invest in new institutions of social solidarity. That is the defensive case of social capital. There is a creative case as well. An ethic of collaboration is central to knowledge-creating societies. To create we must collaborate. (Ibid., p. 13)

MacBeath and Mortimore (2001) provide a stark reminder of the correlation between parental income and school achievement. This reminder is of crucial importance. It is given in the context of the fact that: 'Britain stands out, internationally, along with New Zealand, in having experienced the largest percentage increase in income inequality between 1967 and 1992 (Mortimore and Whitty, 1997, p, 2). Whilst the standard of living in Britain has continued to rise in the last few decades, MacBeath and Mortimore (2001) remind us that since 1979 the number of people living in poverty has increased threefold. The official definition of poverty is living on 60 per cent or less of median household income. In an analysis of poverty levels by the Joseph Rowntree Foundation in 2001 it was found that the New Labour government had had little or no effect by spring 2000 on reducing the level of poverty.

MacBeath and Mortimore reported that the proportion of children living in poor households at the turn of the century was 32 per cent compared to the Economic Union average of 20 per cent and the world average of 40 per cent (Bellamy, 2003). This means that in the UK one in three children were living in households below the poverty level at the beginning of the twenty-first century. The authors reminded us that:

While this does not preclude the possibility of a caring and supportive environment for children, it does significantly weight the odds and affect the balance of priorities in both home life and school life ... The scale of social transformation presents schools and teachers with a challenge on a scale never before encountered nor foreseen ... It is a poverty trap made not simply because people are materially poor but because the quality of opportunity offers no obvious avenues of escape. Even the most brilliant of schools cannot compensate for such a society. (MacBeath and Mortimore, 2001, pp. 3–5)

The desire to demonstrate that schools can make a difference, particularly for pupils from disadvantaged backgrounds, became the starting point of the school effectiveness and school improvement movement three decades ago.

A review by MacGilchrist (1992) of the research literature about the relationship between ethnicity, gender, socio-economic status and achievement revealed a complex relationship between these different factors. It concluded that of the three, social class appears to have the most significant effect. There was considerable research evidence that identified the challenge

15

schools faced of combating the persistent underachievement of children from working-class backgrounds at the beginning of the 1990s.

A decade later an Organization for Economic Co-operation and Development (OECD, 2002) international study of the test results of 265,000 15-year-olds in 2000, known as the Programme for International Student Assessment (PISA), found that whilst British pupils had noticeably improved their ranking in the world league tables for mathematics, reading and science results, there was a glaring gap between the performance of rich and poor pupils. Whilst the UK's performance overall was praised, the OECD warned that there was still a class divide in the education system. Only five of the 32 countries involved in the study had a wider gap between children from professional homes and those from deprived backgrounds. The study found that 13 per cent of UK youngsters either only reached, or failed to reach, the lowest band of attainment (boys 15 per cent, girls 10 per cent). Also, in Britain, children living with a single parent were found to be further behind those from two-parent homes than anywhere in the world other than the USA. This finding was linked to poverty among lone-parent families.

In 2001 the Secretary of State for Education in England and Wales acknowledged these concerns. She reported that only four out of seven pupils of manual workers achieved expected levels in SATs at age 11 compared with six out of seven for children whose parents were in the professional classes. Only 30 per cent of pupils from social groups D and E gained at least five good GCSE grades compared with 68 per cent of children from social groups A and B. The same trend continued at A level. Fifty-six per cent of middle-class teenagers got at least one A level compared with 13 per cent from working-class backgrounds. Similarly, only 13 per cent of working-class students gained a place at university compared with 73 per cent from middle-class families. The Secretary of State conceded that: 'We have not got over that link between social class and educational attainment.'

Reynolds and Teddlie (2001) conducted a review of initiatives to improve schools, in particular, schools that served disadvantaged areas. They concluded that: 'the most persistent finding of all post-war attempts at education reform is that social class inequality in educational qualifications has been largely unchanged by educational improvements on both quantity and quality dimensions' (ibid., p. 333). It is in the context of this finding and against the background of all the changes we have identified and their consequences, as well as criticisms of some of those changes, that we now turn to an examination of the school effectiveness literature and the lessons learnt so far.

2

Reflections on school effectiveness

- The school effect
- The concept of value-added
- Measuring what we value
- Defining achievement
- The characteristics of effective schools
- Criticisms of SESI research
- Questions for discussion

The school effect

School effectiveness research found its origins in the 1960s. It grew out of a concern for equality of educational opportunity and a desire to use schooling to combat social and racial divisions. It had a faltering start. The first two major school effectiveness studies in the USA by Coleman (1966) and Jencks et al. (1972) concluded that the influence of home background was far greater than that of the school. The Plowden Report (CACE, 1967) in the UK added weight to this argument as did those who were claiming that heredity influences were very strong (Jensen, 1969). By the late 1970s, however, the social determinist view was being challenged and a consensus began to emerge that schools can and do make a difference. School effectiveness researchers (Rutter et al., 1979) began to compare schools with similar intakes to ascertain if some were more effective than others and to identify the characteristics of schools that were making a difference (Edmonds, 1979).

The ground-breaking study by Rutter and colleagues paved the way for the school effectiveness movement in the UK. The study set out to compare the effectiveness of ten inner-city secondary schools on a variety of student outcome measures. The researchers identified a range of factors such as academic emphasis, incentives and rewards and general learning conditions, and argued that schools that had a combination of these factors created an 'ethos' that made a positive difference to pupil outcomes.

Since then there has been substantial international research evidence (Mortimore et al., 1988; Scheerens, 1997; Teddlie and Reynolds, 2000) that confirms that there is a school 'effect'. The difference between more and less

17

effective schools is believed to be somewhere in the region of 5 to 15 per cent. For example, the *School Matters* longitudinal junior school study by Mortimore et al. (1988) found that over a three-year period disadvantaged pupils made more progress in more effective schools than similar pupils in the least effective schools. The researchers found that the influence of the school was approximately four times more important than the influence of the home in reading progress and ten times more important in accounting for progress in mathematics. Thomas and Mortimore (1994) calculated the potential significance of these findings for pupils at the end of their time in school. They reckoned that the results could mean a difference for the average pupil of seven grade Cs instead of six grade Es at GCSE.

Just how much effect a school can have and what accounts for these effects have exercised researchers in recent years. A complex picture emerges, one that policy-makers usually choose to ignore. As MacBeath and Mortimore (2001, p. 8) put it: 'The general finding that schools matter is tantalizingly elusive because it leaves a host of unanswered questions.' Some of these questions concern issues to do with where the greatest effects lie. The emphasis for a long time was on the 'school effect'. But we now know that this is a somewhat naive notion because effects can be at different levels both within and beyond the school. MacBeath and Mortimore (2001, p. 9) point out for example that: 'The school as an organisation may add value to that of its individual members or, on the other hand, may subtract value. It may enhance and multiply the skills of its members, or may stifle and inhibit their mutual growth.'

The combined effectiveness of the leadership, management and the general organizational arrangements in the school, and the extent to which they lead to consistency in practice and have a stable effect on pupils as they move through the school, all contribute to the school effect. We will look more closely at the issues of stability and consistency of effectiveness when, in the next section, we examine the complexities surrounding the concept of value-added. In the meantime, a question needs to be asked about the balance between the effect of school-wide policy and practice compared with the effect that individual teachers can have in the classroom. It is a difficult one to answer, not least because trying to 'measure' both consistency of practice and stability of effect over time between teachers is very hard to do. It is particularly difficult in secondary school contexts where pupils tend to move regularly from teacher to teacher as they move from class to class and subject to subject. MacBeath and Mortimore (2001) describe how most research appears to agree that teacher effects are powerful. Creemers (1994) claims that the classroom can have a greater effect than the school as a whole and the Hay McBer (DfEE, 2000) study identified a range of characteristics that effective teachers appear to have. The work of Sammons, Thomas and Mortimore (1994) was able to show that the impact that teachers have in the early years of schooling can carry over into the later years of schooling.

There have also been studies of the effect that departments in secondary schools can have on pupil outcomes. Luyten (1994) found that the effect of subject departments was greater than the whole-school effect. Sammons, Thomas and Mortimore (1997) found that different subjects can have different effects. Whilst a number of studies found a correlation between departmental effects and whole-school effects, it has also been shown that there are often different effects between departments in the same school (Smith and Tomlinson, 1989; Harris, Jamieson and Russ, 1995; Thomas, 1995; Sammons, Thomas and Mortimore, 1997).

The effects that we have discussed so far relate to actions taken by the adults in a school, be they members of the senior or middle management team, individual class teachers or members of support staff. The relationships between these effects are complex. They are likely to become more so as the trend towards schools becoming learning organizations that are strong on teamwork and exercise distributed leadership, gathers momentum. In these institutions it will be very hard to disentangle the significance of any effects at different levels within the organization particularly those of class teachers. This is one of the reasons why the policy of financially rewarding the performance of individual teachers is very problematical.

There is another important contextual factor that research indicates has a significant impact on the school effect. This contextual factor concerns the pupils themselves. There are two key issues here. The first is that a school can have a different impact on different pupils. The second is that the impact of the 'social mix' within the school is increasingly being shown to have an important influence on pupils' progress and outcomes. The Junior School study (Mortimore et al., 1988) confirmed that, overall, an effective school tended to have a positive impact on all the pupils, whereas an ineffective school tended to have a negative impact. Below this generalization lies a much more complicated picture. Some studies have found that schools can have different effects on pupils of different abilities and on pupils from different social, ethnic and gender groups (Willms and Kerr, 1987; Nuttall et al., 1989; Sammons, Thomas and Mortimore, 1997). Longitudinal studies following pupils from primary to secondary school have also shown that progress among different groups varies over time, with some ethnic groups falling behind in primary school, but beginning to catch up at secondary school (Sammons, 1995). The MacBeath and Mortimore (2001, p. 12) research found that: 'the longer that pupils stay in school, the more pronounced becomes the influence of social class'. They ask the question: 'Is this a school effect or a background effect? That is, does the social background that pupils bring with them exert itself more strongly over time, or is a school constructed in such a way as to accentuate the difference progressively?'(ibid.).

They go on to remind us that the interrelationship between social class, ethnicity and gender is very significant and, as described in Chapter 1, there is ample research to back this up (Gillborn and Gipps, 1996; Gillborn, 2002). MacBeath (1999, p. 12) tries to capture some of the issues.

> The experience of a low attaining English middle-class girl with parents of Indian background needs to be probed with a more textured understanding of peer group affiliation, racial and sexual harassment, ascribed roles, sub-cultural tensions and parental and teacher expectations. High achieving, African-Caribbean boys may experience particularly acute difficulties in adjusting to the different expectations of peers, teachers, their families and the group identity which defines them not only as a threat to the authority of teachers but to that of the police and others in positions of power.

School effectiveness researchers have been criticized for not paying attention to the importance of social mix (Thrupp, 2001). Harris (1998) draws on a wide range of research to argue that the peer group to which a pupil belongs has a significant impact on the identity of the pupil as a person and on the pupil's capacity and motivation as a learner. In their description of her work, MacBeath and Mortimore (2001, p. 13) comment that:

> In a large racially and socially heterogeneous comprehensive school what becomes a salient feature of a pupil's self-definition arises from a complex social dynamic, constantly shifting as new relationships form and old ones disappear, as the social mix of the school and peer group changes or stabilises. In Harris' thesis young people's most essential experience of schooling is one of defining and redefining themselves in relation to their peers.

They acknowledge Thrupp's criticism that school effectiveness research may well have underestimated the effect of social mix on pupil outcomes. It would seem that government policy to expand specialist schools and create more faith schools is ignoring these findings too. Thrupp (1999, p. 183) argues that the backgrounds and the communities from which pupils come play a crucial role in defining a school's culture: 'The issue of school mix highlights powerful social inequalities in the provision of schooling.' This view needs to be set alongside our earlier concerns about the widening gap between the 'haves' and the 'have nots' and the fact that a growing number of pupils are becoming disaffected with school.

Teddlie and Reynolds (2000) in their review of the international school effectiveness literature conclude that more attention in the future needs to be paid to a wider range of contextual factors than has been the case in the past. The complexity of these factors means that researchers are recognizing that comparing attainment results across schools is becoming more and more problematical. Comparisons can be useful and raise some interesting issues for the schools concerned. But this is all. No two schools are exactly the same. The validity and reliability of efforts in the UK to benchmark schools by providing them with data that groups them with other schools of seemingly similar intakes in order to then make judgements about pupil outcomes are very questionable. They are questionable not just because of the evidence about the uncertain impact of a wide range of possible effects, but also because of the finding that achieving stability and consistency of effect over time are proving to be elusive particularly when research concerned with the concept of 'value-added' is examined.

The concept of value-added

When identifying the lessons learnt from school effectiveness research it is important to bear in mind the definitions of an effective school given at the beginning of Chapter 1: 'one in which pupils progress further than might be expected from consideration of its intake' (Mortimore, 1991, p, 9) and which 'adds extra value to its students' outcomes in comparison with schools serving similar intakes' (Sammons, Hillman and Mortimore, 1995, p, 3). These definitions have helped us to focus on individual pupils' progress as well as the outcomes of their learning. The emergence of the concept of 'value-added' is embedded within the definitions. It concerns the value schools add to the progress of their pupils. This concept has made a significant impact on schools, particularly in helping staff realize the need to track and monitor pupil progress and not just concentrate on outcomes. This has led to *intelligent schools* developing a range of self-evaluating strategies to monitor progress including the systematic collection of data to provide the necessary evidence of improvement (MacGilchrist, 2000). In primary schools it has resulted in the gathering of baseline data on children when they first begin school, so as to be able to support and monitor their progress from day one.

We welcome these moves, but value-added is a complex concept and in recent years new research has confirmed and added to this complexity. Like many of our colleagues, we urge caution in using and interpreting such data not least because of the use of such data to publish league tables of school performance. It is important to remember that raw results describe the grades or levels that pupils have obtained. They do not describe how well a school has performed. Through the use of value-added results it is possible to demonstrate how effective a school is in promoting pupils' academic attainment. However, even these results need to have a 'health warning' attached to them. They may, for example, mask a high turnover of pupils (Goldstein, 1996). Also, because of the limited number of pupils normally included in the sample, there are inherent limitations built into the technique when using it to make comparisons between schools. This means that in respect of test and examination results the technique of value-added, particularly when using a multi-level modelling approach, can be used as a screening device to identify

21

very low-performing or very high-performing schools. However, it is not able to provide finely graded differences between schools (Goldstein and Spiegelhalter, 1996).

Goldstein (2001) is of the view that publishing league tables encourages schools to adopt tactics to improve performance in the short term and 'play the system'. He challenges the inappropriate use of performance data by government and LEAs which ignores research findings. He concludes that:

> There has been some recognition, within bodies such as QCA and OFSTED, as well as among educationalists at the DfEE, that a higher degree of sophistication is required, that value added data should be encouraged and schemes set in place that would collect useful data and allow more sensitive analyses. (Ibid., p. 442)

It is also important to be cautious about the interpretation of year-on-year value-added data. Initially it was thought that about three years' worth of attainment data could signal a trend with a fair degree of confidence. This was at a time when researchers had no access to substantial longitudinal data on pupil performance. As such data have become available, questions are now being raised about the extent to which schools can and do achieve stability of effect over longer periods of time. For example, Gray, Goldstein and Thomas (2001) found that trends in national performance statistics in the UK during the 1990s suggested that the entire education system was moving upwards. However, a closer examination revealed that what this masked was a variation in performance one year to the next within and between schools. It also revealed that schools followed a complex range of trajectories depending on the particular improvement strategies they were using, with most having bursts of improvement for a few years followed by a plateauing or a decline. We will look more closely at the whole notion of improvement trends in the next chapter.

Gray and colleagues offered a conceptual framework for assessing value-added. They suggested that the data could be looked at from three perspectives. The data could indicate that a school is:

- maintaining its effect from year to year, i.e. the amount of effect remains stable over time;
- increasing its effect over time, i.e. the effect is unstable because it is changing for the better;
- decreasing its effect over time, i.e. the effect is unstable because it is changing for the worse.

The implication of this is that it is one thing to assess a school's effect at any given point in time, it is another matter to try and examine and assess changes in effectiveness over time.

Value-added data are most useful for helping individual schools to pinpoint areas of good practice and aspects of school practice that need to be improved. They enable differential effectiveness to be assessed in relation to groups of pupils and specific subjects and departments. This is important because, as described earlier, research has shown that, on the surface a school's overall results may look impressive, but this snapshot of attainment may well mask noticeable differences in outcomes for specific groups of pupils and subject areas (O'Donoghue et al., 1997; Sammons, Thomas and Mortimore, 1997). As with individual pupil data, it is necessary to look at results over several years to make a more reliable judgement about the stability and continuity of the trends emerging, whilst bearing in mind the findings of the Gray, Goldstein and Thomas research about problems in predicting future perform-ance. It is also necessary to bear in mind the margin of error or uncertainty that can be associated with such results if small numbers of pupils are involved (Goldstein, 1996).

When using value-added data there are a number of other issues that schools need to consider. The technique enables a school to take account of 'givens' that may have an impact on pupil outcomes such as prior attainment, socio-economic status, gender and ethnicity. It is therefore important that these pupil-intake factors are built into the equation. It then becomes possible to use the information gained on individual pupils as an internal screening device.

Value-added data can also be used as a screening device to identify individual pupils whose 'predicted' or 'expected' levels of attainment are very different from those observed. For this to be useful, however, it is pupils' achievements *during* their time in school, for example at the end of a year, not their final end results, which are crucial. This implies a different data collection strategy but one which is potentially more useful than comparisons of whole institutions. Pupils who depart markedly from their expected levels of attainment can be identified and, if necessary, can become the focus of additional support.

It must be remembered, however, that even at an individual level, the reliability of the screening instrument being used will need to be taken into account when assessing a pupil's potential or actual performance. Also, different instruments need to be used in order to assess a range of pupil outcomes. It is important to do this because research evidence indicates that pupils can achieve very differently depending on the outcomes being measured (Mortimore, Sammons and Thomas, 1994). For example, a pupil's attainment may be high but her or his self-image as a learner and/or attitude to school may be very low. Such a finding signals the necessity to develop a range of pupil 'measures' to provide a much fuller picture of a school's effectiveness.

Measuring what we value

In the main, recent comparisons within and between schools using value-added measures tend to draw on a narrow data set of pupil attainment measures. For primary schools, this means SATs results in English, mathematics and science and, for secondary schools, SATs results at Key Stage 3 and GCSE and A/AS level results. As Gray (2001, p. 8) reminds us: 'If other outcome measures are either not measured or seen as less important, rises in one area might be at the expense of performance in others.' This is a timely reminder in respect of the concerns we raised in Chapter 1 about, for example, the narrowing of the primary curriculum following the introduction of the National Literacy and Numeracy Strategies. It moves us on to a broader consideration of educational 'measures'.

A report from the USA called *Education Counts* (1991) stated that we must learn to measure what we value rather than value what we can easily measure. One of the limitations of school effectiveness research is that it is relatively easy, notwithstanding the caveats we have identified, to track progress and assess value-added by using statistical data such as baseline scores and examination results. School effectiveness, therefore, has tended to be assessed on a narrow set of quantitative attainment measures. For example, reading and mathematics test results in the primary school have been used because of the ready availability of standardized tests in these areas of the curriculum.

Maden (2001, p. 305) reminds us that: 'It is also important to take into account what pupils are gaining at school in addition to grades and points scores; most schools have an agenda that goes well beyond – and properly so – what they continue to be judged on.' Using qualitative measures is methodologically much more difficult. Peter Mortimore et al. were among the first researchers to attempt to combine different types of measures to assess the effectiveness of schools. In the Junior School study (Mortimore et al., 1988), as well as testing children's reading, writing, speaking and mathematical skills, they also measured their attendance, self-image, behaviour and attitudes towards different types of school activities. Other researchers have attempted to develop qualitative indicators. For example, John MacBeath et al. (1992) have developed ethos indicators for the Scottish school system. Gray (1995) argues that the effectiveness of schools can best be judged by academic progress, pupil satisfaction and pupil–teacher relationships. The main message from all these studies is the danger of concentrating on too narrow a definition of achievement, i.e. attainment, when assessing a school's effectiveness. It is for this reason, along with the issues raised in the first three sections of this chapter, that there is an urgent need to revisit the values underpinning notions of effectiveness. An examination of these values includes the need to consider what is meant by achievement.

Defining achievement

It is essential for schools to have a broad definition of achievement. David Hargreaves and colleagues (ILEA, 1984) suggested that there are at least four aspects of achievement that a school needs to develop:

- dealing with the capacity to remember and use facts. This aspect concerns the type of achievement that public examinations tend to measure. It emphasizes a pupil's ability to memorize and reproduce knowledge often in a written form;
- practical and spoken skills. This aspect concerns the practical capacity to apply knowledge with an emphasis on problem-solving and investigation skills;
- personal and social skills. The focus here is on a pupil's capacity to communicate with and relate to others. It also concerns personal characteristics such as initiative, self-reliance and leadership potential;
- motivation and self-confidence. This concerns a pupil's self-image and ability, for example, to persevere in the face of failure.

We have become good at measuring the first aspect. We still have a long way to go to 'measure' the other three despite the fact that increasingly employers are pressing for these aspects to be given greater prominence in schools. The four aspects have stood the test of time but, because of the significant changes in information and communications technology that have taken place and because of our growing understanding about the nature of learning, we are not the only people to argue that an even broader notion of achievement and therefore of value-added is needed to reflect these changes.

One such example is from the USA:

> Our conventional definitions of student achievement and assessment are much too narrow to meet the demands of the global economy. In order to succeed as productive citizens in the 21st century, students should graduate from high school with a vast and diverse set of skills and knowledge, including, but scarcely limited to: reading, mathematical and scientific understanding and application, and social studies … we urge federal policy makers to integrate 21st century skills into the definition of student achievement. These 21st century skills must include the technology and digital age literacy, inventive thinking, effective communication, and high productivity skills that will be essential for citizens in the rapidly changing digital age. … We must also ensure that our children have the ability to move beyond basic skills to apply higher order problem-solving skills that will be needed to compete in the new and ever changing information economy. Students must be able to use technology's tools to enhance learning; increase productivity; promote creativity; research topics online; proficiently use web-based tools; evaluate sources; develop problem solving strategies; and incorporate technology into their coursework. (CEO, 2001, p. 6)

Such views provide a challenge for practitioners especially when there is no clear consensus about the purpose of education and, consequently, the content of the curriculum and the focus of assessment. In the final chapter we will propose a change of focus for education. In the meantime the lack of consensus makes it even more important for each school to be quite clear what its aims are and, therefore, the criteria the head and staff will use to assess their own effectiveness.

The characteristics of effective schools

A shared vision and agreed aims have been identified as being characteristic of an effective school. The identification of such characteristics has been another major contribution from this area of research. There are some who would argue that many of the characteristics are obvious, so why make so much of them? This is a good example of the value of research, as often it does confirm what practitioners might say is no more than common sense. But, of course, what is seen as common sense by one group might be viewed very differently by another – the debate about the most effective way to teach children to read is a classic example. The important message about the characteristics of effective schools, in terms of the definitions provided earlier, is that there appear to be a number of characteristics that, when present, make a difference to the life chances of pupils in that school.

Sammons, Hillman and Mortimore (1995) were commissioned by OFSTED to undertake a review of international school effectiveness literature, particularly from the UK, North America and the Netherlands. They were asked to assess whether or not, despite the many differences in approaches to education from one country to the next, it was possible to find distinctive features that successful schools have in common. It needs to be borne in mind that the definition of 'success' that underpinned the review focused in the main on improvements in test and examination performance. The review confirmed that there appear to be at least 11 characteristics that are present in those schools that do add value to their pupils. Table 2.1 reproduces the synopsis provided in the write-up of this literature review (Sammons, Hillman and Mortimore, 1995, p. 8).

There seems little point in providing a description of each of these characteristics because they are well known and remain readily available for practitioners to read about. However, we do want to reflect on these characteristics because we believe that by developing them the evidence is that schools can improve pupils' levels of academic attainment. We asked ourselves three questions:

- Are they all of equal value or are some more central than others?
- Are they important/valid in isolation from, or in relation to, each other?
- How can a school develop these characteristics?

26

Table 2.1 *Eleven characteristics found in effective schools*

1	**Professional leadership**	Firm and purposeful A participative approach The leading professional
2	**Shared vision and goals**	Unity of purpose Consistency of practice Collegiality and collaboration
3	**A learning environment**	An orderly atmosphere An attractive working environment
4	**Concentration on teaching and learning**	Maximization of learning time Academic emphasis Focus on achievement
5	**Purposeful teaching**	Efficient organization Clarity of purpose Structured lessons Adaptive practice
6	**High expectations**	High expectations all round Communicating expectations Providing intellectual challenge
7	**Positive reinforcement**	Clear and fair discipline Feedback
8	**Monitoring progress**	Monitoring pupil performance Evaluating school performance
9	**Pupil rights and responsibilities**	Raising pupil self-esteem Positions of responsibility Control of work
10	**Home–school partnership**	Parental involvement in their children's learning
11	**A learning organization**	School-based staff development

Source: Sammons, Hillman and Mortimore (1995, p. 8)

When considering the first two questions we came to the conclusion that the characteristics are not of equal value, although they are all important. There appear to be some essential characteristics at the core of the *intelligent school* and, if these are not present, then the other characteristics are unlikely to be present either and, even if some of them are, they will be operating in a vacuum. In other words, we believe that some characteristics are of central importance and that the remaining ones arise out of, or are nested within, them. From our experience we would argue that there are four essential core characteristics of an effective school, with one providing the fulcrum for the other three:

- pupils' rights and responsibilities, i.e. their agency and their engagement in learning;
- professional high-quality leadership and management (we have added management because we believe that both are essential);
- a concentration on (pupil) learning and teaching (we have added pupil learning for reasons that will become clear in Chapter 4);
- a learning organization, i.e. a school with staff who are willing to be learners and to participate in a staff development programme.

We would place pupils' rights and responsibilities at the heart of an effective school. In doing this we have drawn on the research available at the time of the Sammons et al. review which emphasized the importance of self-esteem, giving children positions of responsibility and encouraging them to become more independent learners. We have also drawn on subsequent research which broadens what is meant by the rights and responsibilities of pupils. For example, Alderson (2003, p. 2) argues that: 'Adults powerfully influence schools and yet the overwhelming majority of people within schools are the students', 'Although students are seldom recognised as formal members of school improvement teams, all school improvement relies mainly on their work and behaviour' (ibid., p. 6) and 'Just as women's views are largely missing from history, children's views are almost wholly absent' (ibid., p. 8).

Rudduck, Chaplain and Wallace (1996) stress the importance of listening and acting upon pupils' views about learning and teaching and the school as a whole. In the context of inclusion, Ainscow (1999) makes a similar plea. It is the pupils who provide the purpose and focus for the educational offer in the school. The other three core characteristics provide the means of enabling the school to concentrate on that purpose and focus, supported by the remaining seven characteristics.

Our experience is that schools that configure these characteristics in this way have the capacity to develop into very effective institutions in terms of their pupils' progress and achievement. Figure 2.1 illustrates what we mean.

With Figure 2.1 we have tried to create a dynamic diagram as opposed to a static one because schools are ever-changing, organic institutions. We believe that the *intelligent school* is able to bring these core and related characteristics together to provide a coherent experience for pupils in each classroom, department and the school as a whole as part of its vision for its effectiveness.

To seek the answer to the third question – how can a school develop these characteristics to become more effective? – it is necessary to go beyond the school effectiveness literature and look to lessons learnt from the school improvement literature, which we explore in the next chapter. We focus in particular on lessons concerned with the four core characteristics we have identified.

However, before we move to the next chapter, we want to draw attention to the fact that school effectiveness research has not been without its critics.

Figure 2.1 Improving the effectiveness of schools (© B. MacGilchrist, K. Myers and J. Reed, 2004)

Some of the criticisms made are important for practitioners to know about, not least because policy-makers have a tendency to ignore them.

Criticisms of SESI research

Many of the criticisms of SESI research confirm the lesson that *change is complex.* Of particular significance are the criticisms concerned with socio-economic factors and the purpose of education.

Critics remind us of the need to set the research and findings of SESI within the wider context of social inequality. Fielding (1997) argues that school effectiveness research diverts attention away from structural impediments like poverty and inequality. Critics also accuse SESI researchers of not taking the political and social context of their work seriously. Ball (1996) reminds us that quality and effectiveness are not neutral descriptors and Fielding draws attention, as we did earlier, to the problematic notion of achievement.

29

Fielding argues that the preoccupation with 'what works' ignores the question of whose interests shape the nature and purpose of the work. This takes us right back to the key question about the purpose of education. Davies (2001, p. 144) claims that 'school effectiveness supports and furthers the political status quo and will continue to do so until research is able systematically to compare schools on a much wider range of considerations including fostering critically and politically aware citizens'. He argues, as others do, that the current thrust of school effectiveness research has encouraged politicians to perpetuate the myth that if only all our teachers and schools were effective then this would solve the problem of social inequality and reverse the decline in national economic competitiveness for which teachers must take considerable responsibility.

Fielding (1997) is of the view that school effectiveness research represents a particular view of social and political reality and has been responsible for its further growth and dominance. Fielding argues that school effectiveness and school improvement have become too closely linked and are in danger of foundering on checklists and league tables. He is of the view that school improvement is too preoccupied with the processes of improvement and has implicitly accepted the current definition of effectiveness. He criticizes SESI researchers for not challenging or articulating alternative frameworks for schooling or for education per se, and argues that 'schooling is not enough, only education will do'. Fielding is of the view that SESI needs to move on to what he calls transformative education in which:

- education becomes the focus;
- values are explicit and can be contested;
- education is about the development of people in and through the community to develop a democratic society.

He draws particular attention, as we have, to the need for much greater student voice and involvement in education.

In recent years criticisms of these kind have been paid attention to by a number of school effectiveness and school improvement researchers. What is heartening is that increasingly the focus of attention is now moving to the learner and the recognition that, if we really do want to improve our schools, the sensible thing to do is to have as a starting point, as we have argued, learners and their learning. We accept that the SESI movement has contributed to, and supported the government's agenda about standards, accountability, targets and league tables, and this has had some positive benefits. In many respects we would argue that it was necessary for some of the reasons argued by Elmore about the need to do something about loose coupling in the system. However, the time is now right and, indeed, it is essential for us to reassess and realign the focus of SESI. There is a growing movement in the Pacific Rim

countries to recognize the need to foster creativity in learning
writing there are encouraging signs, particularly in the primar·
2003), that creativity is coming onto the agenda in the UK. T
strongly supported and encouraged by the *Times Education·*
its readers.

We would argue that there is also a need now to focus on indiviɑu.
group opportunities to learn – as well as institutional learning. Consequently,
the concept of school and schooling will need to change. We will want to
argue in the final chapter that we need to move from thinking about the *intelligent school*, to thinking about '*intelligent schooling*'. For the time being,
however, we now turn to take a close look at the lessons we can learn from
school improvement research.

Questions for discussion

1 How do you define effectiveness in your school?
2 How effective is your school? Is it equally effective for all groups of pupils?
   How do you know?
3 How do you rate your school on the effectiveness characteristics, particularly the core ones we have identified?
4 What data (evidence) do you use to support, monitor and assess pupil
   progress and achievement? How useful and how accurate are these data?

3
Reflections on school improvement

- What is school improvement?
- Some key messages
- Change takes time
- An individual school's capacity for change varies
- Change is complex
- Change needs to be well led and managed
- Teachers need to be the main agents of change
- The pupils need to be the main focus for change
- Questions for discussion

Fullan (2001a) comments that not all change is improvement but all improvement leads to change. This always brings a wry smile to the face of most practitioners. School improvement literature has burgeoned in recent years and a number of buzzwords have become associated with it – vision, mission, empowerment, collegiality, professional learning communities – to name but a few. Digging below the surface of this jargon, some important messages for practitioners can be found. They are messages that have emerged from a range of sources. Some are as a result of researchers acting rather like 'flies on the wall' and observing and analysing practice in schools that are particularly successful at improving themselves. Some come from observing schools in difficulty. Yet others come from gathering the perceptions of practitioners about how improvements have been achieved in recent years. Before examining these messages, however, it is important to explore definitions of school improvement and to consider what is meant by an improving school.

What is school improvement?

In 1985 the 14 countries involved in an international school improvement project agreed the following definition of school improvement: 'A systematic, sustained effort aimed at change in learning conditions and other related conditions in one or more schools with the ultimate aim of accomplishing educational goals more effectively' (van Velzen *et al.*, 1985, p. 34).

At that time the emphasis moved from a focus on individual teachers' professional development to school-wide improvements with development planning as a process for achieving these. By the end of the decade school improvement researchers and those engaged in school improvement at a local level, be they in schools or in local education authorities (LEAs) were becoming increasingly influenced by findings emerging from studies of effective schools.

This heralded the beginning of the coming together of school effectiveness and school improvement research and resulted in a shift in the definition of school improvement. Hopkins (1996, p. 32) defined it as: 'A strategy for educational change that enhances student outcomes as well as strengthening the school's capacity for managing change'. This definition emphasizes the importance of assessing the outcomes of improvement efforts for the pupils themselves. For the first time, the need to create a much closer link between school-wide improvements and improvements in the classroom was signalled.

This shift in emphasis resulted in a range of school improvement projects initiated by LEAs and higher education institutions (HEIs). It encouraged the creation of centres such as the International School Effectiveness and Improvement Centre (ISEIC) at the Institute of Education, University of London and networks such as The Leadership *for* Learning (L*f*L) Network at the University of Cambridge.

The definitions focus on deliberate action to bring about improvements. They concern process factors and, whilst mention is made of pupil outcomes, no attention is paid to the nature of these outcomes. Since then, however, definitions of school improvement have emerged that make a definite link between process and outcome, thus drawing the school effectiveness and school improvement paradigms even more closely together.

By the end of the twentieth century the academic performance of students had become a key success criterion for an improving school, thus illustrating how school effectiveness and school improvement research had all but merged. The coming together of these two paradigms means that our concern about finding ways to 'measure what we value' is just as applicable to school improvement research as it is to school effectiveness studies. It makes it even more important to examine the values and beliefs underlying definitions of improvement.

In a substantial school improvement study, Gray et al. (1999) premised their study of 12 schools on the notion of an improving school being one that increases its effectiveness over time. It was the first study of its kind to define school improvement in this way. Gray et al. set out to study the schools' rates of improvement in their effectiveness over time using value-added data. They also examined some of the factors and strategies associated with changes in performance. Their definition of an improving school as opposed to school improvement was 'one which secures year-on-year improvements in the outcomes of successive cohorts of 'similar' pupils ... in other words, it increases in its effectiveness over time' (ibid., p. 48) and 'What matters is how much progress they (schools) make from their respective starting points' (ibid., p. 11).

33

As a result of the outcome of this study and subsequent research, Gray (2001) commented that there is a shortage of evidence about the extent to which schools manage to sustain improvement over time. He asked the question: 'Is school improvement a realistic ambition or merely some kind of holy grail?' (ibid., p. 19). Gray went on to remind us that: 'Research on school improvement at present amounts to not much more than a sketch map' (ibid., p. 2) and that there remains 'some fuzziness about when a school is an 'improving' one' (ibid., p. 9). We now want to explore the current state of the 'sketch map' and what we can learn from it.

Some key messages

The literature makes it quite clear that there is no set recipe for achieving improvement. What the *intelligent school* has been able to do, however, is to maximize its improvement efforts by heeding some of the key messages that have emerged from this area of research. We have chosen to concentrate on six interrelated messages as we believe they are particularly helpful for schools:

- Change takes time.
- A school's capacity for change will vary.
- Change is complex.
- Change needs to be well led and managed.
- Teachers need to be the main agents of change.
- The pupils need to be the main focus for change.

Change takes time

> The Chinese Bamboo
> When you plant it nothing happens in the first year, nor in the second or the third or the fourth years. You don't even see a single green shoot. And yet in the fifth year, in a space of just six weeks, the bamboo will grow 90 feet high. The question is, did it grow 90 feet in six weeks or in five years? (Dick, 1992, p. 186).

A superficial quick-fix approach to change may end up being no more than moving the deckchairs around on the *Titanic* (Stoll and Fink, 1996). If a school is serious about wanting to improve learning conditions and, ultimately, the standards of achievement of pupils, then this requires a systematic, sustained effort as suggested in the van Velzen et al. definition. Yet, pupils only get one chance in the reception class, one time in year 9 and only one chance for each year. Time is therefore precious for pupils and if a school needs to improve then it has a responsibility to its pupils to make the necessary changes as soon as possible. This is the challenge for schools – how to bring about change (improvement) as soon as possible but in such a way as to ensure that the improvements are for the better and can be sustained. Stoll and Myers

(1998) have provided substantial evidence to show that a one-size-fits-all approach to school improvement is totally inappropriate. What is needed is a differential approach to improvement that starts from where a school is and puts in place a range of strategies aimed at building a school's capacity for sustaining improvement over time.

Fullan (1992), recognizes this dilemma and encourages schools to 'ready, fire, aim'. His basic message is that change can be messy, that it is difficult to predict exactly how things will go and that rarely does the end result turn out as planned. He is of the view that it is better to get started and then modify and adjust as you go. This reflects the reality facing schools. However, Fullan and other researchers do subscribe to the van Velzen et al. view that improvement requires a sustained effort (Hargreaves and Hopkins, 1991; West and Ainscow, 1991; Harris, 2002). Louis and Miles (1992), who undertook a study of six urban high schools in the USA, introduced the concept of 'evolutionary' planning. They argued that schools need a planned approach to change that is flexible and adaptable rather than rigidly imposed. In other words, a planned approach to change that is long term and flexible will enable, as circumstances change, modifications to be made and unexpected events to be catered for. We argue in Chapter 7 that this is a characteristic of the *intelligent school*.

Throughout the UK and in many other countries worldwide – for example, Canada, Australia and New Zealand – school development planning has been adopted to achieve this kind of evolutionary approach to planning. There appears to be a general consensus that development planning is a strategy for school improvement. However, as the findings of a study of the impact of school development plans (MacGilchrist et al., 1995) revealed, not all plans lead to improvement – more of this later.

As indicated in the previous chapter, there is new evidence emerging from an examination of longitudinal attainment data sets that improvements in student performance comes in short bursts as opposed to a year-on-year continuous upward trend. Gray, Goldstein and Jesson (1996) used a sophisticated value-added technique to look at trends over five years in changes and improvements in pupil performance. In this study, Gray, Goldstein and Jesson drew on the performance data from 34 secondary schools in one LEA covering five successive cohorts of pupils. This, with Teddlie and Stringfield's (1993) work in Louisiana, was one of the first studies to examine longitudinal data sets. They wanted to seek evidence of rates of improvement over time. The timing of their study was interesting in that in 1993/94 Her Majesty's Chief Inspector in his Annual Report (OFSTED, 1995), singled out and named 50 improving secondary schools for praise for the first time. They had all apparently made substantial progress in raising the performance levels of their pupils. There was no way of knowing, of course, whether the pupils in the year under consideration in these 50 schools were achieving more than the previous cohort, or the degree of similarity between cohorts.

Gray, Goldstein and Jesson found that the schools they looked at differed in their effectiveness over time. They concluded that the question as to whether improvement is a continuous year-on-year process or one which goes in fits and starts remains open.

Gray et al. (1999) then identified 12 schools out of the 34 and studied the changes that had taken place in them over the five-year period. They were looking at naturally occurring improvement, not improvements linked directly with external intervention. They used a combination of qualitative and quantitative methods drawn from both school effectiveness and school improvement research. They also used knowledge from these two paradigms to identify factors that might have contributed to the changes and improvement processes in the 12 schools. They looked at changes in a school's effectiveness over time, i.e. from one cohort to the next, something rarely done in previous studies. As before, they were interested in rates of change over time.

They placed the schools in terms of their value-added performance data at the beginning of the study at one of three levels of effectiveness – above average, average or below average – and looked to see whether the schools had made rapid, steady or slow progress. They found that up to three years of continuous improvement at the same level seemed to be the norm after which a school tended to reach a plateau or, as they described it, 'hit a wall'. For a school to move up a level of effectiveness, however, required four or five years of sustained improvement. In practice, they actually found that a five-year run of continuous improvement was quite exceptional. They concluded that there was limited evidence of sustained improvement in attainment over time.

The study provides useful insights about the context and change processes within the schools. It found clear evidence of differential rates of improvement across the schools. Three different approaches to improvement were identified:

- tactics (i.e. quick fixes);
- strategic activities;
- capacity-building.

Nearly all the schools used short-term tactics to improve examination results, for example providing additional support for borderline C/D candidates. These were the sorts of tactics that headteachers often call 'playing the improvement game'. Not surprisingly, such responses did not lead to sustained improvement over time. In contrast, those schools improving more rapidly showed evidence of also using a more strategic approach to improvement. For example, they were involved in developing whole-school policies and were using school development planning to enable them to focus on areas in need of improvement. They were trying to have a co-ordinated approach to improvement with varying success. Only two schools were into capacity-building. They had gone beyond incremental approaches to change and were trying to focus on ways of improving learning and teaching in classrooms. However, in only one of the schools did the research team feel that the practices in place were sufficiently embedded for them to be confident that the school really did have the capacity to improve in the longer term.

The authors looked at the power of contextual factors. They surmised that it may well be the case that schools serving particularly disadvantaged socio-economic communities experience constraints that are *additional* to any shared with schools that have comparably low-attaining intakes. They identified a range of contextual factors that appeared to have a particular impact on rates of improvement. These included: headteachers having to cope with a mix of personalities and attitudes on the staff; the age profile of staff; the turnover of staff; and the competition in the local marketplace affecting the social mix of the intake. They argued that the next wave of school improvement or 'third age' as they called it, needs to focus on classrooms and the improvement of learning and teaching. Important as it is, none of the schools in the study found sustaining a focus on learning and teaching easy. They concluded that: 'teachers are probably the most important resource of all and what is needed is a way of unlocking teachers' interest in changing their performance' (Gray et al., 1999, p. 151).

In a further study, Gray, Goldstein and Thomas (2001) then focused on trying to establish the extent to which sustained trends in effectiveness can be identified, and also the extent to which such trends can reliably predict the future performance of schools. What was particularly significant about this study was that, unlike previous studies, it was based on a very large nationally representative sample provided by the Department for Education and Employment (DfEE). The sample comprised nearly 700,000 pupils representing four successive cohorts in 2,500 institutions. The focus was performance in the years leading up to A/AS levels in a context nationally of very stable A/AS results in England from year to year.

They found that only in a very small minority of cases did schools have consistent trajectories either up or down. Such trends as were identified appeared to be relatively short-lived and to come in bursts, and very rarely went beyond three years. This confirmed the findings of the studies described earlier.

They found that: 'among the small minority of institutions (the top and bottom 5%) where the trends were most evident over 3 years; the most likely outcome for the fourth year was in the opposite direction to the linear trend' (Gray, Goldstein and Thomas, 2001, p. 404). They went on to conclude that:

few institutions, it would seem, have yet managed to lock into cycles of 'continuous improvement' ... The urge to employ the past to predict the future is undoubtedly strong. The present analysis provides some evidence of the likely limitations of such an approach. Whether there are other, more powerful strategies, however, remains a moot point. (Ibid., p. 404)

37

In a subsequent article (2003) the same research team reflect on these findings and pay particular attention to two areas of school improvement research, which so far have not yet really been explored:

- trends in performance over time;
- the incidence of time-lagged phenomena, for example, the gap between a new headteacher beginning and the impact that that person has, or the time it takes for new approaches to learning and teaching to begin to have an impact on pupils' outcomes.

They set the article in the context of the rising national trend in GCSE examination results being (unwisely in their view) extrapolated to individual schools and the consequent expectation that every school is expected to improve its results year-on-year. They drew on their tentative conclusion that schools with improvement 'trajectories' in a consistently upward projection are probably much rarer than is commonly supposed. Where upward movement does occur, it appears to be of a relatively short duration with three years representing a 'good run'; four to five years an exception to the rule. Whilst three years' worth of data is needed to identify a trend, it would seem that for most schools this tends to be the maximum duration of the trend.

So, from the evidence emerging, school improvement appears to come more often than not in short bursts. This means we need to understand what the contextual factors are that are creating this situation – are they long term, medium term or short term? Can particular school improvement strategies buck these trends? Can they counter what appears to be the statistical probability of such variations over time being a factor of life? The *intelligent school* understands that tailored support that takes account of an individual school's context is a key factor. It recognizes the fact that each school's history and context is different.

An individual school's capacity for change varies

No two schools are the same. This is an obvious statement, but worth emphasizing. In their anxiety to improve the system, policy-makers have a tendency to forget this fact. All three authors of this book have been inspectors and advisers. We know from our personal experience that it is one thing to create a policy aimed at improving schools, it is quite another to ensure that all the schools in a district have the desire for and or the capacity to bring about these changes. It is no different for headteachers and their senior management teams. They know, only too well, that sense of frustration when a policy, seemingly agreed by the staff, fails to get put into practice for all kinds of reasons.

The message in the literature, therefore, is that schools cannot be treated as an homogeneous group. Each school's history and context will vary (Reynolds et al., 1996). There will be some factors, be they internal or external, that are simply beyond a school's control. Some of these will be persistent long-term factors such as poverty, geographical location and new legislation imposed from outside. Others will be more medium to short-term factors such as staff turnover and pupil mobility. There will also be personal issues affecting staff such as birth, marriage, bereavement, divorce and illness. The leadership team has very little control over these real-life change issues that can profoundly affect members of the school community. There will be other factors that are within the control of the school to do something about, such as the type of leadership and management arrangements in place, the type of support provided for staff and the teaching methods used.

One of the most powerful messages to come out of the school improvement literature is the importance of a school's culture in relation to change. The culture of a school is seen as the deciding factor when it comes to a school's state of readiness and its capacity to improve. Those who study school improvement stress the importance of identifying the different cultures and subcultures within schools and that understanding a particular school's culture is a vital part of school improvement (Stoll and Fink, 1996). Defining the culture of a school is not easy. It has been called 'the way we do things around here' (Deal, 1987, p. 17).

MacGilchrist et al., (1995, p. 40) argue that 'the culture of an organisation is demonstrated through the ways in which those who belong to the organisation feel, think and act'. The authors identify three interrelated ways in which the culture of a school is expressed in practice:

- *Professional relationships*. For example, how headteachers and staff relate to and work with one another, their attitudes towards the pupils and others connected with the school and the quality of leadership and shared sense of purpose in respect of the school's aims.
- *Organizational arrangements*. For example, people management arrangements in respect of roles and responsibilities, procedures for making decisions, communication systems, pupil grouping and pastoral care along with environmental management arrangements such as the upkeep of the building and playground and the display of pupils' work in classrooms and the public areas of the school.
- *Opportunities for learning* – for both pupils and adults. For example, for pupils, the curriculum on offer, attitudes and expectations about what it is possible for pupils to achieve, equal opportunities concerns and the type of provision for special educational needs. For teachers, their own professional development and their attitude towards their own learning.

MacGilchrist et al. concluded that: 'These three dimensions are a practical manifestation of the underlying beliefs and values of a school community. All three are amenable to change so that, not only are they an expression of the present culture, but they can also help shape and change the future culture of the school' (ibid., p. 42).

The findings of Susan Rosenholtz's (1989) study of Tennessee schools and school districts illustrates these dimensions in practice. She found that the schools in her study tended to fall into two broad categories, 'moving' and 'stuck' schools. Needless to say, it was the moving schools that were successful in improving themselves. They were characterized by shared goals and teachers who were willing to collaborate with one another and who accepted that they still had things to learn whilst at the same time demonstrating a sense of confidence and commitment in what they were already doing. Susan Rosenholtz found there to be a relationship between this type of culture and improvements in pupils' learning. Since this study, further categories of schools have been identified such as strolling, cruising, struggling and sinking schools (Stoll and Fink, 1996). Such descriptions of different school contexts provide evidence of the need to avoid the simplistic notion that schools fall along a continuum from least to most effective. The nine intelligences that we identify in Chapter 7 build on and develop the notion of the relationship between a school's culture and its capacity for improvement.

Change is complex

Again, this finding smacks of common sense but needs to be emphasized. An acceptance of the fact that change is complex is both a reassurance and a challenge for practitioners. Interpersonal relationships and micropolitics cannot be ignored when people and change are concerned. The prospect of change can mean different things to different people and, of course, people may react differently depending on the nature of the change being proposed. For example, some people find change exciting and that it sets the adrenaline flowing. Others may take a much more cynical view and think that if they keep their heads down then the latest idea will die a natural death. For others the prospect of change may be threatening. They may feel de-skilled and dislike dealing with uncertainty. People may, of course, react differently depending on the nature of the change suggested. These are all natural human reactions. What the literature tells us, however, is that real change – real improvement – is more than likely to be associated with some pain and some conflict, especially if it is challenging a person's fundamental beliefs and attitudes. Michael Fullan (2001a) describes at least three different ways in which change can take place simultaneously by introducing new:

- equipment and materials (for example, the introduction of a new mathematics scheme);

- behaviours and practices (for example, a change in the way in which pupils are grouped for mathematics);
- beliefs and attitudes (for example, changing the way in which mathematics is taught).
  [Our examples]

Simply changing the first two without dealing with the third can lead to shallow, short-lived improvements (Cuban, 1988).

Change is also complex because it is not linear or mechanistic. It often happens in unpredictable and, sometimes, unlikely ways. This accords with new thinking about the nature of organizational change and development and we elaborate on this issue in Chapter 7.

The need to distinguish between means and ends is another factor that needs to be addressed. The emphasis in the early school improvement studies, as exemplified in the van Velzen et al. definition, was on concentrating on improving general learning conditions within the school. Particular emphasis was placed on the importance of staff development. Since then there has been a recognition of the need to create a link between school-wide development, staff development and classroom development. The evidence is that this is not easy to do in practice, particularly when it concerns trying to change approaches to teaching and learning in the classroom.

The findings of the school development planning study in which one of us was involved illustrate the importance of this warning (MacGilchrist et al., 1995). The study found that there was only one type of plan that brought about improvements at these three levels. It was the type of plan that was well led and managed, had teacher development built in and, most importantly, had as its focus pupil progress and achievement in the classroom. In other words, school-wide improvements and the staff development programme were ultimately seen as a means to an end. More will be said about this in the final section in this chapter.

Change needs to be well led and managed

When writing about school development planning, Hargreaves and Hopkins (1991) stated that it is one thing to establish a plan for improvement, it is quite another to ensure that the plan is put into practice. They talked about the dangers of assuming that planned action will run on 'auto-pilot'.

In the literature a clear distinction is made between *leadership* and *management*. This distinction is illustrated by the definitions in Table 3.1. Schein (1985, p. 171) sums up the relationship between the two by stating that 'Both culture and structure, leadership and management are necessary if an organisation is to become highly effective'.

41

Table 3.1 *Distinctions between leadership and management*

Leadership	Management
'Building and maintaining an organisational culture' (Schein, 1985)	'Building and maintaining an organisational structure' (Schein, 1985)
'Establishing a mission for the school, giving a sense of direction' (Louis and Miles, 1992)	Designing and carrying out plans, getting things done, working effectively with people' (Louis and Miles, 1992)
'Doing the right thing' (Bennis and Nanus, 1985)	'Doing things right' (Bennis and Nanus, 1985)

Southworth (1995) argues that traditional views about leadership and management are still prevalent particularly in primary schools. Leadership tends to be equated with the role of the headteacher who is deemed to be responsible for establishing the overall aims and purposes of the school and for managing the school with the help of the senior management team. School management is often still perceived as something that happens outside classrooms and to be concerned with systems and procedures often of a hierarchical nature.

Fullan (1992) argues for the need for a significant change in views about the role and purpose of leadership. He draws on the work of those who have studied organizations outside the world of education. For example, Block (1987) argues that organizations need to become much less bureaucratic and hierarchical because bureaucratic organizations encourage staff to look to 'managers' to provide the ideas. They discourage personal initiative and responsibility. He urges a move towards organizations that are led and managed in such a way as to enable staff to play an active part in shaping and improving the organization. In this way, staff are encouraged to learn and develop as practitioners. Bennis and Nanus (1985) studied 90 successful industrial leaders. They found that all were open to learning themselves and, likewise, encouraged and stimulated their staff to learn as well. The culture they fostered was one of trust and good communications about the aims of the organization and the staff in these organizations were responsible and accountable for change. The government's strategy for continuous professional development published in 2001 (DfES, 2001) emphasized the importance of leadership that was distributed between senior and middle management staff. The leadership programme developed by the National College for School Leadership (NCSL) is built on this notion.

Charles Handy (1984) studied schools from the perspective of an industrial management specialist. He identified four types of school culture. The personal, informal *club* culture which revolves around a headteacher who has a network of power which is likened to a spider's web. The *role* culture which signifies a hierarchical role system which has formal procedures for managing the organization. Such an organization is managed rather then led by the headteacher and can be resistant to change. In contrast, there is the *task* culture which is responsive to change in a less individualistic way than a club culture. It is built around co-operative, not hierarchical, groups, and is usually a warm, friendly and forward-looking culture. Finally, there is the *person* culture which is a very individualistic one. The organization is used by each member as a resource for developing their talents rather like stars loosely grouped in a constellation.

Handy found aspects of all four cultural types present in any one school and found, from his study, that no two schools were the same. He argues that the headteacher and senior management team need to be aware of these different types of culture and to use the strengths of each when appropriate. He believes that if schools are to improve, headteachers and their staff need to rethink their approach to leadership and management. He supports the traditional primary school philosophy of an emphasis on teaching pupils, rather than school subjects, and suggests that classroom teachers be valued as managers of learning.

Hargreaves and Hopkins (1991, p. 15) subscribe to Handy's view about management, arguing that: 'Management is about people. Management arrangements are what empower people. Empowerment is the purpose of management.' They criticize definitions of management that focus on structures and procedures. They point out that this can lead to a false divide between teaching and managing, and can perpetuate the notion that 'managers manage and teachers teach'. In other words, teachers are also managers and, at the end of the day, the management of learning and teaching in the classroom is *the* most important management activity that goes on in school. We would argue too, that in the *intelligent school* senior managers see themselves as teachers and learners and as such provide a model for classroom teachers. Roland Barth (1990), for example, advocates that the headteacher should be the lead learner. One London head we know describes herself on the school notepaper as 'headteacher and head learner'.

Fullan (2001a) argues for the need for leadership to be shared across a school and stresses the importance of the development of a professional culture in schools. This kind of culture is one in which there is an openness to new ideas. Staff give and receive help from one another and there is a sense of teamwork which has as its focus improving learning and teaching in the classroom. He sees this as both a strategy and an outcome of leadership and management. Such a view finds much support in the literature. Hargreaves (2003) describes the importance of schools becoming professional learning communities for all those who work and learn within them. Sergiovanni (2000, p. 140) stresses the importance of teachers learning with and from one another to improve learning for pupils: 'Building capacity among teachers and focusing that capacity on students and their learning is the crucial factor. Continuous capacity building and continuous focusing is best done within communities of practice.'

Teachers need to be the main agents of change

Like schools, teachers cannot be treated as a homogeneous group. The staff will be made up of a number of individuals who will bring to any proposed change different skills, knowledge and attitudes depending on their previous experience, their length of time in the school, their status within the school and their own particular concerns and interests, not least in terms of the stage they have reached in their own career as a teacher. There has been some interesting research into teachers' life histories and the changing values and attitudes that teachers have as they move through their career (Huberman, 1988; Sikes, 1992). These studies are a useful reminder for those with leadership and management responsibilities because, as Fullan (1991, p. 117) says, 'Educational change depends on what teachers do and think. It's as simple and as complex at that'.

The challenge for headteachers and their senior management teams is to find ways of bringing the staff on board and getting them committed to and prepared to become involved in change. All three of us have had experience of working with schools on a range of school improvement programmes. Nine times out of ten, the biggest hurdle to be overcome is achieving staff commitment to the change. In our view, without it, long-lasting improvement will not occur.

As far as teachers are concerned, some important messages have come out of the school improvement literature. Good quality, professional working relationships are essential (Nias, Southworth and Yeomans, 1989; Bolam et al., 1993), so too are teamwork (Mortimore and Mortimore, 1991), shared leadership (Chrispeels, 1992; Louis and Miles, 1992) and shared understandings (Rosenholtz, 1989). Another key message is to do with teachers' own learning (Day, 1999). The importance of evidence-based practice involving teachers learning with and from one another through observing and reflecting on their practice has received much attention. A further message is the need to recognize the emotional aspects of change for teachers (Hargreaves, 2003).

Studies of schools and of other types of institutions beyond the world of education (Peters and Waterman, 1982) stress the importance of the attitude of the staff within such institutions towards their own learning and the priority given to staff development. Many studies have demonstrated the relationship between teachers' learning and school improvement (Rosenholtz, 1989; Chrispeels, 1992; Nias, Southworth and Campbell, 1992; Gray et al., 1999).

Strategies for improving staff development programmes have been identified (Joyce and Showers, 1988; Hopkins, Ainscow and West, 1994) as have strategies for encouraging teachers to be more reflective and analytical (Joyce, 1991) and to gain greater control over the change programme themselves. In Chapter 6 we describe in detail practical ways for supporting teachers' learning.

As noted earlier, change can challenge teachers' fundamental beliefs and attitudes, and lead to some form of conflict. It is essential that this normal and typical sign that change is taking place is well led and managed. Understandably, teachers' main concerns are focused on what goes on in the classroom. The vast majority of teachers are hard-working, hard-pressed professionals for whom time is a precious commodity. Their time is mainly consumed in planning and preparing lessons, marking pupils' work and recording and assessing their progress. It is hardly surprising, therefore, that teachers often have a healthy scepticism towards change particularly if 'the management', the government or other 'external agencies' are seen as the sole initiators of change which is likely to result in a further increase in workload for teachers. Our experience is that school improvement efforts that concentrate on the classroom in such a way that teachers experience the benefits of change for themselves and their children are the ones much more likely to be successful (MacGilchrist, 1996). Only time will tell if the government's workforce reform strategy will enable teachers to have more space and time to concentrate on what matters most – pupils' learning.

The pupils need to be the main focus for change

The findings of the study into the impact of development planning (MacGilchrist et al., 1995) brought home the importance of schools ensuring that pupils' learning is the main focus for improvement. Of the four different types of plans, the authors found that only one made a real difference for children. A particularly poignant message from this research was that the type of development plan found in the majority of schools in the study – the co-operative plan – had many of the characteristics identified in the school effectiveness and school improvement literature. In these schools

- there was a willingness on behalf of the staff to work on school-wide improvements, although not all the staff had a 'piece of the action';
- there was strong leadership from the headteacher and the senior management team managed the implementation of the plan very well;
- resources were allocated to the priorities for improvement chosen;
- there was a detailed staff development programme directly linked with the school plan.

However, although it was possible to identify improvements for the school as a whole such as new policy documents and changes in management practices, along with improvements in teachers' own professional development, it was not possible to track these improvements into the classroom for pupils. In other words, it was not possible to find examples of improved learning opportunities for them.

There was only one type of plan – the *corporate* plan – that did make an impact on pupils' learning. The reason for this was that whilst the plan had many of the characteristics of the co-operative plan, it had four vital additional ones:

- The leadership of the improvement efforts was shared amongst a number of teachers.
- Every member of staff had some piece of the action – something within the plan for improvement for which they had specific responsibility.
- The main focus for the plan was pupils' learning – their progress and achievement.
- Strategies for monitoring and evaluating the impact of the plan and for providing data to establish further priorities for improvement were well developed.

Chapter 4 focuses on learning and stresses the importance of children's learning, rather than their performance, being the main focus of attention. Rudduck (2001) offers different strategies for keeping the focus on students. They range from listening to students to treating them as equal partners in the learning process.

1 *Listening to students*: students are a source of data; teachers respond to student data but students are not involved in discussions of data; there is no feedback; teachers act on the data.
2 *Students as active participants*: teachers initiate enquiry and interpret the data but students are taking some role in decision-making.
3 *Students as researchers*: students are involved in enquiry and have an active role in decision-making.
4 *Students as fully active researchers and co-researchers*: students and teachers jointly initiate enquiry; students play an active role in decision-making together with teachers; they jointly plan action in the light of data and review the impact of the intervention.

There is growing recognition that students' perceptions about themselves as learners have a key role to play in school improvement and we discuss this in the next chapter.

Questions for discussion

1 How do your school improvement efforts enable a link to be made between school-wide development, teacher development and classroom practice?
2 What strategies do you use to keep pupils' learning the main focus of your improvement agenda?
3 What role do pupils play in setting your improvement agenda?
4 Are your improvement efforts making a difference for pupils? How do you know?

4

Learning about learning

Learning is nature's expression of the search for development. (Senge, 2000a, p. 57)

In order to help young people to become better learners, the first thing is for all teachers to start thinking, acting and talking as if learning were learnable. (Claxton, 2000b, p. 8)

Learning things is important 'cos I can learn more better (Khalid, year 1)

Introduction

'Knowledge acquired by study', a traditional definition of learning found in the 1991 edition of the *Oxford Dictionary*, is too narrow for the *intelligent school*. A much more expansive view of what it means to study is needed if important forms of learning are not to be excluded from the definition. A broader view would include the natural and spontaneous way that young children learn as well as much of out-of-school learning. Learning, as implied in the discussion about achievement in Chapter 2, is a broader and more dynamic process than just studying and acquiring facts. Human beings have an innate capacity for learning as they live. As Claxton (1999, p. 6) points out: 'Learning is not something we do sometimes in special places or at certain periods of our lives. It is part of our nature. We are born learners.' One of the tasks for the *intelligent school* is to find out what its stakeholders, particularly,

48

the pupils, think learning is about.

A literature review published in 2001 identified different views of what learning is:

- increasing one's knowledge;
- memorizing and reproducing;
- applying general rules to particulars;
- understanding and making sense;
- seeing something in a different way;
- changing as a person. (Watkins et al., 2001, p. 1)

Initial school improvement research concentrated on school level change. Later studies showed, however, as Reynolds (2001, p. 36) points out, that 'the classroom learning level has maybe two or three times more influence on student achievement than the school level does ... . It is clear that the neglect of the classroom level and the celebration of the school level may have historically cost us valuable teacher commitment'. The impact of the classroom environment on pupils' learning and attainment is now taken much more seriously.

The knowledge base about learning has been growing rapidly and many practitioners with whom we have been working have been studying the literature, renewing their understandings, creatively investigating learning in their own schools and examining the implications for their school improvement practice.

The three of us work in a range of different partnerships with practitioners. This work has confirmed for us that effective learning is not a passive process confined to either the classroom or to the process of studying. It is an active process of making meaning that includes questioning, understanding, reflecting and making connections between existing and new information, and, subsequently, being able to use and apply learning in a range of situations. More often than not it involves learning with and from others, which means that much of learning is an interactive, social process.

A model of learning based on the work of Kolb outlining stages of 'planning', 'doing', 'reviewing' and 'learning' is shown in Figure 4.1.

The learning cycle provided by the model in Figure 4.1 demonstrates a *process* of learning, not just its content. We also have known for some time that learning is not only an intellectual process, it crucially involves the development of personal, emotional and social skills, and its success depends on the feelings, motivation and confidence of the learner.

Schools have a primary task of *enhancing and enriching* learning. By its very nature it is not possible to 'do learning' to someone. This is an important message in an era when teaching as telling, and learning as listening, have been in the ascendancy. Watkins (2001, p. 1), reflecting on this point suggested that:

49

Figure 4.1 A model of the learning process
Source: Watkins et al. (2002, p. 1).

> It's surprising how often talking about learning is hijacked by talking about teaching. Perhaps those of you who have been in teaching over recent years will notice as I have the term 'teaching and learning', which often means 'teaching and teaching', or is said so fast that it sounds like 'fish 'n' chips'. We have to have a clear focus on learning.

Watkins (2003) describes what he terms two further 'space invaders' that can get in the way of learning. The first is the tendency to refer to pupils' learning as their 'work'. This is a popular discourse in most classrooms, which have schemes of '*work*', exhort pupils to get on with their '*work*' and do their home'*work*'. The second is the confusion that currently arises between *performance* and *learning*, which we discuss later in this chapter. We would add that there is also confusion between notions of attainment and learning, which we particularly pick up in Chapter 5 when we look at the role of feedback and assessment.

The review of school effectiveness literature in Chapter 2 leaves us in no doubt that schools can make a difference to pupils' chances as learners. Young people can also learn very successfully when not in school. As we mentioned in Chapter 1, the gap between in-school and out-of-school learning and the connection pupils make between them may indeed be growing wider. Outdated assumptions and beliefs about learning mean schools can limit or even damage learning, adding little value, no value or even conferring negative value by damaging the image of oneself as learner. One of the questions for the next decade of school improvement activity will be to ask, 'How do we evaluate the value we are adding as a school to our pupils' learning?'

We want to assert that learning in the *intelligent school* is a continuous, life-long process, which starts well before its pupils arrive at school and continues each day as they walk out of the door and long after they graduate from school. This has profound implications for the organization of a school and the way it provides a nurturing learning environment. As we have already noted, the responsibility a school has is much wider and more awesome than simply raising standards in national assessments. It can provide the beginning or not of an access to lifelong learning for all its pupils. The belief that *everyone* can learn, including profoundly disabled people, is becoming increasingly accepted now across the globe and is an important theme that is explored later in this chapter. This belief is providing an important new basis for educational practice.

For the purposes of this book we focus on the experience of learning that takes place for pupils in school. At the same time we acknowledge the many other experiences of learning that occur beyond the classroom but can be influenced by an enriching diet and experience inside it. We suggest that such learning often involves an unspoken, unwritten and sometimes unconscious PACT between learner and teacher. We pick up this theme in the next chapter. For school learning to be enhanced, useful and interesting for the learner we argue that the *intelligent school* understands as much as possible about the different factors that can influence a pupil's motivation and ability to learn. In the process of doing this it updates and challenges its assumptions and beliefs about the nature of learning. This involves being:

- knowledgeable about learning;
- knowledgeable about learners;
- knowledgeable about learners' experience of their learning.

Throughout this chapter, we reflect on these three themes, together with some of the implications for teachers in the classroom.

Learning as an active process of making meaning

Learning, like other fields of knowledge in our culture, has its own technical language. This includes terms such as '*meta-learning*' and '*metacognition*'. In this section we examine some of the research and theoretical perspectives that have generated these terms.

Through time there have been many theories developed about learning and some common themes appear in the literature. Carnell and Lodge (2002) identify three different approaches to learning. Reception (or instruction), construction and co-construction. At one extreme is reception; the dictionary definition is at the beginning of this chapter. This is based on a model which views learning as the reception of knowledge, the learner as passive and the learning style as fixed and formal. To caricature this approach the learner is seen as empty or passive and the teacher as the one who is active and responsible for 'filling up' the student's mind.

The passive learner responds to input provided mainly by the teacher on whom she is dependent for her learning. Here learning is a simplistic process that is linear and sequential, and little account is taken of what the learner may bring to the experience in the way of existing knowledge, reflective capability, previous experience of learning and preferred approaches. This is not to discount a need to be taught particular skills, listen to a formal presentation or be trained for particular purposes. These forms of learning and instruction are still relevant in appropriate circumstances.

In the past 20 years there has been a significant shift in our understanding of how learning takes place. As Gipps and MacGilchrist (1999, p. 47) point out: 'Recent work in cognitive and constructivist psychology shows learning in terms of networks with connections in many directions; not as an external map that is transposed directly onto the student's head.'

The construction approach acknowledges and respects learners' engagement in the process of their learning and takes account of the inherent complexity of the process. Learning happens in the process of coming to new understandings in relation to existing knowledge. The research literature suggests that this is an active, collaborative process where learners take responsibility for their learning and also learn about themselves as learners. The constructivist approach acknowledges the importance of an interactive social component in learning, in contrast to the reception model that encourages more solitary learning. Maha, a year 6 pupil illustrates this well:

> I learn best when someone explains it to me, then gives me questions based on it so that I can do it by myself and see how it works. Also, if people give me different ways to solve it, I can do them all and see which one's easiest. This extends my knowledge.

The co-construction model is an extension of the constructivist model. It reflects a view that remains under discussion amongst theorists that learning is more likely to occur through social interaction than just in the mind of the individual. It emphasizes the importance of discussion and dialogue between learners and each other, and between learners and their teachers and other adults. Carnell and Lodge (2002, p. 15) state that: 'Dialogue is more than conversation, it is the building of learner centred narrative, (it) is about building and arriving at a point you would not get to alone.'

Resnick (1987) points out that the dominant form of school learning is individual. She contrasts this with work, personal life and recreation which almost always takes place in social settings. Carnell and Lodge (2002, p. 15) suggest that more school learning should be based on dialogue as: 'It has the power to engage learners in learning conversations, keeps them open to new ideas and requires both honesty and trust.'

Annie in year 7 observes: 'You learn more because if you explain to people what to do, you say things that you wouldn't say to yourself, really. So you learn things that you wouldn't know if you were just doing it by yourself.' Bilal in year 6 agrees: 'I learn best in a group so then I can see the different points of view from different people.'

Learning and performance

The research of developmental psychologist Carol Dweck in the field of motivation and personality is of crucial importance to teachers. Her work challenges the view that learning is the same as performance and suggests that they are two different motivational positions. She suggests that people have beliefs about themselves that give meaning to what they do and how they see their world. For the purposes of classroom learning she has distinguished between pupils who are mastery or learning orientated and those who are orientated to performance. Pupils who are learning orientated are more likely to think about their learning and are less in need of proving that they can succeed in formal testing situations or in competition with others. Pupils who are performance orientated tend to equate their grades with their intelligence and in the face of difficulty have fewer strategies to help them to persist in their learning. They give up easily. This Dweck refers to as a position of helplessness and it too can be learnt!

Dweck's research (1999) challenges beliefs about pupils that are still fairly firmly embedded among educators and also in society more widely. These include:

- students with higher ability are the ones with a learning orientation;
- successful school performance is based on a learning orientation;
- students' sense of their own intelligence will give them a learning orientation;
- students who put effort into their work are less intelligent than those who do not.

Watkins et al. (2002, p. 2) summarize the difference between learning and performance orientations in the following way.

A positive pattern: 'learning orientation'	A negative pattern: 'performance orientation'
• belief that effort leads to success	• belief that ability leads to success
• belief in one's ability to improve and learn	• concern to be judged as able to perform
• preference for challenging tasks	• satisfaction from doing better than others
• personal satisfaction from success at difficult tasks	• emphasis on competition, public evaluation
• problem-solving and self-instructions when engaged in task	• helplessness: evaluate self negatively when task is difficult
concern for *improving* one's competence	concern for *proving* one's competence

We have found in our own work that encouraging practitioners to challenge these fundamental beliefs is a good incentive for discussion and change of practice. In several schools in which we have worked recently, the teachers have found that the pupils who do well in end of key stage assessments do not always have a learning orientation. There is a widespread belief that inspectors are looking only at performance data to make their judgements during school inspections. Our evidence suggests, however, that it is often schools with high standards based on pupils' progress in learning that have the most successful inspections.

Teachers from two Buckinghamshire primary schools working with one of us have been researching the learning orientation of some of their pupils. They wanted to find out why some groups of students were failing to make adequate progress and also had poor attitudes to learning. In one school a group of year 6 boys was invited to share their perceptions of learning and describe how they saw an effective learner. It was discovered that these boys were predominantly performance orientated in their learning. This meant that they had a desire to *prove* rather than *improve* what they were doing at school. In the second school teachers discovered through talking and observation that the pupils with a learning orientation were more likely to like learning and being at school than their performance-orientated peers. They were also more likely to compare themselves with their previous performance rather than compare themselves with each other. They also recognized the need to practise in order to get better. Furthermore, the teachers found that several pupils designated as having special educational needs had a very good learning orientation. The two schools have been carrying out beneficial school improvement strategies with both pupils and staff as a result of these findings. This has resulted in improving the learning and attainment of many more pupils.

Meta-learning

Gipps and Murphy (1994) remind us how important it is that learners have a sense of ownership over what they are learning. They need to feel that what they are being taught is relevant to their purposes for learning. Research indicates that effective learners have a learning rather than performance orientation as we have already noted. They also have more complex views of themselves as learners and greater control of their learning. They can set goals, evaluate what they are doing and monitor their learning.

Watkins et al. (2001) distinguish between 'metacognition' which concerns an awareness of thinking processes together with 'executive control' of such processes and 'meta-learning' which is much broader and includes an awareness of goals, feelings, social relations and the context of learning.

Metacognition refers to a second-order form of thinking: thinking about thinking. It is a process of being aware of and in control of one's own knowledge and thinking and, therefore, learning. There are those who see it as 'the engine of learning' (Marzano, 1998).

Carnell and Lodge (2002, p. 18) describe the broader process of meta-learning as: 'Standing back from the content of the learning and evaluating the effectiveness of the processes involved. The social and emotional processes implied here are broader than just 'thinking about thinking.' Developing a capacity to use meta-learning therefore means learners need opportunities to reflect on:

- their goals for learning;
- the strategies they are using to learn;
- how they are feeling about their learning;
- what the outcomes of their learning are.

We can conceptualize meta-learning as another central component of the learning process as illustrated in Figure 4.2. Learners here are reflecting on the *process* of their learning.

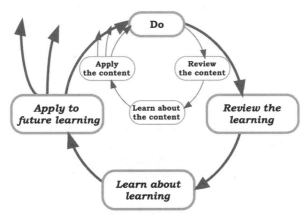

Figure 4.2 An extra cycle in learning about learning
Source: Watkins et al. (2002, p. 6).

Teachers with whom we have been working have been developing successful strategies for enabling pupils to reflect upon and review their learning with each other. Some of the best practice is the use of 'response partners' who discuss their learning with each other and give each other feedback.

The nature of intelligence

Claxton (1999) gives an example from the work of Robert Sternberg et al. (1981) of the unexamined way in which we view intelligence in our culture. Sternberg et al. say:

Suppose that admissions officers to colleges and graduate schools stopped using grade point averages and high scores on IQ-like admission tests to select students, and started using height ... . Under the new system, all the positions in society, which depend on educational success, would soon come to be occupied by taller people. Those at the bottom of the educational, financial and social pile would be shorter. Being tall would come to seem a natural corollary of success, and shortness of failure. As soon as such a society was established, the original arbitrary decision of the admissions officers would come to look like the most natural, obvious, necessary procedure in the world. Because tall people do well, it would be perverse not to select for expensive courses of education and training those people who already have the height qualifications. (Claxton, 1999, p. 30)

In this example, Sternberg and colleagues draw our attention to the arbitrary way in which we define intelligence in both school and society and hence exempt those who on a broader set of indices would be more successful.

Vicky Phillips, a District Superintendent in the USA, suggests that school improvement must be an attempt to build very different types of school communities to those of the past. Schools in these communities are built on a fundamental belief that all students can be successful, overcoming categories of below average, average and above average. The thinking behind the initiatives 'Success for All' and 'No Child Left Behind' in the USA endorses this view.

Our conceptualization of intelligence for the *intelligent school* is that:

- there are many different kinds of intelligence;
- intelligence is not fixed;
- it is possible to learn how to be intelligent and how to live intelligently;
- effort is the basis of intelligent learning.

It is still predominantly the belief in UK culture that intelligence is a fixed commodity; some people have more of it than others. This view can lead to the labelling of pupils based on fixed views of ability particularly in a school system driven by normative assessment results and the publishing of league tables. So, unfortunately, in many schools and classrooms phrases such as 'Well what can you expect from these children?' have not yet totally disappeared from professional vocabulary.

For a long time educators have questioned the value of IQ tests as an adequate measure of intelligence. They are limited because they only test particular abilities such as verbal and non-verbal reasoning, and do so at one point in time. Children labelled 'below average' may well live up to expectations regardless of ability. There are also problems labelling pupils as 'gifted and talented'. For this reason, we are wary of the Gifted and Talented Programme within the Excellence in Cities initiative, whilst in no way wishing to deny that pupils should be given every opportunity to pursue their talents. We believe that all children have talents and therefore we fear that unless this initiative is creatively handled it will merely reinforce the worst prejudices about the nature of intelligence.

Research suggests that intelligence can be expanded through learning in real situations. It can also be enhanced through instruction, self-instruction and experiences that cultivate metacognition. Pupils can be enabled to develop their gifts and talents, particularly if they learn to use effort-based strategies. The implication, as suggested earlier, is that teachers can provide activities that develop and enhance these aspects of intelligence and teach pupils how to develop effort-based learning.

Dweck (1999) suggests that the development of a mastery or learning orientation depends on the way that people understand the nature of their intelligence. She has identified two very different ways that people understand and internalize intelligence. The first is an entity view; the idea that intelligence is something fixed and unchangeable within. For others, intelligence is something that can be developed through learning. This is an 'incremental' view of intelligence and what Claxton means by learning being learnable. Dweck calls this the theory of 'malleable intelligence'.

According to the psychologist, Howard Gardner (1999), all learners have the capacity to develop and extend a number of different aspects of their intelligence. We would caution limiting learners in any way to these and suggest that the following list of Gardner's intelligences are expansive rather than reductive. They are not for either labelling pupils or limiting learning. Believing that all of us have the capacity to develop in all these areas, though some may need more help than others, has an impact on our view of ability and consequently on teaching strategies.

1 Linguistic: the intelligence of words.
2 Logical–mathematical: the intelligence of numbers and reasoning.
3 Spatial: the intelligence of pictures and images
4 Musical: the intelligence of tone, rhythm and timbre.
5 Bodily kinaesthetic: the intelligence of the whole body and the hands.
6 Interpersonal: the intelligence of social understanding.
7 Intrapersonal: the intelligence of self-knowledge.
8 Naturalist: the intelligence of context and environment.
9 Existential: the intelligence of ultimate issues.

The question we should be asking of our pupils is not 'how smart are you?' but 'in what ways are you smart?' (MacBeath, 1997).

Gardner's work has helped educators to see that the content of learning is not just about the types of cognition traditionally associated with school. Goleman (1996) supports this view. He demonstrates the nature and importance of emotional intelligence and the need to become emotionally literate. This means realizing that the mind and the emotions are working in a fruitful partnership when learning is taking place. What Claxton (1999) refers to as drawing on 'the rich mud of someone's experience'. We discuss emotional intelligence in Chapter 7.

Handy (1997, p. 120) argues that: 'Everyone can be assumed to be intelligent, because intelligence comes in many forms.' From his experience of life he makes his own provisional list of 11 intelligences with the proviso that they need not, and usually do not, correlate with each other.

1 Factual intelligence – the facility that 'Mastermind' addicts have developed
2 Analytic intelligence – reasoning and conceptualising
3 Numerate intelligence – being at ease with numbers of all sorts
4 Linguistic intelligence – a facility with language
5 Spatial intelligence – an ability to see patterns in things
6 Athletic intelligence – the skill exemplified by those who excel in sports
7 Intuitive intelligence – an aptitude for sensing and seeing what is not immediately obvious
8 Emotional intelligence – self-awareness and self-control, persistence, zeal and self-motivation
9 Practical intelligence – the ability to recognise what needs to be done and what can be done
10 Interpersonal intelligence – the ability to get things done with and through others
11 Musical intelligence – this one is easy to recognise in opera singers, pianists and pop groups (ibid.).

A combination of the first three intelligences equips us for most tests and examinations. But we are arguing there is more to intelligence than succeeding in formal assessment. From our reading of the literature we have come to see that both Gardner's and Handy's intelligences describe the range of rich and varied outcomes of effective learning. Undoubtedly some of us have both preferences for and elements of aptitude for some aspects of intelligence rather than others. However these are not fixed, they vary at different times of life and can be learnt.

Resnick (1987) identifies a core theory of aptitude underlying most practice in American classrooms. This is generally believed to be hereditary and therefore effort makes no difference to learning; indeed, learning requiring effort could signal that you are not intelligent. Resnick views effort-based learning as the theory replacing aptitude theory. By treating pupils as if they are already smart then they come to believe that they are. They can then be successful. During a recent discussion in a first school Oliver remarked 'If my teacher says that I can do it then I think that I can and then I can!'

Nida, a year 6 pupil in a primary school which has worked really hard at developing a learning orientation in children, sums up effort-based learning rather nicely:

> Learning means that I have put my effort in to do something good and important. When I learn something it makes me feel really proud of myself because I know that I have learnt something new and wonderful. I know that I have learnt something because I haven't done it before, or I haven't done it properly before. I feel that my learning has improved for me because I can set myself goals which helps me to achieve much more, and I can take myself into my visual memory. Knowing that I can learn more makes it more easier not much more harder. It makes it easier because I know that I can do everything if I put a bit of effort into it.

The contribution of neuroscience

Findings from neuroscience are giving us further insights into the nature of learning. While we are still not entirely sure how our brains work, Abbott (1994, p. 63) argues that:

> One major discovery, which has revolutionised the way we think about the brain and how it learns, has been the fact that we know that it has plasticity, which means that the physical structure of the brain actually changes as a result of experience. The brain will change if stimulated through interaction with the environment

and, 'The brain learns when it is trying to make sense; when it is building on what it already knows, when it recognises the significance of what it is doing; when it is working in complex, multiple perspectives' (ibid., p. 73).

Researchers have known for some time that there are 'critical periods' in the development of the brain that require the right kind of stimulation. The work of Marian Diamond (1998) has enabled us to see the importance for brain development of rich, stimulating play environments for young children. She identified several factors in the learning environment that make a difference:

- a steady source of positive emotional support;
- providing a nutritious diet with sufficient protein, vitamins and calories;
- stimulating all the senses (though not all at once);
- an atmosphere free of undue pressure and stress, but with a degree of pleasurable intensity;
- presenting a series of novel challenges that are neither too hard nor too easy;
- encouraging social interaction for a percentage of activities;
- promoting the development of a broad range of skills and interests that are mental, physical, aesthetic, social and emotional;

- encouraging the child to be an active participant rather than a passive observer (ibid., pp. 107–8).

Recent work in the field of neuroscience has also reminded educators of the crucial role that spoken language plays in the cognitive development of pupils at all stages of schooling. Primary practitioners with whom we have been working on school improvement projects with a specific focus on improving learning, have been concerned to ensure that their curriculum is providing sufficient opportunities for speaking and listening alongside the current emphasis on literacy and numeracy. Research in a school one of us is working with has provided evidence to show that a deliberate attempt to enrich young pupils' opportunities for enquiry-based learning through talk and problem-solving has raised standards in both literacy and numeracy. Other schools we know are revisiting the role of drama and role-play in their curriculum for all ages of primary pupils.

The potential of the brain for learning is, in neurological terms, limitless. It is estimated that there are something like 2,000 billion brain cells each of which has tens of millions of possible connectors, or 'hooks', to other brain cells. In other words, there are billions of learning pathways, only a few of which are travelled. The untravelled paths become overgrown and fall into disuse. While this is, in part, a process of ageing, the capacity to learn throughout life, even into old age, depends on knowing how to make use of the brain's untapped potential.

Learning styles

Researchers have also identified different learning styles and these have been of great interest to classroom practitioners. Dryden and Vos (1994) for example, have linked Gardner's work to the way we learn. They believe that each of us has a preferred learning and a preferred working style, and identify at least five style preferences.

Some of us, they suggest, are mainly visual learners: our learning is helped when we see pictures or diagrams. Others learn more by listening or are kinaesthetic learners: we learn best by using our sense of touch or by moving our bodies. Some of us are print orientated: we learn most easily by reading books. Others learn best when interacting with others. They suggest that we can and do use a combination of these strategies to learn, but one approach may be more dominant.

No doubt a contributory factor to some pupils' disaffection at school is that they do not have sufficient opportunity to learn in a way that helps them to access the curriculum. Schools with which we have worked have found that it is useful to be aware of the range of learning styles in their classrooms and, more importantly, for their learners to be aware of these too. Pupils who identify themselves as weak in one or more of the areas need to consider how they develop strategies to be able to learn through these approaches. However, given our argument about both intelligence and learning being learnable, we think these are best treated as a *range of possibilities for enriching learning rather than further fixed views of pupils*. In a culture that is prone to label and categorize we need to be aware of this danger with learning styles.

We prefer to think of different *approaches* to learning. Different learning situations need different approaches. For example, everyone is being given access to becoming a more visual learner in art or when they are out on school trips, whilst physical education (PE) and dance enhance the possibilities for kinaesthetic learning for everyone. Part of this process is selecting the most appropriate approach for the type of learning required. The *intelligent school* enables pupils to maximize the different ways in which they learn and not to be limited by the labels of particular styles of learning.

In this section we have reflected on some current theories and thinking about learning. In the next sections, we consider the nature of the learner herself. We pay attention to individual and group differences and then consider the importance of the perception learners have of themselves.

The nature of learners

Learners come in different shapes and sizes

Some children arrive on their first day of school being able to read. Others do not but will have developed aptitudes in other aspects of the curriculum. Some arrive appropriately dressed, well fed and well cared for. Some are fit and healthy. Some will enjoy sitting down quietly, speaking and listening to each other and the adults in the classroom. Others will prefer to move around boisterously. Different pupils will have had varying opportunities to develop the different intelligences identified by Gardner. The list of potential differences is very long and does not diminish as we get older. The consequence is that all learners will have experienced different learning opportunities and have different learning needs. Some will easily be able to play their part in the learning and teaching PACT (p. 91). Others will need more encouragement. Members of both sexes and all minority ethnic groups will be represented in all these categories.

Girls and boys: some differences

There has been considerable concern recently about the underachievement of boys. As always it is important to look beyond the headlines and ask further questions. Which boys should we be concerned about (some of them are actually doing very well)? What about the girls (some of them are not doing very well)? Class, race and gender are inevitably interrelated and it is very difficult to disentangle the individual effect. For example, when we focus on the achievement of Afro-Caribbean boys we need to consider race *and* gender *and* class issues.

We know that boys and girls can be socialized into different habits and that over a period of time there has been a change in their achievement patterns. For example, before 1988 (and before the compulsory National Curriculum) more boys than girls studied physics and chemistry subjects up to the age of 16. Current statistics show that entries and achievements are broadly even. This would indicate that whatever biological, physiological and genetic differences exist between girls and boys (and the jury is still out on what exactly these differences are) there are other factors at play. It is also important to remember that whatever the findings for the 'average' male or 'average' female there will be huge variations from the mean. So, for example, the average male is taller than the average female. However, the range between the tallest man and the smallest is greater than the difference between the average male and female. The implications for the classroom are that not everyone conforms to expectations and we need to look beyond the stereotype when addressing issues of equity.

Several researchers have argued that males and females tend to respond differently to the same stimuli or situation. Gilligan (1982), for example, demonstrated how girls tend to consider contexts and analyse the 'whys and wherefores' before making a judgement about a moral dilemma, whereas boys are more likely to create and stick to rules when deciding their opinion. It is important to note that Gilligan does not suggest that girls and boys have different abilities, but that they have different ways of using their abilities: that is, different cognitive styles. (See Figure 4.3.)

Calibration, which means making sense of new knowledge, may be very different for males and females as well as for people from different cultures. While there are conflicting theories about why these differences occur there is some evidence that females are more field dependent than males (although there is also criticism of the methodology used in some of the research which demonstrates this). Field-dependent learners are interested in the context and relevance of the issue being discussed. Field-independent learners are interested in concepts for their own sake.

Murphy (1988, p. 169), for example, argues that:

> Typically girls tend to value the circumstances in which activities are presented and consider that it gives meaning to the issues to be addressed. They do not, therefore, abstract the issues but consider them in relation to the content, which then becomes part of the whole problem. Boys as a group, conversely, do consider the issues in isolation judging the context and the content of the activity to be idiosyncratic.

Figure 4.3 Helen Cusack in Myers (1992, p. 133)
Reprinted by permission of Helen Cusack.

Murphy (1988) gives several examples of this phenomenon. One is when primary and secondary age pupils were asked to design a vehicle and a boat to go round the world. As can be seen, the girls and boys in this example had very different perceptions of the same problem:

> The boys' designs were army-type vehicles, sports cars, powerboats or battleships. The detail the boys included varied except the majority had elaborate weaponry and next to no living facilities … . The girls' boats were generally cruisers, the vehicles family transport, agricultural machines or children's play vehicles. There was a total absence of weaponry in the girls' designs and a great deal of detail about living quarters and requirements, including food supplies and cleaning materials (notably absent in the boys' designs). (Ibid., p. 170)

Head (1996) points out that on occasions a field-dependent approach is advantageous and on others a field-independent approach is more appropriate. It is not suggested, therefore, that either way of responding is superior to the other. They are both valuable and sometimes one is preferable in a particular situation. Head (1996, p. 62) argues therefore that:

Field dependence and independence can be seen as value-free terms. In some contexts, for example locating which component of a car engine is malfunctioning, the extraction mode of thinking is needed. In other contexts, for example in environmental biology, the embedding mode is better, as we would need to consider how a change in one part of the eco-system affects other parts.

Learners need to develop both ways of responding. Gipps and Murphy (1994) make the point that those who set and mark test papers need to be aware of the different ways in which pupils could respond to the same question.

Some research by Daniels et al. (1996) focuses on special needs in primary classrooms. It demonstrates how much girls help each other to learn and how much more they do this than boys. The researchers speculate that this may have at least three important consequences. First, it may help reduce the number of girls needing extra support because they can get it from their peers. Second, the support given is likely to be appropriate because the peers know exactly what type of 'scaffold' is needed. And, third, the person giving the support can embed her own learning through the process of teaching someone else. She has extended opportunities to calibrate the information she is passing on.

Boys seem to be more motivated by competition with each other whereas research has found that girls prefer to work in co-operation with each other. Head (1996, p. 64) illustrates this point: 'If two girls are asked to co-operate in painting a picture together they negotiate an agreed plan. Under similar circumstances two boys may simply draw a line down the paper so each has half the page to complete and they then work quite independently.'

Cultural differences depending on ethnicity, country of upbringing and class will interplay with gender differences. So, for example, an upper-class Asian boy reared in Pakistan is likely to perceive the world differently from a working-class Asian boy whose upbringing has been in Tower Hamlets – though they will have race and gender in common. However, Head (1996, pp. 66–7) argues that:

> The distribution of gendered roles in the work place shows broad similarities across many cultures. Although there may be regional variations in social practices in detail nevertheless there are enough underlying structural similarities for the explanatory models to have widespread credence. We might therefore expect both gender identities and preferences in cognitive and learning styles to be broadly similar in most cultures.

Head (1996, p. 68) states that the implication of all this for teachers is that if girls and boys:

> prefer different learning procedures then teachers should be flexible in their choice of teaching and assessment methods. But these gender differences are not absolute, there is considerable overlap between the two sexes and considerable

variation within one group. A flexible approach to pedagogy should therefore be of general benefit to the school population.

Pupils' experience of their learning and the role of their teachers

One of the goals of the work of ISEIC at the Institute of Education has been to re-engage with learners and learning rather than to improve teaching in isolation. This gives a powerful impetus to classroom-based improvement and has the benefit of involving the pupils in the process.

We begin to do this in five different but related ways:

- listening to pupils;
- noting and respecting their perspectives;
- giving their perspectives significance;
- reflecting on the meaning and implications we find;
- taking account of these in further research and action.

Surprising things come to the surface when we do this. Particularly, we learn how articulate and in touch even the youngest pupils can be when they are given time to talk about their learning and their experience of it at school. When asked what the word 'learning' means to them, primary-aged pupils replied: 'trying to achieve something you do not already know'; 'to be taught something and remember it'; 'when you have done something and know it well enough to do it again'; 'working hard'; and 'what the teacher tells you'. It is possible to discern in what they say that they also share the range of conceptions of learning that have been described earlier in this chapter.

Similar responses occur in relation to the question 'What makes a good learner?': 'listen to your teacher'; 'don't be afraid to ask for help'; 'have a go is better'.

We all had teachers that we recall because we remember learning with them. One of us was a head of house, advising year 9 pupils about their option choice, and remembers they would frequently want to pursue a subject because they liked the teacher who was teaching them that subject. The school 'line' was that that was not a sensible or mature way to choose subjects to take to examination level. Choices should be made on rational grounds based on future career ambitions rather than emotional and subjective feelings. Although she endorsed the pursuit of 'balance' and widening pupils' aspirations she always harboured feelings that choices based on teachers rather than subject content were actually just as sensible and rational (Myers, 1980).

As adult learners, the three of us know that we learn better, whatever the topic, if we find the teacher empathetic, interesting and inspiring. We like the teacher to explain the topic well, not to make us feel stupid when we do not understand immediately, and to treat us as someone who may have something interesting to say. We like to be stretched and challenged but also to be allowed to challenge conventional wisdom. We suspect that we are not alone here and that these preferences are common to all ages and stages of learning.

A few years ago, one of us informally interviewed secondary pupils in a number of schools about their views on their education. Their answers to questions about how they learn were almost always the same, whatever their age. They said they learn best with teachers who:

- explain things well;
- listen to them and are concerned about them as an individual;
- show them how to get better;
- keep control of the class;
- have a sense of humour.

In response to a question in a survey asking pupils in one secondary school to describe a good teacher the following were typical responses. A good teacher is someone:

- who helps you do your work;
- who can control the class;
- who listens to me;
- you can talk to and ask them when you are worried or stuck;
- who helps you and teaches you something;
- who is good with kids, can control kids, who knows what they are doing;
- who has a laugh but gets some hard work done.

A year 10 pupil summed up the general feeling: 'A good teacher is someone who, if you don't understand the work, explains it to you patiently. Isn't too strict but when pupils are being pathetic, can control them, and you can talk to and have a laugh with him/her' (Myers, 1996a).

Rudduck, Chaplain and Wallace (1996) have emphasized the importance of asking the learner about her/his needs. They tracked pupils during their last four years of secondary schooling. They claim that although the pupils were very appreciative of the support and time they received from their teachers, they felt that the *conditions of learning* they were subjected to did not adequately take account of their social maturity: 'nor of the tensions and pressures they feel as they struggle to reconcile the demands of their social and personal lives with the development of their identity as learners' (Rudduck, Chaplain and Wallace p. 1). The authors consequently suggest six principles that would make a significant difference to learning. They acknowledge that the conditions are not new and that many schools will have already incorporated them in their practice. However, the importance of these principles, outlined below, is that they are presented from the pupils' perspective; not what we think is good for them, but what they think is good for themselves.

1 Respect for pupils as individuals and as a body occupying a significant position in the institution of the school.
2 Fairness to all pupils irrespective of their class, gender, ethnicity or academic status.
3 Autonomy – not as an absolute state but as both a right and a responsibility in relation to physical and social maturity.
4 Intellectual challenge that helps pupils to experience learning as a dynamic, engaging and empowering activity.
5 Social support in relation to both academic and emotional concerns.
6 Security in relation to both the physical setting of the school and in interpersonal encounters (including anxiety about threats to pupils' self-esteem) (Rudduck, Chaplain and Wallace, 1996, p. 174).

To create appropriate conditions of learning, the authors suggest that we need to consider organizational structures and pupil–teacher relationships. They also argue that in addition: 'pupils need to have a sense of themselves as a learner; status in the school; an overall purpose in learning; control over their own lives; and a sense of their future' (ibid., p. 174).

Rudduck and Flutter (2002) suggest that involving pupils in their learning can help them develop a stronger sense of membership of the organization and a feeling of belonging to it. This is particularly relevant for young people who feel marginalized. They recommend that schools bide by the following principles when consulting pupils:

- that the desire to hear what young people have to say is genuine;
- that the topic is not trivial;
- that the purpose of the consultation is explained to the young people;
- that young people know what will happen to the data and are confident that expressing a sincerely held opinion or describing a feeling or an experience, will not disadvantage them;
- that feedback is offered to those who have been consulted;
- that action taken is explained and where necessary justified so that young people understand the wider context of concerns, alongside their own input, that shape decisions (ibid., p. 3).

Consultation can be about relationships between teachers, pupils and the community, for example what happens about racism, school-level issues such as rewards and sanctions, or at classroom level about learning. Rudduck and Flutter suggest that schools wanting to consult pupils about their learning may wish to raise the following questions with pupils:

- What gets in the way of learning in class and what helps learning?
- What are the qualities of a good teacher?

67

- What makes a good lesson?
- How can feedback be used to improve work?
- Which friends do you work best with and is that different for different subjects?
- Why do boys do less well than girls and vice versa in different subjects?
- What could be done about this? (ibid., p. 3).

Consulting pupils is not always easy and on occasions the messages from pupils may be sensitive to manage. Nevertheless, their feedback is an essential part of school self-evaluation.

The physical, emotional and social environment of school

A perennial topic that is raised when pupils are asked about their school is the state of the toilets. This is not a trivial topic and their condition gives pupils important messages about what the institution feels about them. Appropriate, attractive and well cared for physical conditions support and facilitate learning. The *intelligent school* understands that an attractive, welcoming, comfortable and safe environment, with access to adequate appropriate resources, enables learning to take place and we refer to this again in Chapter 8. Schools that take these requirements seriously will take account of individual circumstances by, for example, considering what is 'safe' for pupils who are racially harassed on their way to and from school, how people whose first language is not English may be encouraged to feel welcome, and how pupils who do not have access to the latest technology at home can have this opportunity during and outside school hours. We can learn in different conditions (and in some parts of the world students have to), but it is much easier to do so when conditions help, rather than hinder, learning. External physical conditions can aid learning but learners also have internal requirements. For example, we are likely to be more responsive to learning if we are not hungry and not cold. Some learners are 'morning people' and some prefer to work late at night (the latter being difficult to cater for in schools that are open 9.00 a.m. to 4.00 pm.). In addition, we have emotional and social needs and preferences: 'Emotion plays a vital part in learning. It is in many ways the key to the brain's memory system. And the emotional content of any presentation can play a big part in how readily learners absorb information and ideas' (Dryden and Vos, 1994, p. 351).

Some learners respond well to a competitive classroom environment, others do not. Some learners prefer to learn on their own and others learn best by working with other people. This preference may have as much to do with the task in hand as with the favoured learning need. Some learners prefer to work in peace and quiet, others like background noise such as music and others like to work in the midst of hustle and bustle. One of our colleagues who has her own office chooses to write her academic papers in the midst of the comings and goings of the secretaries' office. When questioned about this she explains that she cannot work in silence.

Schools may find it difficult to respond to these varied preferences but during the course of the day or the week it should be possible to ensure that learners experience a range of conditions, some of which will suit them more than others.

Conclusion

In this chapter we have reflected on thinking and research about learning, stressed that learners have different learning needs and discussed what learners say they want from their teachers and schools. We have suggested that learning involves a PACT. This PACT is between the learner and whoever the learner is interacting with. We develop this idea further in the next chapter.

In summary, the *intelligent school* is up to date with recent literature about learning and knows how to create contexts for learning. It understands how to motivate and inspire its learners and how to encourage them to participate in learning. Its goals are to help the learner understand how to learn and to *believe that it is possible* to do so. It knows that learners need to make sense of what is being learnt. This will be dependent on many factors such as the learner's prior experiences, her self-esteem, her heritage, her attitude to learning and her attitude to what is being taught. It will also be dependent *on the way* she is being taught. This part of the process has traditionally been in the control of the teacher. Increasingly we are seeing the importance of teaching being much more open to feedback from learners. The teachers themselves need to be learners as well as being knowledgeable about what they are teaching. Their side of the PACT is to be aware of these factors, in order to be able to assess what is needed and to provide the appropriate conditions for learners to continue to develop their learning orientation and love of learning. The following chapter looks at the implications of this for teaching.

Questions for discussion

1 Think of something you have enjoyed learning recently. What were the factors that made your learning work well for you? What did you do?
2 What are the implications of the section on recent research and thinking about learning for your classroom practice? What are the implications for those with leadership responsibilities?
3 In what ways do you prefer to learn? What are the ways you need to develop your orientation to learning? How does this influence your approach to teaching?
4 Do the girls in your classes support each other in different ways from the

boys? If so, does this matter? Can you/should you do anything about it?

5 Ask your pupils what helps their learning. Do their answers surprise you? Do they differ depending on their age or ability (or some other variable such as sex) or is there considerable consensus?

6 Are your approaches to teaching appropriate for your pupils' learning needs? How do you know?

5
Teaching for learning

How much are you prepared to risk of what is familiar, comfortable, safe, and perhaps working well for you, in the name of better education for others? (Roland Barth, 2001, p. 186)

It was easy to show teachers that pupils are constructivist learners. It is another thing entirely to arrange the practical consequences of this for teaching. (Desforges, 2000, p. 8)

The previous chapter discussed learning, learners and learners' perceptions of their learning. This chapter explores the nature of teaching and its relationship with learning. We discuss how *intelligent schools* conceptualize the goals and processes of teaching, the role of the teacher and what they can do to support the development of teaching that will promote effective learning.

There are many interesting aspects to effective teaching. Some of these are connected with teachers' own histories and biographies. We also know that the particular context in which teachers find themselves influences the effectiveness of their practice. Studies have shown that the range of practices between classrooms within the same school can be greater than the differences between schools (Mortimore et al., 1988). In this chapter, however, we focus particularly on the craft of the classroom and what it is that teachers can do there to enable learning to be enriched and effective. The chapter identifies the main features of teaching for learning in order to help readers reflect on the relationship that these have with each other and with learning. We hope in the process to contribute some new insights into the nature of 'craft' knowledge that forms the basis of teaching and specifically supports learning.

Roland Barth (2001, p. 57) usefully clarifies the nature of craft knowledge:

> Telling our war stories was therapeutic, we found a way of cleansing the experience of the week from our lives so we could go home and begin a restorative weekend with our families. Craft knowledge in contrast is something much more than the telling of war stories. It is a description of practice accompanied by an intentional *analysis* of practice.

Teaching and learning

Teaching rather than learning has been the main focus of reform efforts in recent years in the UK. There has been an assumption that teaching will automatically lead to learning and that improving the effectiveness of teachers is the answer to raising standards. The importance of the process of learning has been sidelined. As one pupil remarked to a colleague recently, 'Never mind my attainment, what about my learning?'

Patricia Broadfoot (1998, p. 4) writing in the *Independent* commented:

> And yet it may well be that the mighty edifice of policy initiatives that have been constructed to underpin the process of raising standards in the end achieves little because it has not addressed the one issue that must be central to raising standards – learning. Learning that is, not teaching. Surprisingly, while issues concerning teaching quality and styles have received considerable attention in recent policy debates, learning and the factors that affect it have hardly been addressed.

Popular and polarized views about what constitutes 'good' and 'bad' teaching have abounded. Chris Woodhead, a former Chief Inspector of Schools, contributed to the debate when he suggested, on numerous occasions, that teachers who teach children to read are more important than those who exhibit the characteristics of reflective practitioners.

Discussions about teaching have often been characterized either by opinion or by traditional views of what makes a good teacher rather than by an awareness of what we are beginning to know about the interdependence teaching has with learning. As we saw in the previous chapter, there are new theories and insights into human growth, development and learning that educators need to take into account. There is a growing awareness, too, of the importance of paying attention to the pupils' perceptions of their teachers, their lessons and their learning. Each of these has implications for the design and planning of teaching. We know now that there is no single, simple way to teach because there is no simple way to learn and the teacher's task in the twenty-first century classroom is becoming increasingly complex and sophisticated. Too much of the discussion in the past has tended to focus on *styles* of teaching rather than its purpose.

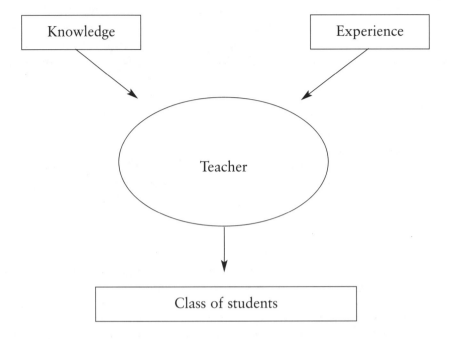

Figure 5.1 The teaching-centred model of schooling in the oral tradition
Source: Branson, 1998 p. 126.

In our view *teaching is the responsibility that schools have for ensuring that pupils are learning about their world, each other, themselves and their learning.* Paul Hirst (1974, p. 105) 30 years ago asserted that: 'The intention of all teaching activities is that of bringing about learning.' He went on to say that this is a simple but crucial idea: 'It involves the claim that the concept of teaching is in fact totally unintelligible without a grasp of the concept of learning' (ibid.).

Branson (1998) suggests that teaching as we know it predates the current knowledge base about learning. He argues that the models of teaching on which our schools are based do not include valid principles of learning. He describes a model of teaching (Figure 5.1) which he terms the 'teaching-centred' model.

He argues that this is the predominant model used in schools in the USA. We would suggest that this model has also been promoted in the UK until recently. He argues that this model has reached the upper limit of what it can achieve and that learning-centred classrooms are capable of achieving much more in terms of student outcomes.

We want to clarify here what we mean by learning-centred classrooms. Sometimes when we are working with colleagues we are told that schools used to be more learning centred or that this was the philosophy advocated post-Plowden Report of the late 1960s. Our response is that the shift from teaching to learning centredness is really only just beginning now and that many schools have through time been *pupil centred* in their approaches and some may have indeed been *learner centred*. However, the notion of learning centredness, where the whole organization has practices and procedures that focus on learning for everyone should, we suggest, be the next phase and focus of school improvement.

Watkins and Mortimore (1999) note that the term 'pedagogy' derives from the Greek and that one of its meanings is an adult having oversight of a child. They too identify the craft dimension of pedagogy and its role in enabling learning: 'Thus the basic premise from which we wish to begin our definition is: "any conscious activity designed to enhance learning in another"' (ibid., p. 3).

But what kind of learning? Roland Barth (2001, p. 54) identifies the limits of much of school learning when discussing approaches that are teaching centred:

> Schools define learning in a limiting, circumscribed, and debilitating manner. 'Legitimate learning' in schools occurs when a student sits at a desk, receives instruction from the teacher, participates in discussions led by the teacher, fills out worksheets of problems devised by the teacher, writes papers required and graded by the teacher, and takes tests, usually constructed and corrected by the teacher. If this is what learning is all about no wonder students burn their books and drop out as learners as soon as they get the chance.

The model of teaching described by Barth is one of transmission rather than construction or co-construction as outlined in the previous chapter. In that chapter we described how recent understanding about learning suggests that successful learners are active, collaborative, reflective and learn about learning. There is often confusion here: this does not mean that the teacher never engages in didactic teaching or instruction, far from it! It means that transmission is not her only way of engaging with the learners and learning or her mental model of how teaching works.

In this chapter we will explore the implications for teaching of more constructive and co-constructive approaches to learning. We propose that the *intelligent school*'s primary task (and not just the task of the classroom teacher but of the whole organization) is to design approaches to teaching which enable these features of learning to occur.

One way to think about teaching for learning is to understand it *relationally*: it is the skills, knowledge and understanding in the mind of the teacher that interact with skills, knowledge and understanding in the minds of pupils. Teaching and learning are like a good relationship; they have their separate and different identities, they have different purposes, and they are also composed of differing elements and technologies but depend for their success and well-being on the way they relate to each other and work together. To add to the complexity of the enterprise, the teacher may be learning, or the pupils teaching, at any one time. They are not role bound.

The features of teaching for learning

From the literature and from our experience of working in and with schools we suggest that there are four main aspects to teaching for learning:

- subject knowledge and making it accessible;
- knowledge of who the pupils are and how they learn;
- facilitating the process of learning and teaching;
- managing the process of teaching for learning.

Each involves knowledge, understanding and skill, and each is dependent for its success on the other three. We now consider these aspects in turn.

Subject knowledge and making it accessible

Knowledge and understanding of the National Curriculum will for some time be a basic requirement for teaching in English schools. Teaching for learning, however, requires more than that. Primary teachers need a grasp of subjects across the key stages if progression and continuity are to be handled appropriately. How the Foundation Stage flows into Key Stage 1 and how aspects of the Key Stage 1 curriculum may still be needed in the early stages of year 3 is an essential skill. As well as requiring subject knowledge in the appropriate key stage, primary teachers need a 'map' of how the subjects fit together in order to achieve balance and avoid overload. More recently they have also needed to be able to incorporate the literacy and numeracy strategies into their curriculum planning.

Secondary teachers need to know where their subject fits into or alongside other subject areas. For example, a mathematics department needs to know how the geographers are teaching data handling and statistics, and it helps an art department to know how the historians refer to the painters in the period being studied. Secondary teachers can also be supported by drawing on and making connections with the content of lessons that pupils are studying both before and after their own lessons. The literacy and numeracy strategies are beginning to require a knowledge of how they can be developed across other subjects: the writing of stories in history, the statistics and numeracy of geography and science. Effective curriculum planning and design is still an essential component of effective teaching, although often overlooked with a curriculum that is mostly prescribed.

Over 40 years ago Bruner (1960, p. 31) argued for a focus on what he then termed 'fundamentals': 'The curriculum of a subject should be determined by the most fundamental understanding that can be achieved of the underlying principles that give structure to that subject.' Preston Feden (1994, p. 20, emphasis added) agrees with this:

> Because truly useful understanding takes time to develop, it is usually not possible for teachers to cover as much curriculum, or as many topics, as they typically attempt ... the point is to lead pupils to a deep understanding of what is covered. Lessons and units of study designed around *core concepts* are more likely to produce conceptual change that moves learners along from novice to expert in subject matter content.

Teaching for understanding is a crucial responsibility. A central task is being able to relate to subject matter in ways that enables genuine understanding and enriched learning. The curriculum needs to be planned in a way that achieves richer learning experiences for the pupils. Such planning needs to ensure that there are different types of experience to enable learning across the curriculum. A recent discussion with primary teachers enabled one of us to make explicit links to designing an inclusive curriculum when one of them said 'every child in this class has a right to access what we are doing'. This is one of the values underpinning teaching for learning. Access for all learners to the curriculum becomes a primary concern.

Effective teaching is characterized by the teacher's ability to plan and facilitate learning experiences in a way that builds on and engages pupils' prior knowledge as well as current experience, both in particular subjects and across the curriculum. 'To prompt learning, you've got to begin with the process of going from inside to outside. The first influence on new learning is not what teachers do pedagogically but the learning that is already inside their heads' (Gagnon 2001, p. 51).

Planning around key themes, skills and concepts can reduce the sense of overload that still pervades the teaching of the National Curriculum. It can encourage greater understanding for pupils and enable them to relate more consciously to their prior learning. It can also enable them to learn about themselves as learners in the process.

In order that pupils can benefit from opportunities to construct and co-construct their learning, they need to develop the skills of carrying out a process of enquiry, whether into a subject topic or the process of learning itself. Pupils not only need to know where to find appropriate information but how to extract, interpret and make sense and use of it. Using and applying what is being learnt in one context to another is one of the characteristics of an effective learner. Learning how to conduct an enquiry involves handling information across the curriculum and across the key stages. Higher-order reading skills, the skill of writing information in the pupil's own words, structuring arguments and asking deeper questions can then all be used in the process of enquiry. This is at the heart of academic study as well as the learning process.

Subject-focused enquiry that enables effective learning may happen in groups or with individual students working on their own. It has sometimes been seen as an alternative to instruction by the teacher, rather than the practice and exploration that pupils need in studying and applying their learning. Rigour has often been lacking in the structuring and teaching of the enquiry process. As a result, the debates about teaching have been rightly critical of classroom activity that has been undemanding and, at times, merely successful in keeping pupils occupied. A recent classroom visit by one of us involved watching a lesson about Shakespeare's England with year 6 pupils. The pupils were involved in multiple tasks each with a different 'subject' focus in order to enrich their learning about this history/literacy lesson. Not only were they able to talk about why they were doing what they were doing, but they also knew how it was helping their learning.

Knowledge of who the pupils are and how they learn

Essential to teaching for learning is the process of enabling pupils to become learners. This means encouraging and equipping them to find out, inquire and develop as a learner whatever the subject matter in hand. Bruner (1996) reminds us that teaching is traditionally based on notions of how the learner's mind works. He identifies a range of what he terms 'folk pedagogies' in the teaching profession and argues that surfacing and examining the tacit beliefs that teachers have about how learning happens is a key to the improvement of teaching. He outlines four main models of how teachers see learners that influence their teaching.

1 Seeing children as imitative learners

This model is based on the view that pupils need to be shown what to do and learn by imitation. This is the basis of apprenticeship and is the 'how to' approach to learning. Whilst essential for some skill-based learning, it does not enable pupils to learn the conceptual underpinnings to more complex forms of understanding and knowing, and thus has a limited place in the teaching repertoire.

2 Seeing children as learning from didactic exposure

There is no doubt that didactic teaching, as part of a repertoire of strategies that operates within a belief system that everyone can learn, has a role to play in the *intelligent school*. This is different to the sole use of a transmission approach, where knowledge is seen as fixed and separate from the learner. This approach is not sufficient for pupils to retain their learning in order then to be able to apply the knowledge they have gained. The difficulty also with the mindset behind this model is that it rests on the assumption that new knowledge is acquired by using mental abilities which pupils either have or have not. What is to be learnt is specified and then assessed. Teaching in this model is not a dialogue 'but a telling by one to the other' (Bruner, 1996, p. 56). In one of our recent projects primary teachers have been investigating their teaching by finding out Key Stage 1 pupils' beliefs about what their teachers expect of them as learners. One colleague in the project has concluded that the children in her class expect to be taught passively what to do and then go and practise it. They do not expect to use their teacher or each other in any way as a resource to further their learning. This is the model of teaching that they have internalized even by age 7. It has challenged the school to try to unpick how they have developed that understanding and what they can do to remedy it.

3 Seeing children as thinkers

Bruner refers to this as the development of intersubjective exchange, a 'pedagogy of mutuality' and there is a direct parallel with the view of learning as co-construction referred to in Chapter 4. The teacher in this model is concerned and interested to know what pupils think and how they think. Understanding is developed through discussion, collaboration and learning about learning. Howard Gardner (1993, p. 253) echoes this when he writes that 'we must place ourselves inside the heads of our students and try to understand as far as possible the sources and strengths of their conceptions'.

4 Seeing children as knowledgeable

Bruner's fourth model of teaching is one that enables pupils to distinguish between personal and canonical knowledge; relating one's own experience and beliefs to knowledge that has a history and that stands the test of time. This approach sees pupils as already knowledgeable and becoming more so through their encounter with ideas, stories and theories that are to be interpreted and understood in relation to their own experience. The year 6 classroom described earlier was very much engaged with these beliefs.

Summing up the four approaches Bruner (1996, p. 65) writes:

Nobody can sensibly propose that skills and cultivated abilities are unimportant. Nor can they argue that the accumulation of factual knowledge is trivial. No sensible critic would ever claim that children should not become aware that knowledge is dependent upon perspective and that we share and negotiate our perspectives in the knowledge seeking process. And it would take a bigot to deny that we become the richer for recognising the link between reliable knowledge from the past and what we learn in the present. What is needed is that the four perspectives be fused into some congruent unity, recognised as parts of a common continent.

Effective teachers can do just that. They know which approach to use depending on the task in hand. They enable their pupils to know what strategies will be needed for that task. The learning process will vary depending on what is to be learnt, by whom and how. It will also depend on the ages of the pupils and their particular stages of development. Experience and research about teaching, together with what we now know about learning, mean that the *learning to be undertaken* rather than our personal preferences as teachers, needs to underpin choices about teaching processes. This is also a challenge to fixed views about teaching styles.

An ISEIC project invited pupils to tell us what their teacher does that helps them learn and what does not help. Pupils from ten primary schools in Dorset reported that teachers who help learning:

- explain things more deeply;
- are not too quick and not too slow;
- do not ignore you;
- give you choices;
- give you ways of remembering things.

And those who do not help learning:

- shout;
- make you sit still for too long;
- give us too much stuff to do;
- speak too fast;
- do not trust you.

When collecting pupils' views about their teachers we have been surprised by how sharp even the youngest pupils can be about what helps and hinders learning and what a good starting point their perceptions are for improving the matches and mismatches in the learning teaching relationship.

Facilitating the process of learning and teaching

The design of learning

Teachers' knowledge about learners and their learning is central to the successful design of learning. The challenge, as Schulman (1987) suggests, is that effective teaching requires subject knowledge to be translated into plans for learning that respond to the pupils and engage them in the process. We know from our knowledge about learning that subject expertise is in itself not enough. Teachers also have to be skilled in designing learning experiences, activities and opportunities for and with pupils.

We have identified four main design components for the learning-centred classroom:

- learning goals linked to prior learning;
- structuring for learning;
- organizing for learning;
- using assessment for learning.

We look at each of these in turn.

Learning goals linked to prior learning

Learning goals are like route planners for a journey. We need to know something about the direction we are going in, the kind of terrain we are likely to cover and how long it might take, in order to make decisions about the equipment and the necessary prior skills and knowledge we need. We have to go through this process to discover the best way to get there. We will not know whether we have arrived even approximately near to our destination without them. We know from the research literature that effective learners need to have the 'big picture' of goals explicitly stated for their learning. The *intelligent school* also knows that pupils need to be able to articulate the purposes of their learning and the ways in which they will achieve these. They need to have some control over the goals rather than second guessing what is in their teacher's head.

So both the teacher and the pupils need to be clear what the particular goals are for a lesson or series of activities. This does not mean that each individual learning activity will always have distinct goals. What it does mean is that activities are taking place in a framework that has purpose and direction that pupils can understand. The goals can be drawn from different aspects of the learning in progress: social and cross-curricular as well as related to the subject. The goals can be identified together with the pupils and mapped into learning plans or schemes for learning. Pupils who were interviewed for an annual school improvement plan review said that 'when the teacher explains what we are learning' and 'when I understand what I am doing' they feel that they can learn well.

The discussion about learning goals has sometimes been confused with discussions about attainment outcomes. Here the term 'learning goals' is used rather than 'learning outcomes' because it is not possible to know precise outcomes for pupils for each individual lesson. There have been many critiques of behavioural objectives in the educational literature, for example, Eisner (1985). However, there is a responsibility to know what the learning outcomes, or achievements are as they emerge to get a sense of what is being learnt by both individual pupils and the class as a whole.

There is also a responsibility within teaching for learning to ensure that the pupils' previous learning is drawn on when current learning goals are being identified. This is often interpreted as an issue about individualizing planning, a daunting prospect given the size of classes and the range of needs the average teacher often faces. If learning goals are seen, however, as something that each pupil has within the overall plan for learning and that they can increasingly set for themselves as they learn how to do so, then this engages them in a crucial learning skill. A learning goal is also perhaps more sensible than a target which suggests a preplanned end point rather than a goal which may change or develop on the way. Teaching for learning has the end in mind, but realizes that it may look different when they and the pupils get there and other goals will have emerged on the way!

Teaching for learning ensures, as we have already noted, that learning plans are inclusive and enable everyone in the class to learn and make progress. The research literature suggests that the pupils' prior experience needs to be related to their current learning activities if there is to be a significant impact on their achievement (Bennett et al., 1984; Galton, 1980; 1989). The challenge is to find ways to enable the pupils to have access to learning whilst maintaining their entitlement to the programmes of study to be covered. Gagnon (2001, p. 52) describes this aspect of constructivist teaching as 'the bridge': 'Traditionally, the opening activity, was designed to set up a lesson, not to find out about prior knowledge. The bridge must link existing student knowledge to new learning. The design of a bridge will determine the quality of the new learning, so it must be thoughtfully planned and documented.'

Gagnon identifies the characteristics of 'the bridge' as the following:

- it surfaces students' prior knowledge;
- it refocuses students;
- it organizes students into collaborative groups;
- it builds community between students;
- it creates a shared understanding and vocabulary;
- it gathers information about what each student knows (ibid., pp. 52–3).

Research studies have demonstrated that teachers too rarely provide children with goals and tasks which are genuinely demanding and open ended. Teachers have been observed spending on average only 2 per cent of classroom time on questions regarded as offering challenge. A year 1 teacher working with us on a learning project in Swansea was concerned to know why her pupils were not asking questions in lessons. On researching this more closely she asked them about their understandings of the importance of questions. She found that the pupils saw questions as an interruption to teaching and did not see that they had a valuable role to play in their learning. When asked

81

'When is it not a good time to ask me a question?' Imogen replied firmly 'In lesson time!' This led the teacher concerned to design a classroom improvement project where the pupils had a clear idea of the use and importance of questions to their learning. This understanding had to be taught.

Structuring for learning

Teaching for learning requires thought to be put into the design of the *structure* of a lesson, activity or series of lessons. Structure has been a particular and important feature of the literacy and numeracy strategies which provide a uniform approach that everyone is required to follow, for example the use of very deliberate introductory and concluding activities. That is not what we mean here. The *intelligent school* uses the notion of structure to facilitate learning. This is achieved by a combination of careful planning and a range of different processes in the classroom that support learning. Some of these processes are derived from the subject material; for example, the teaching of a chronological series of events, the different stages in a science experiment, the cooking of a cake. Others relate more to the process of the learning itself; for example, the need for pupils to have time to reflect on their learning and discuss it with each other. Structure is the way in which the learning experience is thought about in advance as well as at the time, so that it can be a coherent, interesting and accessible experience.

The form of the lesson or activity, whole-class teaching, group or individual work, needs to be thought about. Effective sessions in the classrooms of the *intelligent school* are usually a healthy mixture of the three. A review of effective teaching reinforced this point and identified, as we have already done, a wide teaching repertoire as an essential classroom condition (Mortimore, 1999). What is important is that there is a structured approach with clear reasons for the choice of structure, matched to the learning goals for a particular series of activities. It is not essential that this happens every lesson as sometimes there will be a good reason to start an activity without an introduction, or to end a lesson with a cliffhanger rather than a conclusion. The point is that somewhere in the teaching of the topic, the pupils should have a clear idea about what is going on and why. This will include both explanations and instruction from the teacher, and experience by the pupils of the process of drawing together what has happened, reflecting on it and planning next steps. Criticisms of teaching are often related to the absence of a sufficient structure within the design of the learning for the pupils and hence in the lesson or activity itself.

Organizing for learning

The classroom environment and its organization can either support or hinder teaching for learning. Carnell and Lodge (2002, p. 42) note the complex nature of the classroom and that if we are to promote a rich learning environment for the twenty-first century then we will need to encourage the following:

- a shift in responsibility from teachers to learners;
- a focus on learning and a learning language;
- a shift in the teacher's role from a behaviour manager to a learning manager;
- a move towards the learner's role as a researcher and learning partner with other learners;
- an emphasis on reciprocal teaching and learning;
- a view that the territory of the classroom is a shared learning space;
- more permeable classroom boundaries.

Teachers report that National Curriculum demands have taken up a disproportionate amount of time and in several of the projects in which we have been involved participants have returned to the importance of the classroom environment and its quality. We have reminded ourselves that most of the National Curriculum cannot be covered if resources are not to hand and the pupils are not being taught the skills of how to find and use them. Also, pupils cannot organize their learning and become self-managing if they are not in an environment that enables them to do so.

Given what we know about the social nature of learning, it is important that pupils have opportunities to learn with their peers not just to sit with them at the same table. Pupils interviewed in one of our projects viewed learning as listening to the teacher. Children in year 1 said that it was not the responsibility of their friends to help them learn! They failed to see each other as an important part of their learning.

In contrast, pupils from a school involved in another of our projects which had concentrated on learning about learning had this to say:

When I don't understand the question, I ask my friends if they can help me, not the answer, just explain it to me and giving me a few ideas. (Zara, year 6)

At the table I learn maths with my teacher and when the other children play with me. (Asil, Reception)

What helps me learn is that we have 'prides' which are groups of five mixed children (boys and girls). What helps me is that some times we have to work at a question on a sheet. Everybody writes down their method and explains it to us. Sometimes my method is not the best and there are methods done by my friends that are much easier, so it helps me a lot, especially when other children explain it to me. (Syresh, year 6)

Teaching for learning requires pupils to be grouped in a range of ways and planning how to meet the needs of different groups. Whilst the pupils in a primary class may have a 'base group' to which they belong, they may well come together in different combinations for different activities based on their identified learning needs. Pupil grouping becomes a deliberate part of the learning design. It is flexible, with the primary purpose of enabling learning to take place. The teacher has a clear notion about the nature of the intervention, support and challenge that she is going to provide. This reinforces again the importance of balancing whole-class teaching with group activities, both to support the pupils' learning and also to enable the teachers to get direct rather than second-hand information about the pupils' experience of learning. We referred in Chapter 4 to notions of incremental rather than fixed views of intelligence. We have a concern, especially in a climate of performativity, that both the grouping of pupils and the labelling of those groups by teachers can reinforce fixed views of intelligence by the pupils.

The plan for learning also includes particular opportunities for pupils to practise and rehearse skills and knowledge which they have had a say in identifying and which take place in real contexts. This is not a learning programme for every child planned by the teacher, but it is time when pupils, in consultation with their teacher, can make progress by having the time to consolidate or gain more experience in a piece of learning. Support staff and parents can also be involved in this process.

Finally, there is a need to build into the learning design quality extension activities for pupils to engage in if they finish a particular activity before others in the class. 'Fast finishers' need to be able to move easily to a range of activities that are sufficiently open ended for them to develop their learning and sufficiently structured for them to reinforce what they are learning. The notion of 'match' is not just giving pupils work that is pitched to a level they can meet and then extending learning by giving them more of the same activity. Extended learning needs also to stretch and challenge pupils and give colour and variety to learning. We have had some concern, for example, that pupils known to us have made good progress towards achieving level 4 by the end of year 4. They are then offered a narrow diet that requires them only to keep consolidating that achievement for the whole of years 5 and 6. We do not advocate labelling these pupils in a fixed way as 'gifted and talented'. Instead, we advocate the provision of a broad, balanced and differentiated curriculum where everyone can thrive and make progress.

Assessment for learning

Formative assessment, in the sense of gathering information about learning and giving feedback whilst it is in progress has been seen as a crucial aspect of teaching since the Task Group on Assessment and Testing (TGAT) report was published in 1988. In recent years there has been a great deal of discussion about the role of assessment for learning and the work of Paul Black and

Dylan Wiliam (1998; 2003) is now well known to the majority of practitioners. The Assessment Reform Group (2002) has played a key role in disseminating research findings. Those involved have published research-based principles of assessment for learning to guide classroom practice. Assessment for learning:

- is part of effective planning;
- focuses on how students learn;
- is central to classroom practice;
- is a key professional skill;
- is sensitive and constructive;
- fosters motivation;
- promotes understanding of goals and criteria;
- helps foster know-how to improve;
- develops the capacity for self-assessment;
- recognizes all educational achievement (ibid., p. 1).

Ways of collecting information that are straightforward and realistic are part of the culture of the classroom in the *intelligent school*. Teachers are always adding to a sound knowledge base about their pupils' learning strengths and preferences, as outlined in Chapter 4. This means that classroom life is organized in a way that enables the teacher not just to *support* pupils' learning but also to give feedback on both their performance and their learning. The teacher can then *diagnose* learning responses and needs, and note the progress that is being made. This is the 'feedforward' function of assessment and its presence in practice greatly contributes to effective teaching.

The importance of using assessment information for planning next steps in learning cannot be underestimated. Monitoring and diagnosis, planned as part of teaching and not viewed as something separate, play an important part in learning design and its implementation. The views of learning that we have been developing in the book so far suggest that 'monitoring' and 'diagnosis' are carried out within teaching for learning through dialogue and discussion with pupils. Time needs to be allocated on a regular basis for the teacher as well as the pupils to gather information about the learning in progress in the class. This might be a running reading record jointly conducted with an individual pupil, or particular questions to ask a group at work on a science task.

The teacher we cited earlier who had carried out research into her year 1 pupils' developing understanding of how to use questions effectively for their learning found that she had to quite deliberately plan to set time aside to practise asking questions. This emphasizes the need to find out what aspects of learning need to be introduced and practised. Most important of all is the use that the teacher makes of the information gathered to inform the planning and design of learning. We can begin to see that what distinguishes teaching for learning is that it gives priority to gathering and exchanging as well as imparting information.

Some definitions and practices of assessment for learning however may still give quite an inactive role to the pupils. Ruth Dann (2002, p. 2) says that: 'if assessment genuinely seeks to give some indication of pupils' levels of learning and development in ways which will further advance learning, pupils will need to understand and contribute to the process'. She cites Newmann, Griffin and Cole (1989) as distinguishing between teachers who use assessment to *promote change* from those who use it only to *measure change*. She describes the difference here as assessment *while teaching* as opposed to assessment *by teaching*: 'Instead of giving the children a task and measuring how well they do or how badly they fail, one can give the children the task and observe how much and what kind of help they need in order to complete the task successfully' (Newmann, Griffin and Cole, 1989, p. 77, cited in Dann, 2002, p. 36).

This is at the heart of what it means to teach for learning and changes the way that we think about both the process and purpose of making judgements within teaching. Dann suggests that formative assessment has an immediacy that has not traditionally been a feature of classroom life. Pupils conventionally do their work and then give it to their teacher to mark who in turn returns it some time later. There still may be good reasons for marking pupils' learning in that way, but assessment for learning happens primarily as part of the dialogue between the pupils and their teachers. *The process of learning and not its outcomes alone is what is being developed.*

Developing the skills of self- and peer assessment are crucial to becoming an effective learner. A teacher with whom we have been working recently realized that the year 3 pupils she was teaching had little or no experience of commenting on their own learning, never mind that of their friends! They expected that the teacher would judge how well they were doing. The teacher concerned realized that the pupils needed plenty of structured opportunity to see models of feedback operating between herself and individuals and groups. Then they could gradually build up their skills to support their own and each others' learning. They could not just magically use those skills because their teacher wanted them to!

Having considered the knowledge, skills and understanding that a teacher needs to have about both subjects and the design of the learning process, we now bring these together into action in the classroom and the actual experience of managing the teaching and learning process as it is happening. This is our fourth core aspect of teaching for learning.

Managing the process of teaching for learning

Teaching for learning is at work when the dynamic interaction between them can be sensed and observed. In his search for indicators of effective teaching,

Schulman (1987) observed several teachers over three years and he comments on how both content knowledge and pedagogical strategies necessarily interact in the minds of teachers and in their classroom practice. This answers the old question asked of one of us, 'do we teach subjects or children?' Our reflections in the previous sections suggest unequivocally that the *intelligent school* knows how to do both; and how to bring those two dimensions of teaching for learning into a reciprocal relationship with each other.

There are two main features of the 'here and now' teaching for learning process that contribute to its success. The first is an approach that emphasizes reflection and interaction about the learning taking place as well as instruction. The second is respect for the learners and their learning processes in a way which enables everyone in the classroom to be involved.

Much of the research literature refers to the importance of instructional strategies as a characteristic of effective teaching. These involve *direct* as well as *indirect* instruction; the first attributed to when the teacher is directly teaching pupils and the second when the pupils are working on a task or activity. The 'Three Wise Men' report (Alexander, Rose and Woodhead, 1992) suggested that indirect teaching has been promoted at the expense of direct teaching. A particular example given was an overemphasis on work sheets and scheme books that were not sufficiently linked for the pupils to any practical context or the explicit development of learning strategies. The points that we made earlier about planning and structure for learning provide a counterpoint to that view. However we have also given illustrations throughout this chapter that suggest that teachers could more explicitly *teach and practise* the skills and strategies needed for effective learning, for example, questioning, giving and receiving feedback, talking about learning, and developing a sense of strategies needed for learning and being able to name them. Pupils then have a better understanding of how to learn through activities that they carry out either alone or in groups.

Teaching for learning is essentially a process of two-way communication between pupils and their teachers and the pupils with each other. It makes less distinction between direct and indirect instruction noting that more traditional forms (notably the transmission/reception view of teaching) have tended to be based predominantly on one-way communications. In a classroom there will be different types of communication going on at the same time. Instructional communication has been linked more to the subject matter and the learning process, and interactive communication more to the relationship with the learners. Teaching for learning that is genuinely two-way will involve complex blends of both of these at any one time.

Maha, a year 6 pupil agrees. When asked if there were particular things teachers or support staff or other pupils do to help her learn she had this to say:

Teachers are very helpful. They find the most easiest way to help us in working out a sum. They understand that everyone needs a time to talk to someone about the problem, so in nearly every lesson, they give us a chance to do that. The pupils in my class help me to understand the problem and instead of telling me the answers they explain it very clearly to me. This kind of learning always helps me.

Schulman (1987, pp. 13–14) suggests that, particularly for intellectual development, instructional teaching in most subject matter needs to emphasize four distinct components – comprehension, reasoning, transformation and reflection:

> This image of teaching involves the exchange of ideas. The idea is grasped, probed, and comprehended by the teacher, who then must turn it about in his or her mind, seeing many sides of it. Then the idea is shaped or tailored in communication with the students. This grasping, however, is not a passive act. Just as the teacher's comprehension requires a vigorous interaction with the ideas, so students encounter ideas actively as well. Indeed our exemplary teachers present ideas in order to provoke the constructive processes of their students and not to incur student dependence on teachers or to encourage imitation.

It is here that the process of enquiry described earlier in the chapter comes into play as part of effective teaching. Comprehension is not enough. Teachers need to engage with students in ways that transform their pupils' understandings so that the skills of analysis, hypothesis, judgement and then application can be developed. For, as Bruner (1960, p. 17) asserted in his early writings: 'The first object of any act of learning ... is that it should serve us in the future. Learning should not only take us somewhere, it should allow us to go further more easily.'

What is found in both research and observation is that what is defined as instructional teaching is not the sole domain of the teacher. Quite the contrary. Effective teaching enables what Schulman (1987) describes as the constructive processes of the pupils: it engages them *actively* in learning. This is echoed in the findings of the ORACLE study by Galton and colleagues (Galton, 1980) and in subsequent studies (Galton, 1989). In her review of Galton's work, Gipps (1992, p. 13) comments that: 'What comes through again and again from Galton's work is the importance of *high levels of questioning* and the need to engage in strategies which allow *maximum levels of sustained interaction* with all pupils.'

The fourth instructional strategy Schulman refers to is reflection. As we have already suggested, teaching for learning pays attention to checking with the pupils, examining and articulating what has been learnt, encouraging them to present their thoughts, findings and opinions as their learning goes along in a lesson. The teacher has an important role in summarizing and reflecting on what has happened and encouraging the pupils to do the same. This provides the pupils with the additional skills of being able to talk about learning which supports their engagement with it and deepens their comprehension and mastery.

There is a second set of strategies that effective teachers use which reflects their understanding of both the learning process and the learners themselves. These are about the relationship the teacher has with the pupils, the pupils' engagement with their learning, the respect and the expectations the teacher has for them and the support she offers to them. The *intelligent school* understands the importance of the combined use of these strategies; a theme we develop in Chapter 7. Emotional intelligence is as important in the classroom as much as anywhere else in a school. Hargreaves (2003) notes the importance of a greater emotional emphasis in teaching and the impact that the bond between teachers and pupils can have on pupils' identity and well-being.

Research undertaken more than 20 years ago (Soar and Soar, 1979) showed that both neutral and warm emotional climates have a strong correlation with achievement, whereas a negative atmosphere can be dysfunctional and is likely to affect the pupils' progress. This suggests that the quality of the relationships the teacher has with her class is not just desirable in itself but has an impact on the quality of the learning. This does not mean that pupil–teacher relations are more important than teaching. Both are important. A study by Good and Brophy (1986) found that pupils did not achieve as well if their teacher was attending to her relationship with them at the expense of instructional teaching. This reinforces our earlier view that effective teaching pays attention to both the learners and to what is being taught.

What emerges time and time again from the discussions that teachers on our projects have with the pupils is that the teachers that help them learn best are the ones that respect them. An evaluation study of beginning teachers (Powell, 1980, p. 9) found that more effective teachers 'call their students by name, attend carefully to what they say, accept their statements of feeling, praise their successes and involve them in decision making'. This accords with the finding in the school effectiveness literature that the acknowledgement of pupil rights and responsibilities is a characteristic of effective schools as we explored in Chapter 2.

The humanistic psychologist Carl Rogers (1982) cites some research undertaken in the 1970s by Aspy and Roebuck (1976) which examined teacher behaviour in relation to learning outcomes for the pupils. They found three things that characterized a clear correlation between the facilitative conditions provided by the teacher and the academic achievement of the pupils:

- The teachers displayed their humanness to their pupils and were committed to the pupils' success.
- There was a high level of respect, interest in and acceptance of the pupils.
- The teachers demonstrated an empathy towards the pupils that showed that they cared about the quality of life for them in the classroom.

The pupils, as a result, were more academically successful, had a more positive self-concept, exhibited fewer discipline problems and had a lower absence rate from school. This kind of classroom climate is endorsed by the pupils' views described in Chapter 4 along with the impact of teachers' expectations also referred to in that chapter.

We have argued in this chapter that the pupils' participation in their learning is central to their success and it is a very unintelligent education system that has not grasped that research finding sooner. This is not just in terms of interactive instruction and planned intervention to support learning, important though this is. Our work suggests that achievement is enhanced when pupils are enabled to understand what they are doing and why they are doing it. This relates to issues raised about developing metacognition in Chapter 4 and is an important aspect of what is implied by 'purposeful teaching', also a key characteristic identified in the effective schools' literature.

Returning to Bruner (1996), pupils need to understand and share the intentions for learning that are in the mind of the teacher. Pupils need to feel safe enough and be encouraged to identify their mistakes and use strategies to improve their work so that they, too, can have an active role in classroom assessment. As far as possible they need to be involved not just in recognizing their achievement, but also in diagnosing what they need to do next to improve. That is why the greater emphasis on positive feedback to pupils about their learning through processes of assessment for learning has been so important. The way work is marked is also an opportunity for pupils to gain important insights into both their success and strategies for improvement. Our observations suggest that this process can begin at a young age.

Conclusion: the learning and teaching PACT

This chapter has examined our own experience and that of other practitioners and pupils, together with some of the research findings about what constitutes effective teaching for learning. We have argued that teaching is a complex and sophisticated craft when it is done well. It is composed of distinct but interrelated parts and cannot be separated from its interrelationship with learning.

In Chapter 4 we suggested that effective learning involves a PACT between the learner and the teacher. Figure 5.2 summarizes Chapters 4 and 5 by drawing together the key features of this PACT to illustrate what it looks like in action in the classroom. Figure 5.2 shows what the learner and the teacher bring to the learning and teaching situation and, in turn, what they both need to bring to enable the PACT to have maximum effect.

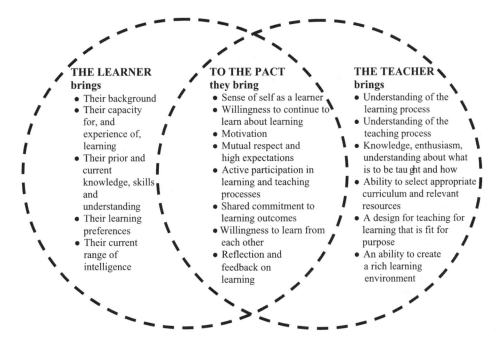

Figure 5.2. The learning and teaching PACT: the interdependence of the learner and teacher. © 2004 B. MacGilchrist, K. Myers and J. Reed

Questions for discussion

1 Do you agree with the characteristics of teaching for learning identified in this chapter? What would you add to them?
2 What guidance is available in your school that supports the promotion of teaching for learning? How can it be improved?
3 Which of the research findings about teaching identified in the chapter do you think would be most helpful to discuss in your school?
4 To what extent has your school identified principles that would support the design of learning activities for the pupils?
5 Do you agree that learning is a PACT between the learner and teacher? How can you develop opportunities to motivate pupils to want to learn with you?

6
Teachers' learning

- Why do teachers need to learn?
- Does professional development make a difference?
- How can teachers learn?
- Where can teachers learn?
- Professional learning communities
- Encouraging learning
- Conclusion
- Questions for discussion and activities

If you are travelling with small children on an aeroplane, the flight attendant tells you in the case of emergency to put the oxygen mask on yourself first in order that you are in a position to help your child. (Barth, 1990, p. 46)

Much I have learned from my teachers, more from my colleagues, but most from my students. (Talmud: Ta'anith, 7b)

We have reflected on learning, suggesting that it is a lifelong activity and examined the characteristics of effective teaching for learning. We discussed the complexity and challenges of teaching effectively given the current climate of high expectations and the multifarious demands placed on teachers. We now focus on teachers' learning. We discuss why teachers need to learn, how they can learn 'on the job', the opportunities that exist for learning outside school and ways to encourage teachers' learning. In conclusion, we suggest that teachers' learning and pupils' learning are inextricably linked.

Why do teachers need to learn?

Most of us would prefer not to be treated by a doctor who is practising exactly as she was taught in her training 30 years ago. Doctors know they need to keep abreast of new medical discoveries and practice from entry into the profession until retirement. Likewise, qualified teacher status (QTS) is a first step in a profession that requires continuous professional development. There are a range of reasons why this is the case.

Teachers need to keep up to date with their area of expertise, subject or focus (e.g. special needs). They need to know about recent research on pedagogy and learning. They need to know about scientific discoveries that are relevant to their role as teachers, e.g. new research about how the brain works. They are required to keep up to date with legislative changes that affect their work such as those enacted at the end of the twentieth century, including the National Curriculum, assessment, inspection, performance management and the key stage initiatives. In addition, their learning needs to be continuous in order to improve classroom practice, contribute to whole-school issues, take on new roles and responsibilities, manage change and acquire new skills. Barth (1990, p. 49) suggests that 'nothing within a school has more impact on students in terms of skills' development, self confidence or classroom behaviour than the personal and professional development of teachers'. Likewise, Joyce and Showers (1988) argue that learning for teachers, can have a significant impact on pupil achievement.

However, learning in the *intelligent school* is more than keeping up to date because you have to, or obtaining qualifications because you must. Learning in this school is about a continual quest to do the job even better and to understand and appreciate the difference you can make. It involves acknowledging, as we said above, that effective teaching is not a fixed set of skills and knowledge but is constantly evolving and adapting to the learning needs of different groups of pupils. We believe that when teachers understand how they learn, they are in a powerful position to help their pupils do the same. According to Barth (2001) there are ultimately two kinds of schools: learning-enriched and learning-impoverished. He believes that the teachers' learning and students' learning are interrelated: 'Teachers and students go hand in hand as learners – or they don't go at all' (ibid., p. 23). Moreover, when teachers present themselves as learners to their students, the modelling role can be very powerful. Pupils are encouraged to realize that learning is not just about passing examinations nor is it something confined to school students: 'The most important responsibility of an educator is to model being an active learner, for only when their role models make their learning visible will students take their own learning seriously' (Barth, 2001, p. 143).

Of course, this applies to all 'educators' including inspectors, headteachers, lecturers and para-professional staff – not only classroom teachers. For this reason, Barth suggests that teachers and administrators should become the lead learners in their school. Reliving the joys and the frustrations of learning is also probably a useful reminder for teachers of the complexities of the process they are constantly encouraging pupils to undertake.

Learning can be exciting and can increase one's sense of self as a learner – important for adults and pupils. It is a continuous process not an event. Teachers' learning should inform school and classroom-based developments. Frost and Durrant (2003) argue the importance of teachers being able to exercise leadership in the pursuit of school improvement. They describe a framework for teacher-led development work which includes clarifying values and concerns, personal development planning, strategic action planning, leading development work and thus transforming professional knowledge.

A culture of enquiry and reflection pervades the *intelligent school* and support for teachers' own learning is fundamental to this culture. It includes individuals, groups of teachers in year or department teams, and the whole school as an institution. In this context, the needs of individuals as well as the institution have to be acknowledged. Individual teachers need to be involved with whole-school learning initiatives. They must also have the opportunity to fulfil their own personal, professional needs. In the *intelligent school* the collective knowledge and expertise within is greater than the sum of its individual parts, and is acknowledged as such.

Does professional development make a difference?

It has always been difficult to be certain that any changes in behaviour and attitudes are solely the consequence of being involved with a particular professional development experience or course. For example, unless people are stranded on a desert island they are likely to come into contact simultaneously with other experiences, which could also affect their behaviour and attitudes. Evaluation forms are often distributed after courses but these will only capture changes that are immediate, not those that are incremental or long term. In spite of the problems of ascertaining the results of professional development, the Evidence for Policy and Practice Information and Co-ordinating Centre (EPPI-Centre) instigated a review of the research on the impact of collaborative approaches to professional development, published in 2003 (Cordingley et al., 2003). The question the report attempted to address was, how does collaborative continuing professional development (CPD) for teachers of the 5–16 age range affect teaching and learning? The complexities of ascertaining the precise impact were acknowledged. It was acknowledged that the link between teachers' beliefs, knowledge or skills, their actions in classrooms in relation to their pupils' actions and pupil learning is complex, dynamic and often not directly observable. Nevertheless 15 studies were reviewed and:

> In all but one of our in-depth studies which were judged to be of medium or higher weight of evidence in relation to the review question, the collaborative CPD was linked with improvements in teaching *and* learning as measured over the period of the intervention; many of these were significant. In the case of the exception, the teachers involved were nonetheless inspired by the power of working with student perceptions about their learning and decided at the end of the first year to undertake another year of action research in order to tackle their agenda in a more focused way. (Ibid., p. 43)

All but one of the studies reported changes in teacher attitudes, and some in pupil attitudes, as a result of participating in the CPD process.

The following were associated with successful collaborative professional development:

- greater confidence, particularly where the teachers were coached in the implementation of new teaching strategies or in tackling new technology;
- enhanced self-efficacy beliefs;
- an increased enthusiasm for collaborative working including overcoming anxiety about being observed and sharing problems;
- greater commitment to changing practice/increased willingness to try out new practices (ibid., p. 45).

Furthermore, a number of the studies reviewed indicated that teachers shared a stronger belief in their power to make a difference to learning at the end of the collaboration, and over half the studies specifically reported an increase in teachers' willingness to take risks, try new things or try things they had previously thought impossible at the outset. In many cases there was initial anxiety about being observed and sharing problems, but this was generally overcome. Indeed, sometimes the positive outcomes only emerged after a period of relative pain and anxiety.

The report suggests that teachers' experiences of collaborative CPD affected classroom behaviours by encouraging increased collaboration between pupils, or between pupils and teachers. There was also an increase in activities that encouraged pupils to question each other, evaluate each others' work and to take greater responsibility for their own learning.

Key features of successful collaborative professional development were identified:

- observation;
- feedback (usually based on observation);
- the use of external expertise;
- processes to encourage, extend and structure professional dialogue;
- scope for teacher participants to identify their own focus;
- an emphasis on peer support rather than leadership by supervisors. (ibid., p. 44)

The review of the studies:

> offers detailed evidence that sustained and collaborative CPD was linked with a positive impact upon teachers' repertoire of teaching and learning strategies, their ability to match these to their students' needs, their self-esteem, confidence and their commitment to continuing learning and development. There is also evidence that such CPD was linked with a positive impact upon student learning processes, motivation and outcomes. (Ibid., p. 8)

How can teachers learn?

Stoll, Fink and Earl (2002) suggest that there are at least seven ways that teachers can move along 'the learning curve'. Most of them conveniently begin with an 'R':

- reflecting – reflecting on experience; an enquiry-minded approach; meta-learning (i.e. learning about their own learning); making a link between own learning and pupils' learning;
- rehearsing and refining – practising and refining teaching skills;
- reading – as an individual or group activity;
- writing – keeping journals/logs of experiences in the classroom;
- researching – researching aspects of classroom and school practice;
- relating – emphasizing mutual sharing and assistance, e.g. team teaching, mentoring, collaborative action research, peer coaching, joint planning and mutual observation and feedback;
- risking – trying out new ideas and taking risks.

They quote a verse from the Sondheim lyric 'Everybody says don't' (from *Anyone Can Whistle*).

> Make just a ripple, come on be brave.
> This time a ripple, next time a wave.
> Sometimes you have to start small, climbing the tiniest wall,
> Maybe you're going to fall, but it's better than not starting at all.
> (Stoll, Fink and Earl, 2002, pp. 87–97)

This advice should not be underestimated. Learning involves taking risks and sometimes putting yourself in a vulnerable position. One of us has regularly been asking groups of teachers and heads to remember the last time they learnt anything. They are then asked to remember how they felt: before the learning took place, during the learning process and after the learning had occurred. Collated lists always look something like:

Before	During	After
Apprehensive	Vulnerable	Elated
Keen	Worried	Excited
Nervous	Frightened	Proud
Anxious	Exposed	Want to tell the world
Embarrassed	Stupid	Fabulous
Worried	Frustrated	Angry

These are words from confident adults who have chosen to learn something and are therefore highly motivated. They all succeeded in their learning too. We can only imagine what it must be like for pupils, who may not be as highly motivated to learn and who may have had unsuccessful experiences of trying to do so. They are asked to put themselves in a vulnerable position every lesson, every day of the school year. It cannot be an easy task for some, especially if there is a culture of 'blame and shame' when failure occurs. We strongly advocate a 'can-do' culture – indeed the *intelligent school* creates a culture where risk-taking is encouraged, valued and rewarded. The school recognizes, as we discussed in the chapter on learning, that a focus on learning rather than performance can encourage excitement and, most importantly, learning from mistakes.

Where can teachers learn?

Learning can take place 'on the job', individually and in groups. It can take place outside the school such as through visits to other schools, in professional development centres and in higher education institutions. It can be a one-off narrowly focused experience; for example, learning how to teach a particular topic better or obtaining specific ICT skills. It can be a long-term goal perhaps leading to accreditation.

Learning on the job

For some staff, at particular times in their career (e.g. if they have child-rearing or carer responsibilities) the only professional development opportunities available to them will be 'on the job'. This makes it even more important to ensure that these opportunities are both of high quality and easily available. Indeed, there are many opportunities to learn on the job – at least 28! They are listed here in alphabetical order. Schools may wish to re-sort them in order of importance:

- action research or *teacher enquiry* based on issues of concern;
- case study meetings – examining specific topics;
- coaching – giving/receiving coaching from a colleague on a particular issue;
- collaborative planning with colleagues in the same or neighbouring school(s) (or even, via the Internet, schools anywhere in the world);
- collaborative projects with colleagues in the same or neighbouring school(s);
- critical friend – inviting someone to be the school's/a department's or team's critical friend and together pursuing improvement;
- demonstration lessons – inviting colleagues to watch a specific topic or class taught;

- discussions – focused discussions on specific topics with colleagues, other professionals e.g. psychologists and education social workers, parents and pupils;
- e-learning, pursued individually, or with colleagues literally anywhere in the world, who share the same interest;
- inviting other practitioners, perhaps an advanced skills teacher to work with you;
- job swapping with a colleague in your school/another school/your LEA;
- job shadowing a colleague, in your school or another school/your LEA;
- mentoring – giving or receiving on professional development issues in general;
- moderating pupils' work;
- observation – inviting a colleague to observe a lesson/observing a colleague's lesson;
- pupils – specifically asking their opinion of the lesson/learning from their discussions about their learning;
- pupils – ongoing dialogue with pupils;
- pupil tracking, following a particular pupil or a class for a day or half a day;
- reading, individually or as a group with one person taking responsibility for teaching the rest of the group the contents of a chapter or paper;
- reflecting on practice, again, individually or with a colleague(s);
- researching, e.g. through use of best practice scholarships (and other similar opportunities) investigating areas of interest or concern;
- self-evaluation – whole-school, section or individual self-evaluation;
- team teaching, involving joint planning and reflection on progress and outcomes;
- team/staff meetings – using meetings to share expertise and practice rather than as a forum to address administrative tasks (important as these are, much could be done by paper or electronically);
- trainees – working with Initial Teacher Education students;
- training each other, e.g. on ICT (trainers often learn through the training);
- video – using video to demonstrate aspects of practice;
- work scrutiny – discussing and analysing selected pupils' work.

Getting groups of staff together can be a wonderful opportunity to encourage learning but sadly many such opportunities are lost in time-wasting meetings that are devoted to passing information down the line. There are other methods of passing on information. Team, department and pastoral meetings can be used effectively for learning – particularly from each other – the value of which is often underestimated. Good practice exists in most schools, yet inservice sessions often consist of bringing in the 'expert' from outside. We are not criticizing this practice, because an outsider's perspective can be very useful. However, as many schools with advanced skills teachers have discovered, inviting teachers within the school to share their experience with colleagues can underline the notion that good practice is valued and acknowledged in the school. Moreover, we learn through teaching. Teaching involves organizing and reorganizing our thoughts in order to explain them in a comprehensible and accessible way to the learner(s). Having to make a presentation to colleagues can, in itself, be a good learning experience. Holding such meetings in the presenter's classroom can add to the experience by giving colleagues opportunities to look at pupils' work, observe displays and consider what it might be like to be a pupil in that room.

Action research and teacher enquiry

Action research can be an invaluable method of learning on the job. It involves investigating an issue in a systematic way through a continuous cycle of reflection and planning, implementing change, reviewing the consequences and reflecting and replanning – 'plan, do, review' is one way of summarizing this approach. The research issue is one that is identified by those involved as in need of attention.

The typical cycle involves:

- identifying the issue;
- auditing and reflecting upon what is already happening;
- planning a piece of development work;
- implementing the action;
- reviewing what has happened;
- replanning the next step.

Teacher enquiry is an aspect of action research that involves teachers, through enquiry, developing the capacity to act strategically in order to make a difference in their school. In the context of teacher leadership, Frost and Durrant (2003) have made this cycle more specific (Figure 6.1).

It can be an individual activity. For example, a teacher may want to discover the differences between male and female contributions in her lessons. Having identified the research issue, she would then plan how to obtain this information. The plan would include the number of lessons to be involved in the study, which classes, the time of day/week and the means of collecting data – for example, by using a tape recorder and observation. The action in this case would be collecting the data. Once collected and analysed, the teacher would replan based on her findings. If she found, for example, that some girls rarely volunteered to contribute to whole-class discussion but were quite vociferous in group work, she would decide whether this was an issue to pursue and then if necessary devise a plan to tackle it. Her plan would start the cycle again. Pursuing action research individually, however, can be lonely and frustrating

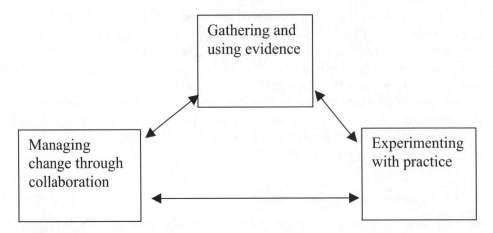

Figure 6.1   Frost and Durrant's action research cycle
Source: Frost and Durrant (2003, p. 2)

and may become disconnected from the rest of the school. The teacher in this situation may also be unaware of, and consequently unable to learn from, other research and experience on the issue being addressed. Teacher enquiry is most beneficial when it includes groups of teachers or even a whole school. When this happens opportunities for collaboration, sharing findings, analysing results and planning future developments can be exciting and invigorating for those involved. Those involved are also much more likely to believe in and consequently carry out any change suggested because of their participation in the process. The *intelligent school* recognizes the importance of such collegial intelligence and its relationship with reflective intelligence, which we discuss in the next chapter.

To be useful, teacher action research like all other research must be rigorous and evidence-based. The work can be accredited as part of a diploma, a masters course or professional doctorate. Schools can also use institutes of higher education to act as critical friends for the initiative by providing: consultancy; school-based in-service training (INSET) on research techniques and the issue being addressed; sharing relevant research; facilitating networks by putting teachers in touch with others involved in similar initiatives; and for external evaluation purposes. The National College for School Leadership actively encourages such practice. It is important that facilitators remember that their role is just that. Teachers should retain control over the initiative.

Each of us have worked with schools in this way, encouraging them to write up their findings and disseminate them via organizations such as the International Congress for School Effectiveness and Improvement (ICSEI). By presenting at an international forum the schools become part of a much wider networked community of learners and researchers. Two of us co-presented with school practitioners at a recent ICSEI conference. As a result, they are now using email to interact with other practitioners from several countries and are exploring possibilities to visit one another's schools.

Learning outside the school

Learning that takes place outside the school should be seen as complementary to the learning described above. Many schools now use in-service training days as an opportunity to arrange joint sessions with colleagues from other schools. This can be cost-effective and has the advantage of facilitating and encouraging cross-fertilization of ideas without necessitating raiding the supply budget. There are times when it is worth finding the money to finance visits to other schools to observe the practice of other teachers. On a school improvement project that one of us was involved in, taking groups of heads and senior staff to visit other schools proved to be an invaluable experience:

> Where possible we travelled together and the ensuing conversation on the forward and return journeys provided opportunities to discuss educational issues in general and what we had seen in particular. Without exception, host schools were generous – both with their time and the sharing of ideas. They were pleased that the work they were doing was being acknowledged, valued and appreciated and said they found the visits stimulating. We found the visits one of the most beneficial forms of in-service experience we had undergone and several ... initiatives were adopted and adapted from initiatives we had observed. (Myers, 1996b, p. 53)

Through the Teachers' International Professional Development Programme (TIPD) (launched in May 2000), professional development opportunities can be experienced abroad as well as in this country. The DfES's international professional development programme is aiming to place 7,500 teachers on short study visits abroad in order to do just this. At the time of writing a new scheme for groups of headteachers, administered for the government by the British Council, is being piloted which involves international visits organized around a theme of mutual interest.

One of us has recently worked with a group of primary schools in a London borough. The LEA was able to obtain funds to enable a teacher from each of the schools to visit a school district in Canada. This visit had a huge impact on the teachers who felt really valued and privileged. They in turn inspired their colleagues back in school to reflect upon the lessons they had learnt and try out new ideas.

Professional learning communities

A strong professional learning community brings together the knowledge, skills and dispositions of teachers in a school or across schools to promote shared learning and improvement. A strong professional learning community is a social process for turning information into knowledge. It is a piece of social ingenuity based on the principle that in Fullan's (2001b) words, 'new ideas, knowledge creation, inquiry and sharing are essential to solving learning problems in a rapidly changing society'. Professional learning communities promote and presume key knowledge society attributes such as teamwork, inquiry and continuous learning. Unlike regimes of competitive and corrosive individualism, which use data for inflicting embarrassment on underperforming teachers, professional communities use data to support and promote joint improvement among them. (Hargreaves, 2003, p. 134)

Successive governments have encouraged schools to compete with each other for pupils and, consequently, resources. This now seems to be changing and there is an increasing emphasis on the advantages of collaboration. Education Action Zones and Excellence in Cities initiatives have encouraged and supported collaboration between schools. The National College for School Leadership's (NCSL) Networked Learning Communities programme is doing the same. Central to the government's London Challenge initiative, spearheaded by Tim Brighouse, is the concept of collegiality between schools. New technology can make collaboration much easier, though time and resources have to be allocated to such schemes.

Teacher and school collaboration is not a panacea to sort out all the problems bedevilling the system at the time of writing. Practical and philosophical issues have to be addressed to give collaboration the opportunity to be successful. Time is the most important resource here, and how it is used is crucial.

There are some good examples across the country of partnerships between LEAs, higher education (HE) and schools that encourage professional development. The General Teaching Council (GTC) is fostering such partnerships through its Teachers' Learning Academy. The ISEIC, for example, has recently been involved in a 'Learning to Learn' project that involved a partnership between five primary schools, the LEA and the Institute of Education. Staff from all the schools exchanged good practice, visited one anothers' schools and, together, as mentioned earlier, visited a Canadian school district. A video of good practice across the schools formed part of the wider dissemination of successful practice to other schools in the LEA. Another project run by the ISEIC has been 'Improvement in Action' which has enabled LEA advisers to update their knowledge about learning and then run locally based projects with teachers in over 70 schools across the country. Leadership *for* Learning (L*f*L) at Cambridge University is involved with similar initiatives. The 'Carpe Vitam' project for example, includes 24 schools in seven countries working together to explore the impact that school leadership has on learning. This project gives teachers opportunities to develop work in their own school and share ideas and good practice with schools from their own and other countries. We explore more formal links between schools in the final chapter.

Many schools now have close working relationships with HE centres that are partners in initial teacher training and these relationships can be extended to support teachers' in-service development. One example of this support is providing mentor training for school-based professional tutors. At the Institute of Education, University of London, professional tutors are offered a range of support in mentoring including school and institute-based accredited courses, subject-related support and consultancy provision. The Institute also offers newly qualified teachers the opportunity to enrol on a Master of Teaching, which is a professional masters course. This enables teachers in the early years of their career to build on their training and learn on the job through researching aspects of their practice and contributing to the learning community which they have just joined.

> Communities of teacher researchers can play an essential role in school reform. Not only does their work add to the knowledge base on teaching, but their collective power as knowledge-generating communities also influences broader school policies regarding curriculum, assessment, school organization, and home–school linkages. Through teacher-research communities, teachers' voices play a more prominent part in the dialogue of school reform. (Cochran-Smith and Lytle, 1993, p. 103)

Encouraging learning

We have discussed why teachers need to learn and where learning opportunities can exist. Nias, Southworth and Campbell (1992) found that teachers who wanted to improve their practice were characterized by four attitudes:

1 They accepted it was possible to improve.
2 They were ready to be self-critical.
3 They were ready to recognize better practice than their own in school and elsewhere.
4 They were willing to learn what had to be learned to be able to do what had to be done.

Promoting and encouraging these attitudes is fundamental to encouraging teachers' learning.

Motivation in teacher learning

Surveys of teacher morale (Sutcliffe, 1997) and numbers opting for early retirement suggest that teacher morale has been fairly low for some time. Being constantly told by the media and some official sources that everything teachers do is inadequate is not conducive to improving morale. And since morale and motivation are linked (Varlaam, Nuttall and Walker, 1992) it is vital that steps are taken to improve this situation. The issue is acknowledged by the government but has not yet been adequately addressed. Years of being told that the state system is failing pupils must have an impact on those who work in the system. In addition, tightly prescribed innovations that leave little room for individual professional discretion, make it difficult for teachers to use their creativity and contribute individual talent.

One of the consequences of league tables and a high-stakes inspection system has been that teachers have been encouraged to play it safe. Performance-related pay has been introduced to improve motivation and 'output'. However, measuring 'multi-task jobs [such as teaching] may be dangerous because they encourage people to focus too much on certain aspects of the contract to the detriment of all the other things that they should be doing' (Prendergast, quoted in Caulkin, 2003, p. 8). Caulkin suggests that 'many incentive schemes are not only damaging of effort and a bureaucratic deadweight: they are unbelievably costly' (Caulkin, 2003, p. 8). He goes on to say that while low pay can demotivate the corollary is not necessarily true. The most important incentive is to allow people to do a good job by involving them in solving problems and making judgements. 'Instead of managing by watching the scoreboard, managers can concentrate on pursuing the ball – the customer. Good work is its own reward. In management, less is more, least is best' (ibid.). Caulkin is writing about business rather than education but we believe that on this subject, the issues are virtually the same. Motivated staff feel able to take risks, are excited and enthusiastic about their job and believe they personally have something to contribute to the school community. We are yet to be convinced that performance-related pay will increase motivation.

The literature on school improvement suggests that teachers need to find both meaning and 'ownership' in order to want to participate in change efforts. Encouraging motivation is a challenge for all managers but we know from various studies that workers are more likely to feel involved and motivated if they are treated in particular ways. The 'Hawthorne studies' that took place in the 1920s are probably the most famous example of this (Mayo, 1930). In this study the women workers improved their output whatever the extrinsic changes that were made to their working conditions – for example, increasing or decreasing light. It appeared that involving them in the decision-making process about the changes proposed was much more important than the changes themselves.

Susan Rosenholtz's (1989) research characterizes schools that encourage 'ownership' as 'learning enriched' and 'moving'. In the 'learning impoverished' or 'stuck' schools which have no such ethos, she found that teachers were more likely not to take personal responsibility for what was happening, blamed others and were too isolated from each other to share in any mutual enterprise of learning.

Earlier in this chapter we mentioned opportunities for teachers to learn on the job. Most of them involve working collaboratively with colleagues. Roland Barth (1990) distinguishes between congeniality (being nice to each other) and collegiality (working together to improve practice). He believes that a number of outcomes may be associated with collegiality:

> Decisions tend to be better. Implementation of decisions is better. There is a higher level of trust and morale among adults. *Adult learning is energized and more likely to be sustained.* There is even some evidence that motivation of students and their achievements rise, and evidence that when adults share and co-operate, students do the same. (Barth, 1990, p. 31, emphasis added)

Hargreaves (1994; 2003) distinguishes between contrived and collaborative collegiality. He sees contrived collegiality as 'usually administratively regulated, compulsory, implementation-orientated, fixed in time and space and predictable' (Hargreaves, 1994, pp. 195–6). Writing about his ideas more recently he suggests that:

> Contrived collegiality neglects, crowds out or actively undermines opportunities for teachers to initiate their own joint projects, shared learning and collective inquiry in such areas as action research, team-teaching, or curriculum planning. By crowding the collegial agenda with requirements about what is to be done collectively and with whom, it inhibits bottom-up professional initiative. (Hargreaves, 2003, p. 130)

Collaborative collegiality on the other hand, tends to be 'spontaneous, voluntary, development-orientated, pervasive across time and space, and unpredictable' (Hargreaves, 1994, pp. 192–3). 'At their best, when teachers' collaborative efforts focused on ways to improve teaching and learning, the effects on pupils' achievement and school improvement were strong' (Hargreaves, 2003, p. 129). However, Hargreaves warns that collaboration is not per se a good thing – it too can be superficial and produce no outcomes. We develop the theme of collegial intelligence in the next chapter.

Roland Barth also refers to the crucial role of headteachers in this process. He believes, as we have mentioned before, that they should be seen as the head learner (Barth, 1990, p. 46) and emphasizes the importance of their behaviour in connection with modelling and passing on implicit and explicit messages to pupils and staff. In this way headteachers set a climate conducive to learning for both adults and pupils.

Working and learning together

Nias, Southworth and Campbell (1992, p. 93) report that teachers and headteachers see professional learning as the key to developing the curriculum and the main way to school improvement. They discovered that:

Teachers, like other adult learners, found some means of learning more congenial and more effective than others. The success of the opportunities to learn, provided, promoted and used by headteachers and others, depended in part on how they were carried out. We found that teachers appeared to make particularly productive use of four types of activity: talk, observation, practice and reflection. (Ibid.)

Effective school-based professional development gives teachers opportunities to do all four of these types of activity. They highlight some of the issues referred to in Chapter 4 where we discussed metacognition – thinking about thinking. In that chapter we emphasized the importance of allowing learners to feel a sense of ownership over what they are learning and giving them occasions to process this learning. Providing these opportunities is an important part of the teacher's job whether the learners are adults or children.

Adults other than teachers

This chapter has addressed the learning needs of teachers but in recent years there has been a significant increase in the number of other adults involved in schooling. These para-professionals have learning needs too, in particular, classroom assistants, learning mentors, bursars, support staff and governors. At the time of writing the government is about to issue a consultation document that addresses the professional development needs of these groups.

Conclusion

In a teacher survey undertaken by MORI for the Teacher Training Agency (TTA, 1995), about the effectiveness of professional development, 89 per cent of respondents said it was useful or very useful but only 26 per cent thought it had a great deal of impact on classroom practice. In the *intelligent school* teachers' learning must ultimately make a difference for the pupils. This does not mean that all learning should be about how to organize the classroom or how, for example, to teach phonics, important though these two issues are. It does mean, however, that the learning that teachers undertake as part of their professional responsibilities should somehow and in some way enhance their teaching more systematically than it has often done. The 28 suggestions for learning on the job offer a range of ways in which professional learning can focus directly on improving practice in the classroom, including through being enthused and excited by some recent academic research on the subject. (Yes this can happen!)

We have discussed the importance of teachers' learning and suggested ways it can be pursued. In all schools, there are individuals involved in some of the processes described above. In the *intelligent school*, however, it is not left to chance. There is an overview of the development needs of all the staff and a plan to meet these needs. This plan contains a balance between individual, group, whole-staff, on-site, off-site, short-term and long-term needs. 'The match between the personal development of individual teachers and the effectiveness of the institution, measured primarily by the quality and amount of learning taking place, becomes a key focus within the school' (Reed and Learmonth, 2001, p. 24).

The *intelligent school* knows why learning is so important. It provides opportunities for learning and provides opportunities for that learning to be put to good use – that is, used intelligently to maximise pupils' progress and achievement.

Questions for discussion and activities

1 Re-sort the list of 28 opportunities for professional development in order of importance for your school.
2 Can you add to the list?
3 What opportunities for teachers' learning are available in your school (on the job and external)? How many of these are there by chance and how many are there by design?
4 Could these opportunities be improved and if so how?
5 How does your school attempt to address the equality issues of professional development?
6 How does your school attempt to address the issues of long-term professional development needs as discussed at the beginning of this chapter?
7 Are there systematic opportunities for teachers' learning to be shared? How could these opportunities be improved?
8 How are the learning needs of adults other than teachers identified and supported?
9 Collate the information about professional development opportunities pursued by staff in the recent past (say three years). What sort of impact has there been on the teachers themselves or any of their colleagues? Is there any evidence of impact in classrooms?
10 How could you use this information?

7

The nine intelligences – a framework for school improvement

- ■ Ethical intelligence
- ■ Spiritual intelligence
- ■ Contextual intelligence
- ■ Operational intelligence
- ■ Emotional intelligence
- ■ Collegial intelligence
- ■ Reflective intelligence
- ■ Pedagogical intelligence
- ■ Systemic intelligence
- ■ Corporate intelligence
- ■ Leading the *intelligent school*
- ■ Questions for discussion

This chapter is central to the book. It explores what we mean by the *intelligent school*. It draws on all the previous chapters to offer a conceptual framework for sustained school improvement.

> If I had one wish for all our institutions, and the institution called school in particular, it is that we dedicate ourselves to allowing them to be what they would naturally become, which is human communities, not machines. Living beings who continually ask the questions: Why am I here? What is going on in my world? How might I and we best contribute? (Senge, 2000b, p. 58).

Senge's wish is premised on his argument (Senge, 2000a), which we discussed in Chapter 1, that there is an urgent need for schools, and the education system as a whole, to move from a nineteenth-century industrial model of learning and teaching to an organic model. This kind of model reflects what we know about living systems and the likely needs of young people growing up in the twenty-first century. Unlike the industrial assembly-line model exemplified by conformity, control, a fragmented curriculum and a standardized product, living systems evolve of their own accord. They are 'composed fundamentally of relationships and the interrelatedness of subject matter' (ibid., p. 44). Senge argues that 'By continuing to prop up the industrial-age concept of schools through teacher-centred instruction, learning as memorizing, and extrinsic control, we are preparing students for a world that is ceasing to exist' (ibid., p. 51).

He believes that the way to combat this is to appreciate that schools are living systems that have learning as their central focus. He argues that in such schools the learning process would come alive. It would become learner-centred learning rather than teacher-centred learning. It would encourage variety, not homogeneity through embracing a range of intelligences and diverse learning styles. It would involve understanding a world of interdependency and change rather than one of memorizing facts and striving for right answers.

Underpinning Senge's argument is an emphasis on the need for schools to lay the essential foundations for learning about life and for lifelong learning to enable the next generation to embrace the challenges, opportunities and uncertainties of the twenty-first century. The pace of change in information communication technologies and the related explosion in the growth of and accessibility to knowledge, which we explored in Chapter 1, add much weight to Senge's argument. The socio-economic issues that we raised in Chapter 1, as well as the events that occurred on 11 September 2001 in the USA and their aftermath, provide an even greater sense of urgency for schools to become the kind of human communities that Senge envisages.

The purpose of this chapter is to take a fresh look at schools as organizations that reflects their dynamic and organic nature. We draw on, and adapt, Gardner's (1983; 1999) notion of multiple intelligence and draw on recent thinking about the nature of organizations to offer a different way of looking at schools as living systems.

Schools that create a sense of community in which the rights, responsibilities and the needs of learners are at the heart of the enterprise appear to be using, in combination, at least nine intelligences. The way in which the term 'intelligence' is used is not straightforward because it is not easily observable and is even harder to measure. March (1999, p. 1) reminds us that: 'the pursuit of organisational intelligence appears straightforward but it is not. Difficulties begin with the concept of intelligence itself'. There are a range of definitions. One that is useful in the context of schooling has been offered by Gottfredson (1997, p. 13) who suggests that:

> Intelligence is a very general mental capability that, among other things, involves the ability to reason, plan, solve problems, think abstractly, comprehend complex ideas, learn quickly and learn from experience. It is not merely book learning ... (or) a narrow academic skill. Rather it reflects a broader and deeper capability for comprehending our surroundings – 'catching on' 'making sense of things', or 'figuring out' what to do.

The nine intelligences we have identified as a result of drawing on the literature in earlier chapters and on our own experience, concern a range of collective capacities that school leaders can foster and develop to maximize the effectiveness of the organization. These collective capacities involve the use of wisdom, insight, intuition and experience as well as knowledge, skills and understanding. The intelligences provide something analogous to the fuel, water and oil in a car. They all have discreet functions but, for their success, need to work together.

Underlying the nine intelligences are a set of values, concepts, principles and attributes that need to be articulated clearly to help address some of the questions we posed in Chapter 1:

- What do we mean by an effective school?
- What does it mean to be an educated person?
- How, through education, can we narrow the gap between the 'haves' and the 'have nots'?

The knowledge about the combined characteristics of effective

- schools,
- improvement efforts,
- learning, and
- teaching

can strengthen a school's capacity to raise standards and enhance pupils' progress and achievement. But, this knowledge is not enough in itself. All important is what a school does with the knowledge; *how* it uses it to improve its own effectiveness. What marks out the *intelligent school* is the ability to apply the knowledge and skills it has to maximum effect in classrooms and across the school as a whole. We would argue that it does this through the combined use of at least nine intelligences which, unlike Gardner's intelligences, are interdependent.

Interdependence is an underlying theme in the literature about organizations. Michael McMaster (1995) suggests that, as a species, we are still bound up in a world view that is mechanistic, reductionist and essentially rational. Many writers, particularly in the fields of organizational transformation and the new sciences (Wheatley, 1992; Senge, 1993; 2000a; Capra, 1996), argue that the views that have been held of how the world works since Decartes and Newton are changing. Increasingly, writers indicate that a renewed sense and understanding of the interconnections of all life is developing. The well-known phrase 'the whole is greater than the sum of its parts' is more true than perhaps the glib way it is often used tends to suggest. The term 'organization' is seen to refer to 'the pattern of connections between parts' (McMaster, 1995, p. 7). A classic example of this concept is the interdependence between teaching and support staff within a school. Both groups have different roles to play but to maximize their effectiveness each depends on the other.

Writing on this theme, David Bohm (1980, p. 1) suggests a need for urgency:

For fragmentation is now very widespread, not only through society, but in each individual; and this is leading to a kind of general confusion of the mind, which creates a series of problems and interferes with our clarity of perception so seriously as to prevent us from being able to solve most of them ... . The notion that all these fragments are separately existent is evidently an illusion, and this illusion cannot do other than lead to endless conflict and confusion.

Those researching in this field are also reinforcing the nature of flux and change at the heart of reality and that 'this means that our understanding is ever changing based on continued inquiry, exploration and dialogue' (McMaster, 1995, p. 4). This resonates with some of the characteristics of the *intelligent school*. McMaster (1995) develops this theme of the relationship between the parts and the whole by using the term *corporate intelligence*. He writes that 'Corporate intelligence emerges when intelligent beings form productive institutions' (ibid., p. 1) and that 'The possibility of a corporate intelligence ... is that more information, more richness of interpretation, more creativity in processing information, and more generative ability can be integrated beyond what any single individual can do' (ibid., p. 3). This applies as much to public sector organizations like schools as to business and commercial organizations.

As we have argued throughout the book, learners and their learning need to be at the heart of schooling which in turn needs to be values driven. The *intelligent school* recognizes this and has a clearly articulated vision underpinned by a core set of values which draw on and relate to the context in which it finds itself. But there is more to the *intelligent school* than this. What it also has is the capacity to mobilize all those within the school to put that *vision* into *action*. It does this in a *systemic* way which enables the school to connect vision to action and vice versa, in such a way that the whole really is greater than the sum of the parts.

The nine intelligences that we have identified can be found in Table 7.1.

Table 7.1 *The nine intelligences*
(© B. MacGilchrist, K. Myers and J. Reed, 2004)

1	Ethical intelligence (EthQ)
2	Spiritual intelligence (SQ)
3	Contextual intelligence (CQ)
4	Operational intelligence (OQ)
5	Emotional intelligence (EQ)
6	Collegial intelligence (CoQ)
7	Reflective intelligence (RQ)
8	Pedagogical intelligence (PQ)
9	Systemic intelligence (SyQ)

The first two intelligences concern the school's vision:

> Ethical intelligence (EthQ)
> Spiritual intelligence (SQ)   = *Vision*

The next six concern how the school puts its vision into action:

> Contextual intelligence (CQ)
> Operational intelligence (OQ)
> Emotional intelligence (EQ)   = *Action*
> Collegial intelligence (CoQ)
> Reflective intelligence (RQ)
> Pedagogical intelligence (PQ)

Systemic intelligence (SyQ) ensures that vision and action work together.

Ethical intelligence (EthQ) and spiritual intelligence (SQ) combine together to represent the vision underlying the *intelligent school*. This vision concerns the values and beliefs about schooling that have as their focus young people and their learning and what it means to be an educated person in the twenty-first century. Contextual intelligence (CQ), operational intelligence (OQ), emotional intelligence (EQ), collegial intelligence (CoQ), reflective intelligence (RQ) and pedagogical intelligence (PQ) combine together to represent the actions the *intelligent school* takes to put the vision into practice, i.e. 'walking the talk'. Systemic intelligence (SyQ) enables this to happen. It is the intelligence that mediates between values and action and makes the necessary connections between the two.

Underlying each of the nine intelligences is a set of concepts, principles and attributes which are identified in Table 7.2. We are not claiming that these are the only defining characteristics of the nine intelligences, but we do consider them to be of fundamental importance. We describe these characteristics through an exploration of each intelligence.

Ethical intelligence (EthQ)

Ethical intelligence (EthQ) combined with spiritual intelligence forms the educational vision that is the driving force for the actions taken by the *intelligent school*. Ethical intelligence and SQ are expressed through the clear statement of values and beliefs incorporated in the school's aims or mission statement. Ethical intelligence concerns the way a school conveys its moral purpose through such interrelated principles as

- justice;
- respect for persons;

- inclusion;
- rights and responsibilities.

Table 7.2 *The concepts, principles and attributes of the nine intelligences*
(© B. MacGilchrist, K. Myers and J. Reed, 2004)

1	Ethical intelligence (EthQ)	– justice – respect for persons – inclusion – rights and responsibilities
2	Spiritual intelligence (SQ)	– search for meaning – transcendency – sense of community – interconnectedness
3	Contextual intelligence (CQ)	– internal – local – national – global
4	Operational intelligence (OQ)	– strategic thinking – development planning – management arrangements – distributed leadership
5	Emotional intelligence (EQ)	– self-awareness – awareness of others – managing emotions – developing emotional literacy
6	Collegial intelligence (CoQ)	– commitment to a shared purpose – knowledge creation – multi-level learning – trust and curiosity
7	Reflective intelligence (RQ)	– creating time for reflection – self-evaluation – deep learning – feedback for learning
8	Pedagogical intelligence (PQ)	– new visions and goals for learning – teaching for learning – open classrooms – going against the grain
9	Systemic intelligence (SyQ)	– mental models – systems thinking – self-organization – networking

Through such principles the school puts its values into action.

The *intelligent school* uses RQ to reflect upon and make explicit the values that inform its everyday work. Haynes (1998, p. 3) reminds us that 'Reflecting on ethical values is of particular importance in education because not only are teachers and administrators beset with moral questions, but now, more than ever, they are responsible for the moral well-being and education of their pupils, the future generation'. As Starratt (1991, p. 187) puts it, 'educators have a moral responsibility to be proactive about creating an ethical environment for the conduct of education'. Haynes agrees: 'There is a need to reaffirm that education is continually about human beings interacting responsibly with each other rather than about those with power controlling others, or those without power acting like automata with neither time nor incentive to make autonomous decisions' (Haynes, 1998, p. 2).

The *intelligent school* understands that its day-to-day practices – sometimes referred to as the hidden curriculum – along with its explicit policies and taught curriculum are not value free. As Tomlinson (2000, p. 2) reminds us, 'irrespective of whether there is a formal curriculum of moral education, teachers inevitably and properly convey moral ideas and principles'. Ethical intelligence is at the heart of learning and teaching because, like SQ and EQ, it is about the development of the whole child.

Both Haynes and Starratt argue for the importance of developing what they call 'ethical schools'. We would argue that to be ethical, schools need to be *intelligent* in order to put such principles as justice, respect for persons, inclusion and rights and responsibilities into action.

Justice

In the *intelligent school* notions of justice apply both to the way individuals, be they children or adults, experience school and to the way the school self-governs itself. Justice is recognized to be a multifaceted concept that involves issues such as fairness and fair play through to a wide range of equity issues. Justice is about, for example, how resources, be they human or physical, are deployed throughout the school. The principle of justice is seen as a good starting point for enabling young people to move beyond notions of justice that relate to them personally to ones concerned with wider notions of social justice and human rights within the context of a democratic society.

The *intelligent school* creates opportunities for children and staff to discuss and reflect upon choices that individuals can and do make and choices that the school community can and does make. This can be done as part of the curriculum through, for example, structured discussion and debates about controversial issues. School councils, assemblies and the use of circle time can all give opportunities for this intelligence to be developed. The *intelligent school* involves pupils, staff and others in decision-making about school policies and in examining the fairness of current practices such as the way pupils are grouped and assessed. It understands that developing an organization premised on the principle of justice must happen within the context of the principle of respect for persons.

Respect for persons

The *intelligent school* conveys respect for persons in everything that it does. This is because it understands that underlying this principle are deep issues such as equal opportunities, the exercise of power, the development of self-esteem and personal confidence, and mutual respect for and between all the children and adults within the school community. For these reasons any manifestation of a lack of respect for people such as bullying (towards children and adults) are not tolerated.

The *intelligent school* demonstrates respect for persons in many ways, for example, through the language it uses, the rewards system it chooses, the practice of ceremonies and the use of displays. As Starratt (1991, p. 197) suggests:

> These are all signs of a school environment that values people for who they are. When youngsters engage every day in such a school community they learn the lessons of caring, respect and service to each other. With some help from peers and teachers they also learn how to forgive, mend bruised relationships, accept criticisms and debate different points of view.

Emotional intelligence and CoQ are an important means of realizing this aspect of moral purpose in practice.

Inclusion

The principle of inclusion concerns all the pupils in the school: 'Inclusive education is not an end in itself ... . It is about the value and well-being of *all* pupils' (Armstrong, Armstrong and Barton, 2000, p. 1).

The *intelligent school* respects diversity and fosters intercultural understanding and tolerance. It advocates equality of opportunity because inclusion is one of its guiding principles. This stems from its concern for human rights and as such, relates very closely with the principles of justice and respect for persons. It sees putting the principle of inclusion into action as the collective responsibility of the whole-school community. This is because the *intelligent school* believes that 'The notion of inclusion ... is about a philosophy of acceptance; it is about providing a framework within which all children [*and adults*] – regardless of ability, gender, language, ethnic or cultural origin – can be valued equally, treated with respect and provided with equal opportunities at school' (Thomas, Walker and Webb, 1998, p. 15, italic text added by ourselves).

115

Evidence from the 'Learning to Learning' project in Redbridge, which had the principle of inclusion at its heart, indicates that schools that focus on learning – for pupils and teachers – can have a significant impact on the progress and achievement of all children, and in particular children with a wide range of special educational needs.

The *intelligent school* thinks through the relationship and tension between inclusion and exclusion. It knows that a crucial part of its focus on learning is twofold. First, increasing pupil participation and engagement with learning and, second, working at reducing pupil exclusion from learning. As Ainscow (1999, p. 218) reminds us: 'Inclusion is a never ending process, rather than a simple change of state, and is dependent on continuous pedagogical and organisational development within the mainstream.' For this reason the *intelligent school* draws in particular on PQ and OQ to put the principle of inclusion into practice.

Rights and responsibilities

Ethical intelligence is characterized by a concern to ensure the right of access for *all* pupils to a broad and balanced curriculum. By all, we mean every pupil in the school system, not just the pupils in our own school. The *intelligent school* consequently would do nothing that would deliberately harm the education of children in other schools such as sending buses into other catchment areas or poaching teachers in shortage subjects. *Intelligent schools* collaborate with each other in order to share scarce resources to the benefit of all pupils. *Intelligent schools* are concerned about future pupils as well as those currently in education. They are aware that some decisions they have to make (for example whether or not to sell off playing fields, whether or not to get involved in private finance initiatives – PFI) will have an impact on schooling in their neighbourhood in the future and consider the ethical issues accordingly.

The notion of entitlement is integral to this intelligence. Support for learning is highly valued and there is an understanding about the nature of learners, what learners need and want and how to embrace these diverse needs within the school community.

As indicated in Chapter 2, taking account of pupils' rights and responsibilities has been identified as a characteristic of an effective school. Rudduck, Chaplain and Wallace (1996, p. 1) as a result of their research of secondary school pupils' views about schooling, argue that 'What pupils say about teaching, learning and schooling is not only worth listening to, but provides an important – perhaps the most important – foundation for thinking about ways of improving schools'.

The *intelligent school* encourages pupils to comment on and reflect upon learning and teaching. It knows as Rudduck, Chaplain and Wallace (1996, pp.

116

177–8) found that 'Pupils are urging us to review some of the assumptions and expectations that serve to hold habitual ways of teaching in place … . We have to take seriously young pupils' accounts and evaluations of teachers and learning and schooling'. The *intelligent school* uses a wide range of strategies to listen to and understand and respond to young people's views about themselves as learners and about the ways in which the school can best support them.

Rudduck, Chaplain and Wallace (1996) found that schools were not recognizing the maturity of young people and the complex demands facing them in their social and personal development and the relationship between these and their identity as learners. They concluded that there is a need for schools to examine critically the values and assumptions embedded in their social structures and day-to-day practices. They used the feedback from the pupils to identify six conditions for learning from the perspective of the pupils:

1 *Respect* for pupils as individuals and as a body occupying a significant position in the institution of the school.
2 *Fairness* to all pupils irrespective of their class, gender, ethnicity or academic status.
3 *Autonomy* – not as an absolute state but as both a right and a responsibility in relation to physical and social maturity.
4 *Intellectual challenge* that helps pupils to experience learning as a dynamic, engaging and empowering activity.
5 *Social support* in relation to both academic and emotional concerns.
6 *Security* in relation to both the physical setting of the school and in interpersonal encounters (including anxiety about threats to pupils' self-esteem) (ibid., p. 174).

These principles are embedded in the working practices of the *intelligent school*. Through CQ, the *intelligent school* understands that, as Rudduck, Chaplain and Wallace (1996, p. 172) put it,

> The culture of childhood and adolescence has been redefined (and not for the first time in social history) through the conditions of unemployment, single parenting, family break down and poverty. We need to try to understand where young people are coming from and how such understanding can help us with the task of school improvement.

Ethical intelligence is not just about pupils' rights. It is also about their responsibilities as learners within the school community. We tried to capture this in our concept of the teaching and learning PACT in Chapter 5. In Soo Hoo's (1993, p. 386) words: 'Students' placed in positions of responsibilities and shared authority could [*can*] actively investigate what was [*is*] working and not working for them as learners' (words in italics added by ourselves).

117

The *intelligent school* also applies these same principles to the adults in the school community through the use of EQ, RQ and CoQ. It enables them to exercise their rights and responsibilities and for the teachers, in particular, this has an important impact on PQ.

Cambron-McCabe (2000, p. 276) reminds us that 'teaching is a moral undertaking'. It is important therefore for teachers to have time to think about and discuss how they teach and the aims, purposes and underlying values and moral principles of their teaching. 'Through reflective questioning the teacher can conscientiously engage with moral dimensions of schooling connected to his or her relationship with the students and their access to knowledge' (ibid., p. 277). 'Our choice of teaching methods and school designs is an ethical decision' (ibid., p. 278).

Schools with ethical intelligence have high self-esteem as an organization, which is not the same as complacency. They rarely feel totally satisfied about what they are doing and usually have ideas about how they can do even better next time. Sara Lawrence Lightfoot (1983, p. 310) found that 'This more modest orientation towards goodness does not rest on absolute or discreet qualities of excellence or perfection, but on views of institutions that anticipate change, conflict and imperfection'.

Spiritual intelligence

Spiritual intelligence (SQ) values that in our experience which is neither tangible nor measurable. It concerns the capacity to enable profound learning to occur (West-Burnham, 2003).

Burns and Lamont (1995, p. xiii) describe spirituality as

> A source of creativity open to us all. It brings that quality of aliveness which sparks inquiry, ideas, observations, insights, empathy, artistic expression, earnest endeavour and playfulness. It opens us to life and to each other. Spirituality is a thread that runs through our life, bringing hope, compassion, thankfulness, courage, peace and a sense of purpose and meaning to the everyday, while reaching beyond the immediate world of the visible and tangible. It drives us to seek and stay true to values not ruled by material success.

It is values such as these that combine with EthQ to underpin everything that the *intelligent school* does.

We have applied the concept of individual spirituality to the school as a whole. We have done this in the knowledge that the nature of spirituality and spiritual development in the context of education are complex issues that have attracted much debate (Best, 1996; Brown and Furlong, 1996; Priestley, 1996; Hay and Nye, 1998; Wright, 2000; Alexander, 2001). Mott-Thornton (1998, p. 69) is of the view that spirituality is 'an essential aspect of human life that schools are inevitably concerned with'. Priestley (1996) agrees and argues that

118

spirituality is at the heart of education. Best (1996, p. 346) warns, however, that 'It is the poverty of so much of contemporary policy-making, constrained as it is by a preoccupation with "efficiency", "performance indicators", "league tables" and the other trappings of the market mentality, that such thinking (for example, as described by Burns & Lamont) is stunted and actively discouraged'. In a similar vein Prentice (1996) urges that the prime concern of education must be to cultivate the human spirit as opposed to an approach that focuses on a specialist and fragmented curriculum.

Zohar and Marshall (2001, pp. 3–4) argue that there is emerging evidence to indicate there is intelligence in the form of spiritual intelligence (SQ).

> SQ is the intelligence with which we address and solve problems of meaning and value, the intelligence in which we can place our actions and our lives in a wider, richer, meaning-giving context, the intelligence with which we can assess that one course of action or one life-path is more meaningful than another.

Zohar and Marshall go on to say that in their view 'SQ is the necessary foundation for the effective function of both IQ and EQ. It is our ultimate intelligence' (ibid., p. 4) and 'it is a third kind of thinking that places actions and experiences in a larger context of meaning and value' (ibid., p. 87).

Hay and Nye's (1998) three-year research into young children's spirituality would seem to provide strong support for the concept of SQ. They found that children are capable of having profound beliefs and meaningful spiritual experience from a very early age. They argue that spiritual awareness is a natural human predisposition but then explore the challenges facing an educational system which wishes to take spirituality seriously. They claim that the data from the children underline their conviction that spirituality is entirely natural: 'It grows out of a biological predisposition which can either be obscured or enhanced by culture … Spirituality is the bedrock on which rests the welfare not only of the individual but also of society and indeed the health of our entire planetary environment' (ibid., p. 153).

Schools with a developed sense of spiritual intelligence seek to know themselves at a deep level. They are the kind of schools that ask the sorts of questions Senge identified in the quote at the beginning of this chapter in their exploration of fundamental issues. Spiritual intelligence requires schools to be deeply honest and aware of themselves and as Zohar and Marshall (2001) argue, 'to stand up to what they believe in'.

It is possible to identify at least four interrelated concepts that underpin SQ:

- search for meaning;
- transcendency;
- sense of community;
- interconnectedness.

Search for meaning

Pascall (1993, p. 2) argues: 'Spirituality has to do with the universal search for individual identity – with our responses to challenging experiences such as death, suffering, beauty and encounters with good and evil. It is to do with the search for meaning and purpose in life and for the values by which to live.'

OFSTED recognizes the importance of spirituality. An OFSTED (1994, p. 8) report suggests that: 'Spiritual development relates to that aspect of inner life through which pupils acquire insights into their personal existence, which are of enduring worth. It is characterized by reflection, the attribution of meaning to experience, valuing a non-material dimension to life and intimation of an enduring reality.'

Spiritual intelligence encourages children to think creatively and to use their imagination. It helps to draw together imagination and experience. Spiritual intelligence involves, therefore, the capacity to exercise empathy and reflectiveness. As Hay and Nye (1998) suggest, SQ is the capacity to provide a range of opportunities for spiritual development such as

- helping children to keep an open mind, e.g. by creating an environment in which children are encouraged to express their ideas and develop their self-confidence and sense of self worth through, for example, the use of circle time;
- exploring alternative ways of seeing things through, for example, metaphors and ambiguous figures (ibid., p. 170).

Transcendency

Through SQ the *intelligent school* helps children (and staff) to think beyond the here and now. Priestley (1996, p. 25) asserts that

> A curriculum which prepares children only for the present world is a betrayal. Change is not an option, it will happen with or without us. It is a moral option of whether that change is for the better or for the worse and education is the vehicle which will help determine that course.

Hay and Nye (1998, p. 172) support this view and argue that 'Spirituality by its definition is always concerned with self-transcendence. It requires us to go beyond egocentricity to take account of our relatedness to other people and the environment'. Spiritual intelligence involves the need to provide children with 'the necessary scaffolding of language and cultural understanding that will enable them to come to grips with their spirituality – that is, their understanding of themselves in relation to the rest of reality' (Hay and Nye, 1998, p. 173). To enable this to happen, Wright (2000) argues for the need for schools to develop a 'spiritual literacy' as a matter of urgency to enable pupils to transcend the here and now and consider the ultimate meaning and purpose of life. As Priestley (1996, p. 25) puts it 'Spirituality invites us to look beyond to a world which might be brought into existence but is not yet with us'.

Sense of community

Spiritual intelligence is characterized by a fundamental valuing of the lives and development of all members of a school community. Everyone is seen to matter and to have something to contribute. Bradford (1999, p. 55) is of the view that 'The school has a significant part to play in promoting all components of human spirituality by the way it values pupils in its mission statement and by the way this is applied and implemented across the life of the school'.

As Hay and Nye (1998, p. 155) put it, schools need to provide 'a social context which gives permission for an open acceptance of spirituality'. Thatcher (1999, p. 223) develops this argument and states that 'an education environment informed by spirituality will take community seriously. It will promote learning together as a shared experience'. Similarly, Alexander (2001, p. 140) argues for the need for 'Intelligent spirituality which entails discovering ourselves in learning communities devoted to a higher good'. At the heart of the *intelligent school* is the development of a learning community with RQ, CoQ and EQ playing a key role in this process.

Spiritual intelligence also recognizes the need to balance the busy life of a school community with times of peace and an opportunity to be in touch with ultimate issues. Fisher (1999) argues for the need for schools to create a community of philosophical enquiry. Such enquiry leads to 'a focus on the underlying concepts of daily experience such as time, space, truth and beauty. As children probe these concepts they learn how to ask relevant questions, detect assumptions, recognise faulty reasoning and gain a sense of competency in their ability to make sense of the world' (ibid., p. 65).

The ethos of the school plays a key role in fostering spirituality and this includes both the physical as well as the social environment. Adult role models in this process, such as the quality of relationships between, for example, teachers and support staff, are all important. As Thatcher (1999, p. 222) argues, 'schools need to provide a safe, psychological environment in which children can "play out" and express strong emotions or incidents that may be frightening to them'. 'An education environment informed by spirituality will take community seriously. It will promote learning together as a shared experience' (ibid., p. 223). In this context, the *intelligent school* recognizes that the ways in which pupils are grouped are all part of SQ because schools have the power to transform relationships.

Spiritual intelligence is fundamental to the development of the individual and the school community as a whole. In combination with EthQ it forms the foundations of the *intelligent school*. Together they enable the school to become living systems as described by Senge at the beginning of this chapter.

Interconnectedness

Mott-Thornton (1998, p. 69) describes spirituality as:

> That quality of being, holistically conceived, made up of insights, beliefs, values, attitudes, emotions and behavioural dispositions which both informs and may be informed by lived experience. The cognitive aspects of our common spirituality can be described at any particular time as being a 'framework' of ideals, beliefs and values about oneself, one's relations with others and reality/the world.

This view is premised on the notion that the individual is part of a wider inter-connected world. Hay and Nye (1998, p. 174) agree and argue that 'Spiritual education as the under-pinning of the curriculum acts as a permanent reminder of the absolute necessity to aim for coherence'.

The *intelligent school* recognizes the need to ensure that spirituality is an integral part of the whole curriculum. It heeds the kind of warning given by Hay and Nye that 'the fragmentation of the school curriculum for the sake of efficiency, specialization or the need to improve exam results is potentially very damaging' (ibid., p. 173) for the development of SQ, because as Myers (1997, p. 175) points out, 'The spiritual health of the school community cannot be assessed in any straightforward manner ... . Easily measured attainment targets notoriously have a backwash effect on classroom practice'.

The *intelligent school* understands, therefore, the holistic interconnected nature of spirituality. It understands, as Bhindi and Duignan (1997, p. 126) put it, that spirituality involves individuals and groups experiencing 'a sense of deep and enduring meaning and significance from an appreciation of their interconnectedness and interdependency, and from their feelings of being connected to something greater than the self'.

Contextual intelligence

Contextual intelligence (CQ) involves the capacity to read, understand and interpret at least four dimensions of the environment in which a school functions:

- internal;
- local;
- national;
- global.

The internal context

Drawing on EthQ and EQ in particular, the *intelligent school* is expert at reading the qualitative aspects of its internal context. It understands the impact of past history on present working practices. It can take an objective look at the culture of the school as expressed through the quality of the professional relationships between all those working in and visiting the school, the school organizational arrangements and opportunities for learning as described in Chapter 3. It is aware of the meaning and nuances behind rituals such as celebrations, outings, remembering birthdays and particular events, both happy and sad. It is aware of its current staffing profile in terms of stability, turnover, experience, expertise and age profile and, as far as is realistic, it engages in succession planning in respect of anticipating future teaching and support staffing needs.

It has an excellent understanding of and relationship with the pupil population. It knows the pupils very well. It is very aware of the pattern of successive intakes, turnover, behaviour problems, referrals, special educational needs and disciplinary action, and any changes in the pupil profile that occur. It can read the extent to which the school 'feels' and acts like a community whilst at the same time respecting individual differences and special needs.

Equally, the *intelligent school* has very good relationships with parents and carers. It understands their aspirations, their social and cultural diversity and the particular challenges facing them. It strives to work in a learning partnership with them. This is characterized by a genuine respect for and responsiveness to parents. The *intelligent school* aims to ensure that the make-up of the governing body will enable it to draw on a wide range of expertise from the community. In order to benefit from this expertise it endeavours to create an excellent working relationship with governors.

It has a good understanding of the site and the educational advantages and disadvantages of the premises and potential areas for improvement and expansion. It is very aware of the importance of the quality of the learning environment. It understands the explicit and implicit, positive and negative messages that the environment can transmit so pays close attention to detail. For example, it pays attention to the quality of displays, the signage, the availability of photographs of staff and pupils, the cleanliness of the toilets, the lack of graffiti and litter, and the quality of play space and sports facilities. It is also aware of the importance of the accessibility of the secretary or bursar and the headteacher, and the need to ensure that visitors feel welcome when entering the school. It regularly seeks feedback from staff, children, parents and visitors on these matters.

An integral part of the learning environment is the quality of learning resources available. The *intelligent school* recognizes this and keeps these under review. An audit of learning resources is a regular event and staff actively seek to augment learning resources in liaison with governors. Staff and governors are encouraged and enabled to understand the school's financial position. Key staff understand any past budgetary difficulties and are able to read the present budgetary situation and assess the extent to which the school gives good value for money.

As well as qualitative aspects of the context, the *intelligent school* has learnt to be adept at reading its quantitative context and assessing the relationship between these. Keeping an overview of pupils' progress and achievement and assessing the value added by the school to pupils' overall achievement has become a vital capacity, particularly in order to keep a balance between the demands of the performance culture and its related targets and benchmarks and the school's own values and beliefs expressed through SQ, EthQ and EQ. The *intelligent school* uses SATs and examination results and Pre-Inspection Context and School Indicator Reports (PIXIEs) and Performance and Assessment Reports (PANDAs) in the context of the school's overall aims and objectives. It uses PQ and RQ to track pupil progress in a rigorous, systematic way so that together the staff, pupils, governors and parents can read and understand the patterns emerging.

The *intelligent school* recognizes that to understand the internal context an external perspective is really helpful, therefore, the outcome of OFSTED inspections, LEA reviews and the use of external consultants are all important sources of data to draw on, to gain maximum understanding of the internal effectiveness and efficiency of the school.

The local context

No school is an island and the *intelligent school* recognizes that an essential part of contextual intelligence is having a detailed understanding of the local context in which the school is actually situated. This concerns the capacity to have an overview of the community the school serves: its socio-economic and cultural make-up; its aspirations and particular challenges; and any demographic changes that have or are likely to occur. It also concerns the capacity to understand the local education authority or district in which the school is located: the quality and range of its services; its approaches to pressure and support; income streams and overall budgetary health and efficiency. It involves networking and seeking collaborative arrangements with other schools in the area over, for example, pupil transfer, possible teacher exchanges and the sharing of expertise and facilities. It also involves an awareness of the availability of staff training and continuing professional development opportunities in the area, the local teacher and support staff supply and recruitment situation and cultivating and using the local press. The *intelligent school* has an 'entrepreneur' feel about it and it is always seeking creative partnerships and opportunities for augmenting the school's resources and opportunities for learning within the local community that it serves. This includes recognizing the need to have a very good knowledge of, and relationship with other local services and facilities, including the business community and the potential partnerships that these services can provide.

The national context

In the last 15 years the national context has increasingly made a direct impact on schools. In the late 1980s and early 1990s government policy led to a national framework being put in place for the curriculum and the assessment of pupils and the inspection of schools. The trend towards central control has increased since New Labour came into office in 1997.

The *intelligent school* demonstrates the capacity to interpret and absorb national requirements and opportunities for development into its working practices without sacrificing its own vision and beliefs. This is no mean feat, particularly when government policies have challenged ethical intelligence as described in Chapter 1. The *intelligent school* has the confidence and creativity to translate national initiatives in ways that strengthen rather than diminish the school's educational offer. The *intelligent school* scans the political landscape so that it can be forewarned as far as is possible of events and issues that are likely to impact on the school in the near future. It understands the potential ramifications of the budget, pay reviews, appraisal and performance-related pay. It keeps up to date with topical issues and anticipates possible reactions from the government to, for example, media pressure over particular concerns and any potential income streams arising from these. The *intelligent school* is opportunistic and seeks to develop national as well as local networks. It is aware of, and keeps up to date with, national bodies such as the GTC, NCSL, unions and research and national networks provided by universities such as ISEIC at the Institute of Education and Leadership *for* Learning at Cambridge University. Using the Internet to assist with all this has increasingly become common practice and an essential part of everyday school life.

The global context

As described in Chapter 1, the global context in which we all work is changing and evolving at a rapid rate and it is the dimension of contextual intelligence that the *intelligent school* recognizes cannot be ignored. The issues discussed at the 2002 international world summit on sustainability of the environment are a case in point and an understanding of global issues and concerns is integral to the development of SQ, EthQ and EQ. The *intelligent school* addresses these 'big' issues so that the pupils can become fully involved in discussing and acting upon global matters in such a way that they can sustain their interest and involvement in these as they move into adulthood.

In summary, contextual intelligence is the capacity of the school to see itself in relationship to its local and wider community and the world in which it is a part. The *intelligent school* has a capacity to 'read its overall context' in a way that it is neither overwhelmed by it, nor distanced from it, but instead is in a healthy relationship with it and is proactive and responsive to both its positive and negative aspects. It recognizes the complexity of the context in which the school works and can work with that complexity. It understands that the different dimensions of the context in which it works can and does create conflicting demands and a degree of uncertainty, hence the need to be flexible, creative and adaptable to create a framework that enables a systematic sustained approach to development over time.

Operational intelligence

It is one thing to have a clear vision based on an explicit set of values and beliefs. It is quite another, however, to realize that vision in practice. Operational intelligence (OQ) plays a key role in this process. Whilst systemic intelligence enables the essential flow between vision and action, the *intelligent school* understands that operational intelligence provides a much needed implementation framework. This framework involves:

- thinking strategically;
- having a planned approach to development;
- putting in place an enabling set of management arrangements;
- ensuring that leadership roles are distributed throughout the school.

It will be seen from the core concepts underlying the implementation framework that our definition of operational intelligence goes way beyond day-to-day management issues. There are those who argue that there is a need for a clear distinction between strategic and operational management (Middlewood and Lumby, 1999; Bush and Coleman, 2000; Fidler, 2000; Mintzberg, 2002). We do not find these arguments particularly helpful. Instead, our experience of *intelligent schools* is that arising out of their systemic intelligence they use a range of implementation strategies which, when used in combination, provide them with a framework to operationalize their vision for the school.

Thinking strategically

The first of these strategies is strategic thinking. We agree with West-Burnham et al. (1995) that there is a lack of consensus in the literature about what strategic thinking means. As Weindling (1997, p. 220) points out, 'The business literature uses a variety of terms such as "strategic management", "strategic planning" and "strategic thinking". But in essence, strategy is the process by which members of the organization envision its future and develop the necessary procedures to achieve that future'.

We do not want to get embroiled in debates about terminology. Instead, from our experience *intelligent schools*, thinking strategically, recognize that if they are to put their vision into action they need to operate simultaneously

126

at different levels. In other words, they need to use a combination
term, medium-term and long-term strategies to achieve their vis'
school. Gray et al. (1999) in their in-depth study of 12 schools dun..
1990s, which we described in Chapter 3, identified strategic thinking as one
of the three approaches to school improvement they observed in the schools.
They found that schools improving more rapidly were using a combination of
medium-term strategic thinking with short-term tactics.

A salutary lesson from the research was that even the schools using a combination of strategic thinking and tactical approaches found it difficult to sustain the developments on which they were working. Because of, for example,
the demands they placed on staff and the departure of key staff. The research
team found only two schools that were not only using tactics and strategic
thinking but were also into long-term 'capacity-building': 'These two schools
had gone beyond incremental approaches to change and were engaged in
some organisational restructuring with enhanced learning as an intended outcome' (ibid., p. 146). These schools were focusing on pupils' learning and
teachers' learning and using a wide range of strategies to maximize the use of
and sharing of internal expertise together with drawing on external advice and
expertise.

As a result, Gray et al. found that 'In only one of the two schools however did
the school's practices seem sufficiently well embedded for us to be confident in
talking about its *capacity* to improve. It would seem unwise to rely too heavily
on approaches to change which assume that such a capacity is widely in place'
(ibid., p. 146). This is an important finding in the context of our concept of the
intelligent school. Too often in the school improvement literature, capacity-
building is discussed in the absence of specific strategies for enabling this to happen. We agree with Fullan (2001a), that capacity-building is also an operational
issue. In other words, it involves 'walking the talk'. The *intelligent school* recognizes that operational intelligence provides the framework for implementing
change, but it is only when it is used in combination with PQ, RQ and CoQ
which all have learning as their focus, that action leading to sustained, long-term
improvement can become a reality. This is confirmed by Gray et al. (1999, p.
146) who found that 'Schools which had developed policies for supporting
teaching and learning and which have begun to focus on ways of tackling the
processes of teaching and learning improved more rapidly'.

They concluded that 'The development of greater awareness of "learning
level" strategies will probably be crucial to the next phase of school improvement' (ibid., p. 147). They cautioned that the schools they observed did not
find this easy. What marks out the *intelligent school* is that it recognizes this
challenge. It knows that to bring about change and improvement over time,
there needs to be a balance between the use of tactical, policy development
and capacity-building strategies. It is explicit as to what that balance is at any
one time and why. This then enables a strategic approach to improvement and

the establishment of a development plan with an accompanying action plan that incorporates these three levels of operation.

Development planning

Development planning, or improvement planning as it is sometimes called, has been long established in schools as an improvement strategy and, as described in Chapter 3, research into its use indicates that some plans are more effective than others and that not all plans lead to improvement (Hargreaves and Hopkins, 1991; Wallace, 1994; MacGilchrist et al., 1995). The *intelligent school* uses development planning not just to work on school-wide policy and practice, but also, and most importantly, to make a direct link between learning and teaching in the classroom. Hopkins and MacGilchrist (1998) describe the strategies schools use to do this. They argue that a key to achieving this link was the nature of the management arrangements in the school.

Management arrangements

The *intelligent school* recognizes that as part of its implementation framework it needs to think carefully about the management arrangements it puts in place. As Hopkins and MacGilchrist (1998, p. 413) argue: 'In schools that are improving, the activities of management are strongly directed at classrooms and in secondary schools, subject departments. Energies are concentrated on developments related to improving the quality of teaching and learning and to the raising of expectations.'

The point being made is that management arrangements cannot function in isolation from classroom practice and children's learning. The arrangements in place need not only to enable the school as a whole to run smoothly, but also to support directly and indirectly teachers and others in bringing about improvements in the quality of teaching which is itself directly linked to identified plans for improvement in the quality of children's learning experiences and their progress and achievement.

Distributed leadership

The *intelligent school* recognizes that the ownership of any development plan and the rationale for the management arrangements will depend on the extent to which teachers and others have been involved in identifying the priorities for improvement. Pedagogical intelligence, RQ and CoQ will all contribute to this identification process. An important aspect of management arrangements is the particular roles and responsibilities held by staff. The *intelligent school* understands that when considering roles and responsibilities it is important to share or distribute leadership responsibility throughout the school as discussed in Chapter 3. The *intelligent school* recognizes that this avoids a culture of top-down change and instead creates a culture in which teachers are given real leadership roles in which they can assume a professional responsibility and accountability for implementing a priority in the development plan. MacBeath (1998, p. 108) argues that 'Implementing "distributed leadership" must be worked through in appropriate ways in different countries, but we are firmly of the view that in a collegial setting, such as a school, moving in this direction is essential'. Collegial intelligence has a key role to play in this process.

Emotional intelligence

Emotional intelligence (EQ) is concerned with a school's capacity to allow the feelings of both pupils and staff to be owned, expressed and respected. Such a capacity should extend to parents and the community as a whole. Goleman (1999, p. 317) describes emotional intelligence, or EQ as it has come to be known, as 'the capacity for recognizing our own feelings and those of others, for motivating ourselves, and for managing emotions well in ourselves and in our relationships'.

Goleman (1999) argues that EQ is distinct from, but complementary to intelligence quotient, known as IQ and that EQ is a basic requirement for the effective use of IQ. From his studies of successful organizations, he concludes that EQ is more important than IQ in determining the performance of an organization. He is of the view that an organization high in EQ can maximize its intellectual capital. Such an organization enables staff to feel that what they do is worthwhile and valued, which in turn results in a motivated workforce that has a high achievement drive. Putting a school's vision into action must have an emotional dimension.

Goleman describes an organization low in EQ as having a 'weakened immune system'. On the other hand, an organization high in EQ can benefit from: 'An inoculation that preserves health and encourages growth ... If a company (or school) has the competencies that flow from self-awareness and self-regulation, motivation and empathy, leadership skills and open communications, it should prove more resilient no matter what the future brings' (ibid., p. 312). The *intelligent school* recognizes that it needs to value and cultivate its emotional competence.

Emotional intelligence has become a fashionable topic in the world of education, particularly since Goleman (1996) applied the notion to schools and to the education of young people. There are researchers who warn against some of Goleman's claims about EQ (Petrides and Furnham, 2001; Roberts, Zeidner and Matthews, 2001) and who remind us that EQ is difficult to pin down and even harder to measure. Nevertheless, it appears that EQ is at least as important as IQ within an organization, but that the differential performance between organizations cannot be explained by EQ alone. This supports our own view that the *intelligent school* draws on at least nine intelligences to maximize its effectiveness, but that developing EQ is of fundamental importance in this process.

Salovey and Mayer (1998) argue that people differ in their capacity to understand and express emotions. They are of the view that 'such differences may be rooted in underlying skills that can be learned' (ibid., p. 315). Drawing on the features of EQ identified by Salovey and Mayer and by others (Gardner, 1983; 1999; Goleman, 1996; 1999), there appear to be at least four concepts (or capabilities) that underpin EQ:

- self-awareness;
- awareness of others;
- managing emotions;
- developing emotional literacy.

These concepts apply to individuals, teams and the school as a whole.

Self-awareness

Self-awareness in this context is about developing shared values requiring organizational self-awareness, which in turn relies on the degree of self-awareness of its members. Gardner's (1983) notion of intrapersonal intelligence is a useful link here. It concerns the capacity to be aware of one's own feelings, the causes of feelings and the recognition of the potential influence that emotions can have on decision-making. Goleman (1999, p. 318) also points out that self-awareness is about having a 'realistic assessment of one's own abilities and a well-grounded sense of confidence'.

Awareness of others

Awareness of others is connected with Gardner's notion of interpersonal intelligence. It concerns the importance of interpersonal relationships throughout the school. This involves the relations between pupils; between adults; and the interactions between the adults and pupils. It involves the capacity to empathize with others by 'sensing what people are feeling, being able to take their perspective, and cultivating a rapport and attunement with a broad diversity of people' (Goleman, 1999, p. 318). It concerns being a good listener, knowing the right questions to ask of others and, as a consequence, it involves trust, openness and good communications. It concerns the capacity, therefore, to 'handle emotions in relationships well and accurately read social situations and networks; to interact smoothly; and to use these skills to persuade and lead, negotiate and settle disputes, for cooperation and team work' (ibid.).

Managing emotions

Managing emotions appears to have three distinct, but linked skills.

- management of emotions;
- management with emotion;
- management through emotion.

The management of emotions concerns what is often called self-regulation, which Goleman (1999, p. 318) describes as learning how 'to handle our emotions so that they facilitate rather than interfere with the task in hand; be conscientious and delay gratification to pursue goals; and to recover well from emotional distress'. In practice, it is about how people, adults and children, treat each other in the school, the headteacher being an important role model here. It can relate to a school's behaviour management policy and the practical strategies it uses to help children to self-regulate their own behaviour. For example, a group of schools with which one of us has been working, encouraged the children to set their own ground rules for behaving and learning in the classroom, which included making all classrooms, and the school as a whole, a 'no put down zone'. This ensured that individuals exercised self-control in how they responded to and respected the views and emotions expressed by others.

Management with emotion involves the skill of using intrapersonal and interpersonal intelligence to motivate others. It focuses on the importance of those in leadership positions demonstrating vision, self-belief and determination, putting the concerns of others first and encouraging others to persevere in the face of setbacks and frustrations. It requires an awareness of the impact that not just words, but also non-verbal signals, can have on the motivation of others. It concerns, therefore, an understanding that 'you are what you do', and that actions can have as much, if not more impact, than words alone. Sensitivity is at the heart of this aspect of EQ.

Management through emotion concerns the ability to recognize the emotional strengths of individual members of staff and to use these when bringing staff together and building teams. Effective teamwork requires group identity, a collective self-belief and mutual trust. Thinking through the composition of teams, including the recruitment of new staff, are important elements of EQ. An emotionally literate school can increase job satisfaction and encourage teacher retention.

Developing emotional literacy

As already indicated, EQ can be learnt. An important part of that learning process is to do with the way things are communicated and the extent to which staff and pupils grasp, not just what needs to be learnt and taught, but why. Boyatzis (2000, p. 117) argues that 'Emotional intelligence is contagious, as is the lack of it'. He stresses the importance of leaders and teachers modelling emotionally intelligent behaviour. Goleman (1999) warns that schools tend to ignore emotional intelligence and focus instead on academic intelligence. This behaviour is difficult to avoid when governments focus on a narrow attainment rather than a broad achievement agenda. Goleman (1999, p. 27) argues that emotional intelligence represents a set of traits that can matter immensely for the personal destiny of young people. We concur with his view that 'Emotional literacy implies an expanded mandate for schools... . Teachers need to go beyond their traditional mission and people in the community need to become more involved with schools'. He argues that we need to 'rethink the notion of the "basics" in education: emotional intelligence is now as crucial to our children's future as the standard academic fare' (ibid., p. 313).

Goleman (1996) stresses that emotional literacy can be taught and must not be left to chance. The *intelligent school* recognizes that developing emotional literacy is helping children to learn the essential lessons for life. For pupils it plays a key role in becoming an educated person. *Intelligent schools* are using a wide range of strategies for assessing and developing emotional literacy. For example, they are using 360-degree feedback involving key stakeholders, in particular, children, teachers, support staff and parents. Videos of lessons are proving helpful as a focus for discussion as are mentoring and coaching, with the latter being recognized by the National College for School Leadership as of growing importance in leadership development.

These four concepts underpinning EQ have significant implications for the content and processes of learning and teaching and the way in which a school is led and managed. Goleman (1999) argues that EQ is a vital capacity for learning and a key characteristic of effective leadership. The *intelligent school* understands that this means that the model provided by teachers and leaders is all important. 'An emotionally intelligent organization needs to come to terms with any disparities between the values it proclaims and those it lives' (Goleman, 1999, p. 281). The *intelligent school* attempts to practise what it preaches.

Collegial intelligence

Collegial intelligence (CoQ) plays an important role in helping the other intelligences to develop and flourish. Writing about leadership, Senge (2002, p. 4) suggests: 'The capacity of a human community – people living and working together – to bring forth new realities is a simple definition of leadership that also points to the interplay of individual and community.' This interplay between the individual and the community is at the heart of collegial intelligence. The *intelligent school* uses CoQ to achieve a shared sense of purpose and commitment to change and improvement. Networking and learning from each other is not only encouraged within the school but also between schools – locally, regionally, nationally and, even, globally.

Collegial intelligence relates closely to reflective and pedagogical intelligence. Staff working together is an important aspect of collegial intelligence but only an aspect. Pupils need to be involved here too. Saunders (1999, p. 425) suggests that

> if we attended to issues of equity and democracy better, particularly in the sense of really listening to what young people themselves say about what they value and dislike about their schools, about what inhibits or helps their genuine involvement in learning, perhaps we might find a way of getting to grips with the 'long tail' of underachievement.

For the *intelligent school*, good relationships and exchange of experience do not stop at the classroom door but are positively encouraged across the school and, indeed, are essential to building the school as a healthy, sustainable community. While students are developing the skills of learning to learn, they are doing so with each other and with their teachers in a range of settings, and their teachers are also learning about learning.

Senge (1999) says there should be no one driving a school, rather there are many people tending to the garden. As we described in Chapter 6, many school improvement studies confirm the centrality of collegial intelligence. Hargreaves (1994, p. 186) states that 'if one of the most prominent heresies of educational change is the culture of individualism, then collaboration and collegiality are pivotal to the orthodoxies of change'. He then, as outlined in Chapter 6, conducts a careful critique of the dangers of collegiality when much of the change that schools are engaged in is conducted from outside. However, the *intelligent school* takes charge of its own agenda and pace for change and collegial intelligence is crucial for that to take place.

The four aspects of collegial intelligence are:

- commitment to a shared purpose;
- knowledge creation;
- multi-level learning;
- trust and curiosity.

Commitment to a shared purpose

Collegial intelligence is not just the capacity of staff and pupils to come together and support each other, important as that is as a starting point.

'Congenial' becomes 'collegial' because of a shared and agreed purpose. The *intelligent school* is learning focused and learning enriched. Regardless of role, deeper learning is what all its members are striving for. The first task of collegial intelligence is to foster and promote the commitment of everyone to this purpose.

Knowledge creation

Collegial intelligence also has a harder edge to it. It involves the development of social learning that enables the core functions of a school and their related technologies to be articulated, developed, transported and used. Louis (1998) says that this collective use and creation of knowledge is what enables a school to move beyond learning that rests with individuals. Knowledge creation has traditionally been seen as an individual act by either a teacher or a pupil in a school. Increasingly, it is being understood to be a social process within a school. Critical enquiry and classroom research in a school are less effective if they are carried out by individuals on their own. The use of CoQ is required to make the results of new knowledge known, available and to support its application in practice. Here we can then see the interrelationship between pedagogical, reflective and collegial intelligence as they work together to produce even greater intelligence in a school. Hargreaves (2001b) has also identified the 'knowledge creating' school and argues that these schools can assess their intellectual capital and know how to create, validate and disseminate new knowledge. Without collegial intelligence this could never happen. The Networked Learning Communities initiative from the National College for School Leadership is promoting this model of school change.

Multi-level learning

Collegial intelligence, as we have already argued, does not just operate on the one dimension of teachers working together. It is a much richer, more complex set of capabilities that reflect the change from school structures based on 'single cell classrooms' to classrooms becoming interdependent parts of a whole. Understanding collegial intelligence alerts us to the potential and demands of working together in order to connect individual, team and organizational learning and to breathe life into the rhetoric and exhortation to schools to become 'learning communities'.

Senge (1995) has identified the crucial role that colleagues he terms 'local line leaders' play in business organizations with which he works. These would be the equivalent of middle leaders in schools. He goes so far as to say that 'Nothing can start without committed local line leaders' (ibid., p. 4). He identifies their significant responsibilities and 'bottom-line' focus and identifies their key role as sanctioning 'practical experiments and to lead through their active participation of those experiments' (ibid.). This is a change from the traditional role of the curriculum leader in a school as one who simply has subject knowledge to impart, to a model where, in the *intelligent school* these colleagues are leading in creative experimentation and the creation of new knowledge about what works or does not in learning and teaching and then assessing its impact.

Senge does not rule out the contribution that executive, or senior colleagues can make within learning organizations. However, he gives them quite a different focus to the traditional 'captain of the ship' role of hierarchical leaders. He has come to see that 'local line leaders' can benefit from the role of their executive colleagues as protectors, mentors and thinking partners.

The significance of CoQ within the *intelligent school* is that it can enable these different 'levels' to operate together and strengthen each others' functioning, to truly become 'distributed'. A quite different view to the twentieth-century approach to school leadership that we are leaving behind.

Trust and curiosity

Elmore (2000) argues that the 'loose coupling' of classrooms from each other and the school as a whole is one of the main reasons that it becomes hard for schools to become open systems with shared beliefs and agreed norms about classroom practice. This culture is very old and in many schools still deeply entrenched. Cochran-Smith and Lytle (1993) identify four obstacles to teachers researching their practice together. One of these is teacher isolation and another they refer to as 'occupational socialization'. This is a belief that 'asking questions and being uncertain are inappropriate behaviours for all but the most inexperienced teachers and even they have only brief periods of grace during which they may ask a limited number of questions' (ibid., p. 87).

Reed and Learmonth (2001) have identified negative and positive cultural features of 'organizational health' in a school as Table 7.3 illustrates.

Table 7.3 *Aspects of organizational health in schools that supprt teachers' development and learning in Reed and Learmonth (2001, p. 21)*

Negative	Positive
The classroom is an independent area	The classroom is part of the whole school
Teaching is 'routinized'	Teaching has a flexibility of approach
Teachers feel isolated	Teachers have a sense of agency
Delivery of the curriculum is the dominant approach	There is a design approach to learning, based on a detailed analysis of pupils'
There is little or no sense of control over impacts	learning needs and stages of development
	There is a sense of control over impacts

The *intelligent school* uses and creates collegial intelligence to foster teacher and pupil agency, to overcome teacher isolation and to take charge of change. Senge (1995) argues that when there is a more collaborative and distributed approach to leadership then change is more likely to take place from a committed position rather than one of compliance, and that fear and defensiveness are less likely to flourish.

Tightly controlled top-down performance management systems do not foster a culture of trust. O'Neill presenting the BBC 2002 Reith lectures on the topic of trust in the public sector shows that this concern is not confined only to education.

> We may constantly seek to make others trustworthy, but some of the regimes of accountability and transparency developed across the last 15 years may damage rather than reinforce trustworthiness. The intrusive methods that we have taken to stem a supposed crisis of trust may even, if things go badly, lead to a genuine crisis of trust.
>
> If we want to avoid this unfortunate spiral we need to think less about accountability through micro-management and central control, and more about good governance; less about transparency and more about limiting deception. If we are to restore trust we shall have to start communicating in ways that are open to assessment … . (O'Neill, 2002, pp. 99–100)

Reflective intelligence

A publication commissioned by the National Union of Teachers (MacBeath, 1999, p. 9) states that: 'In teaching, as in many professions, the commitment to critical systematic reflection on practice as a basis for individual and collective development is at the heart of what it means to be a professional.'

The four aspects of reflective intelligence (RQ) are:

- creating time for reflection;
- self-evaluation;
- deep learning;
- feedback for learning.

Creating time for reflection

Schools are very action orientated. Making choices and decisions quickly and efficiently is part of their role and finding time to reflect often feels like an impossibility. Barth (2001, p. 228) echoes that when he says 'the general feeling is that there is not time for reflection in school. We are too busy and reflection requires a slower, more thoughtful frame of mind'. The *intelligent school* knows that it is really important amidst the bustle and busyness of school life to find time for reflection. In Chapter 4, when we discussed research about learning, the value of reflection emerged as of great importance. Opportunities for reflection are vital to effective learning. Trying to learn without having the time to think about what is happening, and why and how it is happening, is like trying to run when your lungs have not got the oxygen they need. It does not work!

So it is at the whole-school level. If we are to genuinely put the rights and responsibilities of our pupils at the heart of the enterprise, if this is the real aim of our schools, then teachers, support staff, parents and governors need not just to be *learners* at the individual level, they need to be *learning* too: learning together, reflecting together critically about what is happening and whether it is working in relation to shared criteria. Because there are so many other calls on colleagues' time this process needs prioritizing and managing if it is to happen and if it is to happen well, and if it is to happen critically.

Self-evaluation

In Chapter 4 we saw what a crucial role reflection plays in learning. Reflective intelligence is active when schools have the capacity to think about what they are doing, pose questions and seek considered ways of answering them through the use of evidence. It involves a realization that reflecting either alone or with others, even very informally, usually produces new information about what is happening, how colleagues are feeling, what the pupils are telling their teachers, the nature of particular incidents in school and so on.

The *intelligent* aspect to this process is precisely what happens to that information. This is why this intelligence appears in the action rather than the vision dimension of the intelligences. There are literally hundreds of times each school week when interpretations are being made about what an event or issue means. Decisions are then made about what to do. Schools are in the learning business and need a way of handling the complexity of all the 'data' that comes their way. The process needs a systematic dimension to it. *Intelligent schools* utilize self-evaluation strategies in order to reflect on their progress. This involves deciding what data needs to be collected, for what purpose and then interpreting and converting this into evidence that can be shared and used to inform action.

Because of the complexity of school life not everything can be thought about at once even though it often seems that is what is required! There has to be a selection made about what to focus on and a justification for that selection. For example, a group of Somerset headteachers with whom one of us worked reflected on the extent to which the aims of their school were being realized. They then revitalized and renewed the process of achieving their aims as an important agenda for self-evaluation along with meeting current quality assurance and accountability priorities.

The *intelligent school* uses reflective intelligence to make informed choices and to create a rationale from inside the school as well as from outside about what it wants to monitor and evaluate and why. It is a cyclical, relational set of practices and capabilities with the quality of the learning, progress and achievement of the pupils as its central concern. MacGilchrist (2000) distinguishes between three different but interrelated levels of evaluation that would be operating in the *intelligent school*:

- *'Macro' self-evaluation* which draws on contextual intelligence to ask questions and collect data about its 'big picture' operations and overall effectiveness;
- *'Means-end' self-evaluation* which focuses on the extent to which plans and activities organized for improvement purposes are actually having an impact on the progress and learning of pupils;
- *'Micro' self-evaluation* that focuses on the quality of processes in the classroom.

Each of these feeds the reflective intelligence of the school, operating and drawing on the evidence being generated by the other two aspects to provide a rich picture of exactly what is happening. This leads to much deeper and enlivening understandings of the purposes of school evaluation than some current more mechanistic models suggest.

Deep learning

Reed and Learmonth (2001) discuss the difference between 'shallow' and 'deep' school improvement arguing a case for both. They are of the view that the dominance of the performance and accountability agenda is tipping the balance too much in the direction of the shallow. The same is probably the case with school evaluation. Clarke (1999) cautions us against practice that leads to avoidance and superficiality. Reflective intelligence leads the *intelligent school* to ask increasingly deeper and deeper questions about the school that can be investigated successfully by an increasing number of both adults and children in the school.

Reed and Street (2002), suggest there should be a distinction between *school* evaluation and school *self*-evaluation. The authors argue that a review of the literature suggests that there has been plenty of evaluation activity conducted by schools but that it has tended to be outcomes driven, essentially related to attainment, and often prompted more by external demands, particularly inspection, than by a genuine interest in using reflective intelligence for the internal purposes described above.

The authors identify five outcomes of successful school self-evaluation that illustrate the use of reflective intelligence to bring about deep learning. They suggest that schools that are successfully using self-evaluation techniques are able to:

- develop an ethos where pupils and colleagues experience evaluation as a motivating and empowering activity;
- create their own knowledge about learning and teaching by finding out and reflecting on what is taking place in classrooms and link that to their understanding of where the school is;
- develop their skills in giving and receiving feedback and ensure that the feedback informs their future action;
- develop their leadership and management practices so that they are enabling, encouraging and supporting students and staff in focusing on the core purpose of learning;
- ensure that everyone is participating in the process and action is resulting (ibid., p. 5).

Feedback for learning

The *intelligent school* ensures that reflective intelligence works with pedagogical intelligence to put pupils' learning at the centre of its enquiries. At the interface between these two intelligences is the critical contribution of the use of feedback for learning by teachers and children alike. The *intelligent school* knows that successful school self-evaluation is very dependent on effective processes of formative as well as summative assessment. What the pupils say about their learning, how successful they are and the extent that they are learning how to learn are all indicators of an *intelligent school* in operation. Integral to its success is its capacity to collect and critique the extent to which this is happening, for which pupils and when.

Leeuw (2001) draws attention to the *reciprocity* needed for successful reflective activity in school. He argues that the willing participation of those involved is critical to its success and the more that it is a two-way process, the more likely it is that the findings from evaluation will be used. He suggests that a culture of *trust* is a crucial factor in encouraging feedback to occur.

Reflective intelligence has a clear sense of the importance of collecting the perceptions of pupils as well as teachers and other stakeholders to get an accurate picture of its operations. Reciprocity has been at the heart of one of the projects that ISEIC has been working on with Slough LEA. Questionnaires have been sent to a sample of each stakeholder group in the participating schools in order to discover the perceptions they each have about a range of the school's functioning. Those working on the project have then been practising their reflective intelligence by discussing and interpreting the data produced and the appropriate direction that school improvement might need to take as a result.

In a Dorset project the teachers have been beginning their investigations into their pupils' learning by reflecting on what the pupils say in response to the following questions: What makes a good lesson? Who is a good learner in this school? What does your teacher do to help you learn? This model of getting feedback begins to get at information that is not always observable.

Reed and Stoll (2000) explore the contribution of feedback at the organizational level of a school. They suggest that feedback has four main functions in organizational learning and we would suggest these are very pertinent to the *intelligent school*:

> Feedback has a *bridging* function when it can link otherwise separate or disparate information and bring these into a useful relationship with each other. Feedback has an *illuminative* function when it sheds light on problems and conundrums that seem otherwise insoluble and enables a school to move forward. Feedback has a *challenging* function when it enables the reframing of information in a way that brings new meaning to bear. Feedback can *renew purpose* when it re-connects a school to its primary task of educating young people and is reminded that they are the primary motivation for all organisational learning. (Ibid., p. 141)

Pedagogical intelligence

Pedagogical intelligence (PQ) is a school's capacity to combine the knowledge and know-how it has about learning to create an environment that engages and challenges pupils. It is the capacity to act on the knowledge and understanding about learning to develop a programme of appropriate teaching. Pedagogical intelligence is at work where the relationship between learning and teaching is regularly being reflected on, strengthened and developed. Pedagogy should never be an orthodoxy that remains unexamined.

In the introduction to this chapter reference was made to Senge's argument that we need to move to a more organic understanding of schools as organizations and away from the predominantly linear and mechanistic model that we have at present. In the *intelligent school* the dynamic relationship between learning and teaching is recognized and in evidence. The *intelligent school* has a deep grasp of the uniqueness of both learning and teaching and the nature of their interdependence and how they work in action together.

Pedagogical intelligence has the following aspects:

- new visions and goals for learning;
- teaching for learning;
- open classrooms;
- going against the grain.

New visions and goals for learning

Chapter 1 described how, at the beginning of the twenty-first century, schools operate in a complex world that is full of paradox and change. We argued that pupils need to become confident, self-fulfilled lifelong learners and that this might mean that schools need to be organized and structured on the basis of new metaphors that replace the mechanistic utilitarian ones of our founding fathers. New directions for schools involving them in more complex, inclusive goals are an exciting prospect. We explore this further in the final chapter.

The need for new visions for learning provides pedagogical intelligence with its *raison d'être*. In order successfully to mobilize their pedagogical intelligence, schools need to utilize their contextual intelligence. They need to be able to 'read' their environment and discern the influences on the lives and learning of their pupils. Learning and teaching need to be 'fit for purpose'. In this sense pedagogical intelligence and contextual intelligence work together in order to ensure that a school is responding to the learning needs of its pupils. Ireson, Mortimore and Hallam (1999, p. 220) define fitness for purpose as 'an alignment between the needs of the learner, the desired learning outcomes and the tasks and activities designed by the teacher to achieve those outcomes'.

Teaching for learning

Goals for teaching and learning are put into practice at the 'microlevel' of the classroom. In Chapter 4 we outlined research that a school can draw on in order to ensure that effective learning is taking place. In Chapter 5 we made the point that teaching is a combination of knowledge, skills and operational practices that do not work independently or stand alone. It is also completely dependent for its success on the relationship it has with learning and learners. Teaching for learning occurs, as identified in Chapter 5, when learners are engaged, their learning preferences and background respected and developed, and when information gathered with them about learning is being utilized. Pedagogical intelligence is a way of seeing this reciprocity between learners and teachers. It is learning and teaching in action which we tried to capture in our notion of the learning and teaching PACT in Chapter 5.

Open classrooms

The social and complex nature of effective learning and teaching means that classrooms can no longer operate in isolation. This was highlighted by Elmore in Chapter 1. He argues that for deep change to take place in schools, the 'instructional core', i.e. the classroom, needs to be open to scrutiny. He suggests that for too long classrooms have operated in what he terms a loosely coupled system and that they now need to be more open. We also discussed this proposition when describing the nature of collegial intelligence. When we see collegial intelligence in operation with pedagogical intelligence, it describes not just staff working together but pupils and teachers fully engaged across open boundaries enlivening and enriching their learning.

Going against the grain

An important part of pedagogical intelligence is taking risks and trying out new ideas. Regrettably the high stakes accountability culture founded on target-setting and on performance outcomes that currently prevails in England has discouraged experimentation and creativity in the relationships between teachers and their pupils. This is despite the fact that, as we have demonstrated, research evidence and the wisdom of the profession tells us that risk-taking is essential to learning, and creativity is the lifeblood of good teaching.

As Fullan and Hargreaves (1998, p. 49) argue: 'It is time we had a new kind of accountability in education – one that gets back to the moral basics of caring, serving, empowering and learning.' We have argued throughout this book that an emphasis on performance without attending to learning will not achieve the goals that we need for education in the twenty-first century. Instead, what we need is learning-centred classrooms, which are not to be confused with child-centred classrooms. The *intelligent school* understands this. It has the confidence to stand by its core values and to 'go against the grain' of notions of pedagogy that are simply teaching centred. It gives teachers permission to experiment. Pedagogical intelligence combines with reflective intelligence to gather together the pupils' views and experiences of their learning. It uses these as a guiding principle in teaching for learning.

Systemic intelligence

At the beginning of this chapter we referred to Peter Senge's wish that schools should be based on living systems instead of the nineteenth-century assembly-line model we have at present. McMaster (1995) discusses systemic intelligence (SyQ) as a way of thinking about the interrelationships and patterns that enable flow and connection between the parts that make up an organizational whole. For us, SyQ is what enables the other eight intelligences to work together.

The intelligences are interdependent, interrelated and have overlapping characteristics. Pedagogical intelligence depends on contextual intelligence and neither of them can function without ethical intelligence, which forms their purpose and direction. Pedagogical intelligence is also found in reflective intelligence, and they both rely on operational intelligence to help them realize their potential. Likewise, emotional and spiritual intelligence depend very much on each other. These are just some of the examples that demonstrate the interdependent nature of the intelligences. SyQ ensures that the individual intelligences operate in an open productive relationship with each other.

The four attributes of systemic intelligence are:

- mental models;
- systems thinking;
- self-organization;
- networking.

Mental models

A mental model is like a mind map that informs the way we view the world. Mental models derive from the assumptions, beliefs and attitudes that people hold. They can be articulated and shared in order to enrich the life and function of an organization or they can remain hidden and cause barriers or unexplained conflict to arise.

Senge (1993, p. 174) describes how

> New insights fail to get put into practice because they conflict with deeply held internal images of how the world works, images that limit us to familiar ways of thinking and acting. That is why the discipline of managing mental models – surfacing, testing and improving our internal pictures of how the world works – promises to be a major breakthrough for building learning organisations.

The *intelligent school* is able not just to understand its own thinking but to challenge its assumptions and prejudices. It draws on its reflective intelligence to do so. Unexamined mental models get in the way of change. Senge stresses, however, that the aim is not to achieve congruence of mental models but the best model for the task at hand. A number of different models can exist together at the same time.

The *intelligent school* understands that when mental models and belief systems are examined there is a greater chance that both change and coherence can come about in the school. Throughout the previous chapters we have noted various ingrained beliefs in the education world that at the moment stop many of our schools from becoming places of innovation and transformation. In Chapter 4 we saw how mental models about learning are often deeply ingrained and hard to surface. Beliefs, for example, about the nature of intelligence and ability underpin a school's culture and can undermine even the best efforts to enable the students to be better learners. We saw how mental models that are based in deficit thinking, i.e. what can you expect from these children, affect our young pupils' chances in school. Teaching, as we saw in Chapter 5 is still dominated by a mental model of transmission. The role of the teacher is largely seen as to tell the students what to do. A mental model

143

that learning will only happen if a teacher is present also prevents a broader, richer less dependent view of learning developing in our culture. In Chapter 3 we saw how mental models of school improvement that have been reduced to performance outcomes can paradoxically limit a school's chance of becoming a learning organization. These are just a few examples of the mental models that prevail in current educational thinking which can limit a school's transformational potential.

Senge (2000a) draws attention to what he refers to as 'industrial-age' assumptions about learning and schools:

- Children are deficient and schools fix them.
- Learning takes place in the head, not in the body as a whole.
- Everyone learns, or should learn in the same way.
- Learning takes place in the classroom not in the world.
- There are smart kids and there are dumb kids.
- Schools are run by specialists who maintain control.
- Knowledge is inherently fragmented.
- Schools communicate 'The Truth'.
- Learning is primarily individualistic and competition accelerates learning.

He suggests that most educators would not necessarily agree with these assumptions but that they somehow continue to prevail in educational environments.

Systems thinking

Systems thinking, argues Senge (2000a, pp. 52–3),

> starts with the assertion that the fundamental nature of reality is relationships not things ... unlike machines, living systems continually grow and evolve, form new relationships, and have innate goals to exist and to recreate themselves. They are neither predictable nor controllable like machines, though they have patterns of behaviour that tend to recur and their future development can be influenced.

Senge believes that a more relational or systemic view of schools as living systems would bring learning to life. When learning is alive, learner-centred rather than teacher-centred learning abounds. Variety and interdependency become the norm. If schools were really to behave as living systems then two particular changes would be evident. The first would be the examination of mental models. The second is that schools would become a more visible part of the web of relationships in which they are set, which means they would serve a wider constituency.

There is sometimes confusion about what is meant by 'systems thinking' because the word 'system' often has instrumental and mechanistic connotations. We are referring here to a body of thinking, writing and discussion that has been around for most of the last century but has been little applied to public service organizations, especially to education systems. O'Connor and McDermott (1997, p. xiii) in their useful introduction to the field refer to a system as 'Something that maintains its existence and functions as a whole through the interaction of its parts' and that 'their behaviour depends on *how the parts are connected* rather than what the parts are' (ibid., p. 3, italics added). They stress that: 'Systems are interwoven with everything we do and in order to gain more influence over them, to gain a better quality of life, we need to understand how they work' (ibid., p. 4).

Systems *thinking* they describe as:

> Look(ing) at the whole, and the parts, and the connections between the parts, studying the whole in order to understand the parts. It is the opposite to reductionism, the idea that something is simply the sum of the parts. A collection of parts that do not connect is not a system. It is a heap. (Ibid., p. 2)

To illustrate this point they distinguish between a 'system' and a 'heap' (Table 7.4).

Table 7.4 *Differences between a 'system' and a 'heap'*

A system	A heap
Interconnecting parts functioning as a whole	A collection of parts
Changed if you take away pieces or add more pieces. If you cut a system in half, you do not get two smaller systems, but a damaged system that will probably not function.	Essential properties are unchanged whether you add or take away pieces. When you halve a heap, you get two smaller heaps.
The arrangement of the pieces is crucial.	The arrangement of the pieces is irrelevant.
The parts are connected and work together.	The parts are not connected and can function separately.
Its behaviour depends on the total structure. Change the structure and the behaviour changes.	Its behaviour (if any) depends on its size or on the number of pieces in the heap.

Source: O'Connor and McDermott (1997, p. 2)

The difference between a 'system' and a 'heap' could easily be applied to a school. If classrooms are perceived as a collection of parts then joined up thinking about the quality of pupils' overall learning experience as they move from class to class or lesson to lesson is prevented. Systems thinking is a crucial aspect of SyQ. It enables 'joined up thinking' and coherence to become a reality.

Peter Vaill (1996) identifies an important connection between the process of learning and systems thinking that lies at the heart of SyQ. He interviewed successful learners and says that:

> What is fairly obvious from the way these people talked about their learning is that the process of becoming increasingly competent amounts to an increasing understanding of a subject in what can be called systems terms. Whatever it is they have become good at is not fragmented for them, not isolated from its environment, not isolated in time or space. They know the relevant elements and their interelationships intimately. These learners have a feel for the *meaning* of the subject beyond its technical detail and its formal structure. They have operative knowledge about this system, which is to say they know how to get this complex something to work in the way that they intend ... . (Ibid., p. 111)

This could be a description of an *intelligent school* in action! It also shows the way that learning and systems thinking are part of each other.

Self-organization

Margaret Wheatley (1992) has been clarifying the notion of self-organization by applying some of what we know from ecology about the functioning of the natural world to the workings of human organizations. She refers to the capacity of the self-organizing organization to renew itself. Self-organization in this sense is the power of those within a school to take the direction and destiny of the school into their own hands and make sense of it in order to bring the necessary changes about. 'We are beginning to see organisations that tap into this property of self-organising or renewing systems ... both types of organisation avoid rigid or permanent structures and instead develop a capacity to respond to a need. When the need changes, so does the organisational structure' (ibid., p. 91).

Self-organization as a property of an *intelligent school* suggests the power of the school to adapt to its environment in order to achieve its goals. Garmston and Wellman (1995, p. 8) suggest that: 'If adaptivity is the central operating principle for successful organisations and for successful schools, then we must search for sources of energy to vitalise this process.'

Goleman (1998, p. 298) describes the process of being engaged in continuous and overlapping feedback loops (reflective intelligence), gathering information from within and without (contextual intelligence) and adjusting operation (operational intelligence) accordingly: 'Systems theory tells us that in an environment of turbulent change and competition, the entity that can take in information most widely, learn from it most thoroughly, and respond most nimbly, creatively and flexibly will be the most adaptive.'

Networking

Developing systemic intelligence enables us to understand first that a school is not just a collection of parts. Its parts and subsystems cohere to make up the whole. Second, it is dependent on an accurate reading of the environment for its existence. Third, all a school's systems, operations and key players are dependent on each other for their own success. Therefore, a key attribute of systemic intelligence in action is building networks and making partnerships.

The use of, and understanding about, networks have developed rapidly in the past 20 years as the world we live in has become more open and complex. Mental models have changed adapting to more flexible ways of running organizations. The Networked Learning Communities initiative from the National College for School Leadership, has encouraged schools to work together to develop themselves as a network. This approach means schools have to be more open, relying on trust and influence rather than position and status. The *intelligent school* knows that networking is very important between teachers within the school as well as between schools. Askew and Carnell (1998) describe the work of teachers who are studying and developing aspects of their school and its learning. Shona has responsibility for staff development and says the following:

> Although I work with people across the entire organisation, I need people to talk things through. So I've set up a small working group which helps me with ideas. I am also working more with people of a similar role in other organisations. Networking is very important. We share lots of ideas and strategies; we contact each other regularly to find out what we are doing as a response to external initiatives … . Email is great for keeping in touch and for debating the ideas in the reading and discussing how it relates to our practice. (Ibid., p. 147)

Through the use of this aspect of systemic intelligence the *intelligent school* maximizes its ability to make full use of internal and external networks.

Corporate intelligence

The *intelligent school* is a dynamic learning community. Its systemic intelligence ensures that there is constant growth and improvement through the use of reinforcing feedback loops because connectivity lies at the heart of SyQ.

Collectively, the nine intelligences represent the corporate intelligence of the *intelligent school*. Figure 7.1 represents this dynamic relationship. The figure is made up of a series of reinforcing feedback loops. In systems dynamics these represent growth, improvement and transformation. They are shown by the arrows all going in the same direction, to illustrate the learning built into the system. If any part of the system is missing or weaker than the others this delays growth or, even worse, sets up a downward spiral.

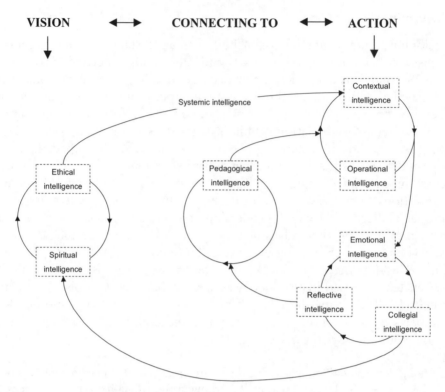

VISION ⬌ **CONNECTING TO** ⬌ **ACTION**

Figure 7.1 Corporate intelligence – the *intelligent school* in action
© B. MacGilchrist, K. Myers and J. Reed, 2004

The vision intelligences are on the left with the action intelligences on the right. The action intelligences work within their own feedback loops. Contextual intelligence and operational intelligence (together) feed into emotional intelligence as the overarching necessary intelligence for collegial intelligence and reflective intelligence. These three together create the teamworking/learning community linchpin. Reflective intelligence feeds into pedagogical intelligence. This is where improvement/transformation is happening with regard to the core purpose of learning and teaching. This in turn feeds back into contextual and operational intelligence, thereby completing the action loop.

None of this is possible without the vision loop, made up of ethical intelligence and spiritual intelligence. These two intelligences are in constant interaction with one another. Ethical intelligence is feeding into contextual intelligence on the grounds that the vision must operate within context otherwise there will be no buy in. Collegial intelligence feeds back into spiritual intelligence, first to get alignment and, secondly, to get distributed leadership based on a sense of community. The whole system is underpinned by systemic intelligence represented by the solid curves in Figure 7.1. It is this intelligence which ensures that vision connects to action, and vice versa.

Leading the *intelligent school*

The nine intelligences have at least three important implications for school leaders. As we have argued, they are interdependent. They have maximum impact when used in combination. They each have the potential to be developed and improved. The challenge for school leaders therefore is to establish a collective understanding of the range of intelligences being used and identify those that need to be developed further. This needs to be done within the context of Dweck's (1999) notion of incremental intelligence whereby everyone recognizes it is possible to improve.

Providing the kind of leadership that uses systemic intelligence to connect vision to action requires a move away from currently held views about the characteristics of effective leadership being promoted, for example, in England. It requires a view, and an exercise of leadership, that is far removed from a technicist, competency-based model of school leadership. It is the kind of leadership that Bhindi and Duignan (1997) describe as 'authentic': 'Authentic leadership is centrally concerned with ethics and morality and with deciding what is significant, what is right and what is "worthwhile"' (ibid., p. 120); 'Leadership is authentic to the degree that it *is* ethical action' (ibid., p. 121); 'Authentic leaders help build and sustain strong organizational visions' (ibid., p. 125).

It is the kind of leadership that creates a human community through the development of EthQ, SQ, EQ and CoQ, and the application of these intelligences through learning and teaching and the work of the school as a whole. Such a community does not have performance outcomes as its driving mantra; rather it is a community that has profound, long-lasting learning at its heart.

Questions for discussion

1 How intelligent are you as a school? Can you do an audit to help you answer this question?
2 How can the nine intelligences be developed and embedded?
3 Are there some that need more attention than others?
4 How dependent are they on key individuals who may move on?
5 Are all schools able to manifest all the intelligences equally? Do they need to?
6 What role do those with leadership responsibilities have to nurture and develop the *intelligent school*?

8
A postscript

In the last chapter we presented nine intelligences which underpin the *intelligent school*. In this chapter we will consider the notion of *intelligent schooling* of the future. We discuss how times are changing, and how they are not. The most worrying constant is that in spite of numerous 'reforms' the link between poverty and low educational achievement continues to challenge us. This is a consistent message from education research. In this postscript, we raise questions that need to be asked about schooling and suggest aspects of the public education system that need to be discarded as well as aspects that should be retained, retrieved, reassessed and taken forward into the future.

Second guessing

As discussed in Chapter 1, globalization, new technologies, new patterns of working and changing expectations are all affecting the way we do things and how we behave. Futurologists are predicting fascinating futures for us some of which have a direct impact on schools and schooling. The OECD (2001) has suggested six different scenarios. Miller and Bentley (2003) discuss their four scenarios, one of which includes schools without pupils, in a paper commissioned by the National College for School Leadership. All these possibilities merit serious attention. In this chapter we offer our version of what could happen. We are aware that second guessing the future is notoriously difficult as some infamous examples demonstrate:

The abdomen, the chest and the brain will forever be shut from the intrusion of the wise and humane surgeon. (Sir John Eric Ericksen, British surgeon, appointed Surgeon-Extraordinary to Queen Victoria, 1873)

Heavier-than-air flying machines are impossible. (Lord Kelvin, president, Royal Society, 1895)

Who the hell wants to hear actors talk? (H.M. Warner, Warner Brothers, 1927)

This 'telephone' has too many shortcomings to be seriously considered as a means of communication. The device is inherently of no value to us. (Western Union, internal memo)

There is no reason anyone would want a computer in their home. (Ken Olson, president and founder of Digital Equipment Corp., 1977)

Source: www.cupola.com/html/wordplay/timely1.htm

It is risky putting your thoughts in print. We hope ours will not come back to haunt us like the examples above. In spite of the risks, we believe that educators have to make some educated guesses in order to prepare for whatever is waiting for our current and future pupils. The one thing that does appear to be certain is that change is inevitable – schools cannot stay as they are. The previous chapters have demonstrated that we are critical of the recent emphasis on targets and performativity. Consequently, for us, change is welcome as well as unavoidable. However, not all that has happened or is current is bad. It is important to acknowledge and build from what is good, what we want from schooling and ensure that this is taken forward into 'the brave new world'. Perhaps the biggest challenge facing school leaders is not leading the change but managing the transition through understanding the importance of continuity. Most importantly, *intelligent schools* and *intelligent schooling* need to be explicitly underpinned by core values.

Changing times

In the twenty-first century *intelligent schooling* has to take place in a global context. Some years ago, in 1964, Bob Dylan alerted us to *'Times they are a-changin''*. A few years later, 1970, Toffler, author of *Future Shock*, wrote: 'the human system has difficulty accepting the rate of change that exists in the western culture'. One wonders what his prognosis would be about the rate of change in the last few years.

Much has been written about this, for example:

- changes in family structures and family life;

- flexible working hours and portfolio careers;
- advances in technical and medical spheres;
- the global economy;

all of which have an impact on schooling (Davies and Ellison, 1998; Stoll, MacBeath and Mortimore, 2001). Changing times require new knowledge and skills. We know that some companies are now wealthier than some nation states, that globalization has made some modern icons literally worldwide (Madonna, MacDonald's, Nike and Coca Cola to name a few). We are becoming used to having services available on call '24/7'.

Education is not the only sector where improvements are constantly sought. For those of us in the UK lucky enough to have them, our homes and gardens are, according to popular television programmes, constantly requiring 'makeovers'. Our expectations of living, life-choices and patterns are increasing as the world is changing.

Changing schools?

It has often been said that if a surgeon from the nineteenth century visited a hospital of the twenty-first century, he (and it almost certainly would be a 'he') would recognize virtually nothing, whereas a school teacher from the same era would feel pretty much at home in most schools today. This is a little unfair and there have been significant changes that have improved schooling. However, in general, schools have not yet adapted enough to our changing world and many of the changes that have taken place have not led to improvement.

We quite properly want an increasing number of pupils to gain qualifications, but in our view there has been too much concentration on the utilitarian aspects of education to the detriment of a wider remit. Many teachers feel constrained by the curriculum and assessment regulations. As we write, the proposed change to Key Stage 1 assessment arrangements with a more significant role for teachers' assessment is to be welcomed. In our experience, in spite of the best efforts of their teachers, many pupils are bored with the curriculum and find school an irrelevant experience. Indeed, as we discussed in Chapter 1, at the beginning of this century, OFSTED reported that there were more than 10,000 pupils who had simply opted out and were unaccounted for.

We know that some pupils are motivated to continue with their studies even if they are not engaged with the work. This may be for a range of reasons, for example:

- at some point they have 'bought into' the values on offer – they either agree with them or do not question them;
- they enjoy some part of school experience;

- they have experienced academic success and get enjoyment from that;
- they can *connect* succeeding in school with reward later. They may find work/school 'boring' but are prepared to put up with it in order for delayed gratification. These pupils are likely to have a long-term view.

However, for a significant number, when faced with a record of failure through the assessment system and a curriculum that appears to have no relevance to their lives, they are more likely to 'switch off', truant or be disruptive. Pupils from low-income families, sometimes grappling with day-to-day survival, often see no relevance in their schooling. As discussed in Chapter 1, it is not surprising that the gap between the 'haves' and the 'have nots' continues to rise.

The state sector is suffering from the narrowness of the curriculum diet; the concentration of assessment *of* rather than assessment *for* learning; and admission procedures. An *Observer* journalist writes about her experience as a parent of a year 6 pupil:

> Next week, many children will sit tests to try and get into selective state schools. One of my friends describes applying for these over-subscribed schools (there are only 164 of them in the country) as harder than getting into the Chinese Civil Service. ... among the middle classes, tutors are the norm and the atmosphere at primary school is reminiscent of a last year at university. Most parents despair of this pressurised culture ... yet every night, like reluctant race horse trainers, they encourage them [their children] to sit down and work at old exam papers ... . In our borough, the situation is particularly severe because most of its secondary schools are failing (dilapidated, under funded and distinctly second choice, some are like latter day secondary moderns), and parents are desperate to get round this problem. Some will find the money to educate their children privately ... But even those who have no grander aim for their children than the best of the local comprehensive school may be disappointed. It, too, is over-subscribed ... . choice is a mirage. For the vast majority of parents, and for every kind of reason – financial, geographical and academic – we don't have the power to choose. (Kellaway, 2001, p. 29)

As Kellaway says, those disappointed with their 'choice' of secondary school who can afford it, can send their children to private schools. Increasingly there is another choice for those that cannot afford it or do not believe in private sector schooling – home schooling.

Home schooling

With new technologies, home schooling is increasingly being seen as a viable alternative to formal schooling. Anyone with a television, and a computer with Internet access can now easily procure their education at home. Videos, CD-ROMs and Internet sites abound offering the National Curriculum and much more. It is now comparatively easy to organize an attractive and fulfilling curriculum not bound by national requirements for curriculum or assessment. As an increasing number of parents work from home it is going to become easier to organize adult supervision for individuals or small groups of young people living near each other. They can find specialist tutors available via the web and the telephone.

We are already seeing a rise in numbers of those who are being educated in this way: 'The rapid growth of home-schooling in the US is draining funds from hard-pressed school districts ... . An estimated 1.5 million American children were said to be "home-schooled" in 1998 and their numbers are thought to be rising by 15% each year' (Budge, 2000, p. 26). No official figures are kept in the UK but according to the 'Home Education' web site, currently (2003), 1 per cent of children may be schooled at home (*c.* 85,000 children of compulsory school age) and this proportion is rising rapidly in some areas and for some groups.

We are not trying to argue the case for doing this and are well aware of the downside of educating young people away from their peers. But we are also aware of how much easier it is going to become to home-school. For example, within weeks of the outbreak of SARS and of having to close schools and confine pupils at home, a virtual school was established in Hong Kong for all pupils who had access to the Internet. One implication of developing technologies in the UK is that if more and more middle-class families become dissatisfied with state schooling and they find it increasingly feasible to home-school, we will see a rise in the number of middle-class children being educated this way. The effect in some communities would be that public sector schooling remained mainly for the deprived and disadvantaged. If we are to resist this and other depressing scenarios where deprivation and disadvantage are compounded rather than reduced by the education system, we need to ask some fundamental questions about schooling and its purpose.

Intelligent schooling is not just about educating the academically interested or able. Public examinations are important and most people who are reading this book will at some point in their lives have done well and passed many. We do have a responsibility to help all our pupils do well with regard to formal qualifications but, as we asserted in Chapter 4, schooling must support the *learning* (not just examination success) of *all* pupils.

Intelligent schooling is about learning for life. A report for UNESCO described four aspects of learning (Delors et al., 1996):

- *learning to do* – the competence to deal with many situations and to act creatively on one's environment;
- *learning to live together* – developing understanding of others and appreciation of interdependence, to participate and co-operate with others;
- *learning to know* – acquiring a broad general knowledge, the instruments of

understanding, and learning to learn;
- *learning to be* – developing greater autonomy, judgement and personal responsibility, through attention to all aspects of a person's potential.

If schools were able to address all these aspects we would indeed be equipping our youngsters for life.

Alternative possibilities

> You see things: and you say 'Why?'. But I dream things that never were: and I say 'Why not?' (Shaw, 1921)

We want young people to grow into active and responsible citizens in their society, respecting themselves and each other. We believe that schools have a special and particular role to play in this process and it is one of the most important justifications for making education compulsory and paying for it out of the public purse.

As discussed earlier, the Internet, digital technology and resources such as CD-ROMs, have meant that schooling from home for individuals or small groups of young people has never been easier to organize. It could be argued that young people may get access to better quality resources and higher calibre teaching this way than at their local school. This gives us reason to address a range of questions. Primarily, what is – or could be – the advantage of schooling? What is its 'unique selling point', i.e. what can (or could) schools do better than any other method of educating young people? We also need to think about what we value and what we want to take forward into the future.

Some questions to consider

- What are the arguments for bringing young people together for their learning?
- What is better learnt in class groups/other groupings?
- What kinds of learning can best be achieved interacting with a 'live' teacher?
- Could some learning be more productive on an individual basis or in small groups (virtual or real) with a virtual teacher?
- Is the answer the same for all types of learning and for all subjects, e.g. history, chemistry, PE, art?
- Is the answer different depending on the age, stage of the pupils or their gender?
- Is the answer different depending on the previous learning experiences of the pupil?
- If we believe pupils' learning experiences are enhanced through participation in group experiences, does the group have to be 20–30 students of the same age?

- Do we need to bring them together on the school site five days a week between 9.00 a.m. and 4.00 p.m.?
- Why is the school year *190* days, divided into three terms, between September and July? (We know why it used to be – in order that children could help with the harvest – but this is not very important for most young people or their families today.)

And, of course, most importantly,

- How do the answers to the questions above affect the role of the teacher and the organization of the school?

We think these are some of the questions that need to be asked and critically addressed during the next decade. We hope that the nine intelligences will contribute to this discourse. For example, *intelligent schools* use their contextual and strategic intelligences to take cognizance of the changing world. They will be aware of what can and should change in the current context and will be looking ahead in order to plan for the future. In consultation with the local community and other schools, some changes could be made now. Other changes may have to wait for legislation.

Learning as a social activity

The importance of the social aspects of learning manifested when young people come together is sometimes forgotten. Most pupils enjoy coming to school to make and meet friends. Indeed, one of the re-occurring findings of the Keele University surveys on what pupils thought about their school was that they liked school but disliked their lessons! Learning at home on your own, as an alternative to learning at school, could be a very lonely experience. Most of us enjoy the idea of belonging somewhere and having a connectedness with other human beings. For young people, *belonging* to a school is an important way to become a member of a community outside the immediate family and to start to establish an independent identity. It is also important to remember that for many young people, school provides the only stability they experience as they grow up.

In her article reviewing the literature about students' sense of belonging, Osterman notes: 'There is little evidence demonstrating that the sense of belonging is directly related to achievement, but there is substantial evidence showing or suggesting that the sense of belonging influences achievement through its effects on engagement' (Osterman, 2000, p. 341). She concludes that:

> The research tells us a number of things. The first is that the experience of belongingness is associated with important psychological processes. Children

who experience a sense of relatedness have a stronger supply of inner resources. They perceive themselves to be more competent and autonomous and have higher levels of intrinsic motivation. They have a stronger sense of identity but are also willing to conform to and adopt established norms and values. These inner resources in turn predict engagement and performance. Those students who experience a sense of relatedness behave differently from those who do not. (Ibid., p. 343)

Osterman says that these students have more positive attitudes toward school, their teachers, classwork and their peers: 'They participate more in school activities, and they invest more of themselves in the learning process. They have a stronger sense of their own social competence, and they are more likely to interact with peers and adults in prosocial ways' (ibid.).

School level

It appears then, that encouraging pupils to feel part of the school community is important for a range of reasons. Without attempting to replace youth clubs, schools could examine their provision for social learning opportunities. What sorts of learning opportunities are provided that enhance affiliation to the school as an institution and encourage bonding between pupils and their school? What opportunities do pupils have to get to know and learn with pupils from different year groups? Examples of such activities would include visits, residential trips and opportunities to represent the school through sports events, drama, debates, etc. Pupils who feel they matter as individuals and who feel their voice as a group is listened to, are more likely to want to belong to the institution. 'Teachers play a major role in determining whether students feel that they are cared for and that they are a welcome part of the school community' (Osterman, 2000, p. 351). As we agreed in Chapter 4, schools need to ask themselves how much say the pupils feel they have in the way the school is managed, as well as how much stake they have in their learning and how it is organized.

We are suggesting that learning with others is a significant factor of schooling that we want to see maintained in any future notion of schooling. However, 'the others' do not always have to be of the same age. For example, in some situations, pupils could be grouped according to interest or talents (as they often are for extra curricular activities). The community schools of the 1970s (some of which have survived into this century) provided opportunities for adults to learn alongside the young, and advocates of these schools were enthusiastic about the social benefits of this system. As far as we know, knowledge and technology are going to continue to increase as least as rapidly as at present. We are all going to need to constantly update our skills and knowledge. We could do this through a private provider but it might be more sensible to benefit from the facilities offered at our local school. This could mean schools becoming the focus of learning for the community, not just for young-sters of compulsory school age.

There are implications here for the furnishings and fabric of school buildings. As mentioned earlier, people fortunate enough to have their own homes are spending more money than ever before on home improvements. People who are increasingly trying to improve their home environment are not going to volun-tarily visit a school building that is dowdy and dirty or has outdated equipment. If schools are to become the focal point for learners of all ages, the facilities have to be better than most individual homes can provide. They must be furnished with state-of-the-art ICT, eating and leisure facilities. More of this later.

Classroom level

Learning can be a social activity in classrooms too. Whole-class teaching, group and paired work can all encourage trust, confidence and listening skills. Trust and confidence are encouraged by generating the groups' own version of 'Chatham House Rules' (i.e. respecting confidences that are disclosed in the discussion). Good teachers know how to encourage the shy to speak and the confident to listen. The use of humour is often the glue that helps bond a group with their teacher. Group identities are frequently formed on the basis of how the class interacts with its teachers.

In a research project focusing on consulting pupils about their learning, pupils from a mixed-age class (years 5 and 6) Cambridgeshire primary school discussed why they liked working in groups and demonstrated how astute they are about choosing partners to work with depending on the subject and the task:

Katy and Sabrina (year 5)
We looked at each other's work and decided what needed improving – we agreed with most of what each other said.

Ryan (year 5)
I have problems in literacy so it's good to work with someone – working with Lewis makes me feel more confident. He helps me with my spelling I help him with his maths.

Samantha (year 6)
(In maths group) I sometimes get lost 'cause they're a lot brainier than me – they stop and explain and don't rush on ahead. If we don't understand we can go over it again – sometimes in whole class you feel silly if you put up your hand – it's easier in a group.

Lewis (year 5)
It's good working in groups – we help each other – we don't tell (each other)

the answer but explain what to do. I'd choose people (to work with) who come up with good ideas and concentrate. (Myers, 2001)

Opportunities for this sort of interaction would be possible for 'home schoolers' to arrange – but perhaps not easily. Social learning is one of the 'unique selling points' of schools but perhaps one that is not considered or celebrated enough.

The timetable

Working together as a large group does entail bringing the students together at the same time in the same place, but this does not necessarily have to happen all day and every day. Mike Tomlinson who was at the time just finishing his term as Her Majesty's Chief Inspector of Schools, told the Social Market foundation that 'conventional timetabling was madness'. He stated that 'the secondary curriculum is designed to facilitate teaching rather than learning' (Canovan, 2002, p. 16).

He has also suggested that:

- the secondary curriculum has failed to motivate all pupils;
- the burden of assessment has limited teaching and become overly demanding for both pupils and staff;
- performance data puts the emphasis on what was measurable, undervaluing 'crucial' other curriculum elements;
- the qualifications framework means that pupils find it hard to change if they have embarked on the wrong course;
- too often schools fail to give pupils good advice on future options;
- timetabling fails to get the best out of pupils;
- there is a lack of support from parents (Mansell, 2003).

We do not need to seek permission or wait for legislation to do something about timetabling.

> The programmes of study for National Curriculum subjects set out what the majority of pupils should be taught during each key stage. It is for schools to decide how to organise time within the key stage. It is not necessary, for example, for pupils to study all National Curriculum subjects each week, term or year and a school may decide to concentrate on particular subjects during particular terms or particular years. (QCA, 1999, p. 3)

Stopping and starting every 40 minutes does not help what Csikszentmihalyi (1990) calls 'the flow'. We could already be offering French immersion courses or history study weeks. Taking a day to paint a picture or participate in a drama workshop could be a much more fulfilling experience than the current one that most pupils are offered.

Working together

Many schools have, in spite of various governments, found ways to collaborate rather than compete with each other. This sane activity is now encouraged by the current government through, for example, Education Action Zones, Excellence in Cities, beacon schools, the National College for School Leadership's Networked Learning Communities and the Leadership Incentive grant.

At the time of writing, for a fee of £2,850, a private company cited in the *Times Educational Supplement* will:

> supply a qualified tutor to give a weekly one-hour video-conference lesson to five AS-level students for the duration of the course. The tutor will set and mark all work, which is based on a self-study pack supplied to each student. Extra students cost £450 per head. For £4,125 the company will also supply a video-conferencing system, replaceable within 24 hours if it breaks down. All the school has to do (apart from pay) is ensure that students turn up to their lessons, spend at least three hours a week on self-study, and email their assignments directly to the tutor, or hand them in to the school's link teacher to send on. (Gold, 2002, p. 14)

As the technology exists that enables private companies to provide this service to schools, it would be possible for schools to provide this sort of support for each other. School A has a strong geography department. Schools B and C are strong in science and the arts respectively. They agree to be the *lead* providers in these areas for each other. Pupil learning can still take place at the pupil's own school, *the link* school (although, if the other schools are in the near vicinity, visits would be possible). All schools would have a lead role and a link one, reducing the likelihood of hierarchy and its spin-off effects on recruitment and retention (staff and students). The schools working together would harmonize their timetables to facilitate learning exchange. This system would allow schools to develop subject strengths but, unlike the specialist school system, pupils would not be expected to decide their own specialism at the age of 11 as, whatever their own school's strengths, all pupils would benefit from specific expertise in all subject areas through link-ups as described. In fact the schools could review which subjects they lead in every year, giving more staff opportunities to lead and to focus on different aspects of their job. If organized on these lines, the particular expertise of each school should make no difference to its own pupils.

As well as organizing pupil learning, the lead school could take the responsibility for teacher learning, in the particular area of expertise. Working this way would enable teachers to develop links with colleagues in other schools, virtual and real. We would like to see local schools retaining their own identity but working together for the benefit of all young people in the area. This would entail schools planning together to share out resources, human and material in the most effective way.

Schools will need to ask themselves what extra they are providing. Why would it be better for a pupil to study geography via distance learning through their link school rather than independently at their own home (or through another private provider such as the local supermarket)? Presumably the answer would have something to do with the expertise of the on-site teachers (particularly expertise with regard to understanding the learning process), the support (moral and technical) that the link school offers and the social possibilities that schools can provide.

The 24-hour school?

Most schools operate a timetable between 9.00 a.m. and 4.00 p.m., though many are open long after that for extra curricular activities. The 9–4 day has been a long tradition for formal learning and there were good reasons for it. These were approximately the hours that the rest of society operated under. This is increasingly no longer the case as we appear to be moving to a 24-hour society (Kreitzman, 1999). We are becoming used to visiting supermarkets or contacting our bank at any time of the day or night. The 24-hour provision, flexi-time and the increased possibilities of working from home derived from new technologies mean that workers are, more and more, working less traditional hours. If this trend increases, will it still make sense for schools to operate a rigid 9–4 day?

There are many possible versions for a 24-hour school. One ground rule must be that, however it is organized, it must not mean that already over-worked and hard-pressed teachers are asked to work longer hours. Work–life balance issues are taken seriously in the *intelligent school*. Those that want to must be able to continue to work traditional hours but opportunities would be available for those that prefer a more flexible timetable.

One version of the 24-hour school that would be possible to introduce now would be for young people of compulsory school age to have priority access to the facilities between 9 and 4, with the school open to the community for the rest of the time. In some areas no one would want to use the school during the night except perhaps virtually (e.g. access for insomniacs to learning materials on the school's web site), but in other areas where there are significant numbers of shift workers this may not be the case. Workers may prefer to take their early morning or after-work swim/work-out at the school rather than at the local health club. Families may enjoy meeting at the school restaurant for an early supper before embarking on either a joint or individual course offered in the evening. These scenarios would be dependent on the school having the state-of-the-art facilities mentioned earlier. Keeping the plant open and in this state all year round would, of course, have cost implications but some would argue that it is very expensive not to have the specialist facilities of schools available more widely.

161

Schools and schooling

We see school as an individual unit becoming the local neighbourhood link into the world of learning. To make the best use of our resources, particularly the human ones, schools must work together and, as noted, there is already a welcome trend in this direction. We believe collaboration could be taken much further. Indeed, in the future, older pupils could be enrolled at their local school where some of their learning will take place. Other learning opportunities, facilitated and guided by the school, could take place from home and other non-school venues, e.g. museums. Some learning will be through other schools and organizations, nationally and internationally. There will be a mix of virtual contact and face-to-face contact. Some learning will be individual and some with groups of varying sizes depending on needs of the situation. Decisions will be affected by the age of the pupils, their experience of learning and available opportunities. Central to these decisions will be what young people themselves feel they need and want.

This scenario means that pupils will no longer be limited by being associated with only one school. Their local link school will offer a sense of belonging and community but will be a starting not a finishing point. Their experience will be of schooling not school.

Throughout this book we have been advocating a learning-, rather than assessment-led, education system. Our learning-led system is underpinned by the vision intelligences – ethical and spiritual – that incorporate a sense of justice, respect for young people and a desire to ensure that *all* young people are served by the system. In this vision, young people see themselves as partners in their education and so have responsibilities in this process as well as a right to an education.

The current high stakes, assessment-led system has patently not reduced the link between poverty and low achievement in schools. We need urgently to rethink schools and schooling. We hope that the intelligences described in the previous chapter will contribute to this process.

Activity

Making changes

Before embarking on change it is often worth carrying out a forcefield analysis. What is helping and encouraging change? What is hindering it?

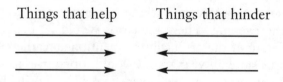

Things that help   Things that hinder

For example, a group of staff in a school may fill in the forcefield as follows:

Things that encourage change:	*Things that hinder:*
Increased knowledge about how the brain works and how we learn.	Who is responsible for the pupils when they are not in lessons?
Dissatisfaction amongst pupils and staff with the curriculum and assessment.	Monitoring individual pupils' curriculum and progress.
Possibilities brought about by new technologies.	Concern about adverse affect on teachers' conditions of service.

The next stage is to attempt to address the items that appear in the right-hand column of the list.

Points for discussion

Describe *intelligent schooling*:

- for pupils;
- staff;
- parents.

References

Abbott, J. (1994) Learning makes sense: re-creating education for a changing future. *Education 2000*, 21st Century Learning Initiative. www.21learn.org

Ainscow, M. (1999) *Understanding the Development of Inclusive Schools*. London: Falmer Press.

Alderson, P. (2003) *Institutional Rites and Rights: A Century of Childhood*. London: Institute of Education.

Alexander, H.A. (2001) *Reclaiming Goodness*. Notre Dame, IN: University of Notre Dame Press.

Alexander, R., Rose, J. and Woodhead, C. (1992) *Curriculum Organisation and Classroom Practice in Primary Schools: A Discussion Paper*. London: HMSO.

Armstrong, F., Armstrong, D. and Barton, L. (2000) *Inclusive Education: Policy, Contexts and Comparative Perspectives*. London: David Fulton.

Aronowitz, S. and De Fazio, W. (1994) The new knowledge work, in A.H. Halsey, H. Lauder, P. Brown and A.S. Wells (eds), *Education: Culture, Economy, Society*. Oxford: Oxford University Press.

Askew, S. and Carnell, E. (1998) *Transforming Learning: Individual and Global Change*. London: Cassell.

Aspy, D. and Roebuck, F. (1976) *A Lever Long Enough*. Washington, DC: National Consortium for Humanizing Education (PO Box 1001).

Assessment Reform Group (2002) *Assessment for Learning: 10 Principles*. Cambridge: University of Cambridge, School of Education.

Ball, S.J. (1996) Recreating policy through qualitative research: a trajectory analysis. American Educational Research Association Annual Conference, New York, 8–12 April.

Bath, R. (1998) Vision and school improvement, in F.W. Parkay (ed.), *Improving Schools for the Twenty-First Century*. Gainesville, FL: University of Florida.

Bath, R. (1990) *Improving Schools from Within*. San Francisco, CA: Jossey-Bass.

Bath, R. (2001) *Learning by Heart*. San Francisco, CA: Jossey-Bass.

Bellamy, C. (2003) *The State of the World's Children*. New York: UNICEF.

Bennett, N., Desforges, C., Cockburn, A. and Wilkinson, B. (1984) *The Quality of Pupil Learning Experiences*. London: Lawrence Erlbaum Associates.

Bennis, W. and Nanus, B. (1985) *Leaders*. New York: Harper and Row.

Bentley, T.P. (1998) *Learning Beyond the Classroom: Education for a Changing World*. London: Routledge.

Best, R. (ed.) (1996) *Education, Spirituality and the Whole Child*. London: Cassell.

Betts, P. (2002) Europe's low-tech schools, *Financial Times*, 13 March, p. 8.

Bhindi, N. and Duignan, P.A. (1997) Leadership for a new century, authenticity, intentionality, spirituality and sensibility. *Educational Management and Administration*, vol. 25, no. 2, pp. 117–32.

Black, P. and Wiliam, D. (1998) *Inside the Black Box*. London: School of Education, Kings College.

Black, P. and Wiliam, D. (2003) The development of formative assessment, in B. Davies and J. West-Burnham (eds), *Handbook of Educational Leadership and Management*. Harlow: Pearson.

Block, P. (1987) *The Empowered Manager*. San Francisco, CA: Jossey-Bass.

Bohm, D. (1980) *Wholeness and the Implicate Order*. London: Routledge and Kegan Paul.

Bolam, R., McMahon, A., Pocklington, K. and Weindling, D. (1993) *Effective Management in Schools*. London: HMSO.

Boyatzis, R. (2000) What if learning were the purpose of education? Developing the whole person and emotional intelligence. *Leading Edge, Journal of the London Leadership Centre*, vol. 4, no. 2, pp. 116–31.

Bradford, J. (1999) *Caring for the Whole Child: A Holistic Approach to Spirituality*. London: Children's Society.

Branson, R. (1998) Teaching-centred schooling has reached its upper limit: it doesn't get any better than this. *Current Directions in Psychological Science*, vol. 7, no. 4. pp. 126–35.

Broadfoot, P. (1998) A nice little earner. Education Supplement, *Independent*, 3 December, p. 4.

Brown, A. and Furlong, J. (1996) *Spiritual Development in Schools*. London: National Society.

Bruner, J.S. (1960) *The Process of Education*. Cambridge, MA: Harvard University Press.

Bruner, J.S. (1996) *The Culture of Education*. London: Harvard University Press.

Budge, D. (2000) A loophole for bigotry to crawl through. *Times Educational Supplement*, 10 November, p. 26.

Burns, S. and Lamont, G. (1995) *Values and Visions, Handbook for Spiritual Development and Global Awareness*. London: Hodder & Stoughton.

Bush, T. and Coleman, M. (2000) *Leadership and Strategic Management in Education*. London: Paul Chapman Publishing.

Caldwell, B.J. and Spinks, J.M. (1998) *Beyond the Self-managing School*. London: Falmer Press.

Cambron-McCabe, N. (2000) Schooling as an ethical endeavour, in P. Senge, *Schools that Learn*. London: Nicholas Brealey.

Canovan, C. (2002) School escapes timetable madness. *Times Educational Supplement*, 12 April, p. 16.

Capra, F. (1996) *The Web of Life*. London: HarperCollins.

Carnell, E. and Lodge, C. (2002) *Supporting Effective Learning*. London: Paul Chapman Publishing.

Caulkin, S. (2003) Keep it simple – not stupid. Business Section, *Observer*, 23 February, p. 8.

Central Advisory Council for England (CACE) (1967) *Children and Their Primary*

Schools (Plowden Report). London: HMSO.

Chief Executive Officers (CEO) (2001) *Education Technology Must Be Included in Comprehensive Education Legislation.* Forum policy paper. Washington, DC: CEO.

Chrispeels, J. (1992) *Purposeful Restructuring: Creating a Culture for Learning and Achievement in Elementary Schools.* Lewes: Falmer Press.

Clarke, P. (1999) *Learning Schools, Learning Systems.* London: Continuum.

Claxton, G. (1999) *Wise Up: The Challenge of Lifelong Learning.* London: Bloomsbury.

Claxton, G. (2000a) Integrity and uncertainty – why young people need doubtful teachers, in C. Watkins, C. Lodge and R. Best (eds), *Tomorrow's Schools: Towards Integrity.* London: RoutledgeFalmer.

Claxton, G. (2000b) What would schools look like if they were truly dedicated to helping all young people to become confident, competent lifelong learners?, in B. Lucas and T. Greany (eds), *Schools in the Learning Age,* pp. 5–12. London: Campaign for Learning.

Cochran-Smith, M. and Lytle, S.L. (1993) *Inside/Outside: Teacher Research and Knowledge.* New York: Teachers College Press.

Coleman, J. (1966) *Harvard Educational Review,* Special Issue, vol. 38, no. 1, pp. 7–22.

Cordingley, P., Bell, M. Rundell, B. and Evans, D. (2003) *The Impact of Collaborative CPD on Classroom Teaching and Learning,* in Research Evidence in Educational Library. London: EPPI-Centre, Social Research Unit, Institute of Education.

Creemers, B.P.M. (1994) *The Effective Classroom.* London: Cassell.

Csikszentmihalyi, M. (1990) *Flow: The Psychology of Optimal Experience.* London: Harper Perennial.

Cuban, L. (1988) Why do some reforms persist? *Educational Administration Quarterly,* vol. 24, no. 3, pp. 329–35.

Dalin, P. and Rust, Val D. (1996) *Towards Schooling for the Twenty-first Century.* London: Cassell.

Daniels, H., Hey, V., Leonard, D. and Smith, M. (1996) *Gender and Special Needs Provision in Mainstream Schooling.* ESRC Report no. R000235059.

Dann, R. (2002) *Promoting Assessment as Learning.* London: RoutledgeFalmer.

Davies, B. (2001) *Rethinking Schools and School Leadership for the 21st Century: Changes and Challenges.* Inaugural professorial lecture. Hull: International Leadership Centre, University of Hull.

Davies, B. and Ellison, L. (1998) *Strategic Direction and Development of the School.* London: RoutledgeFalmer.

Day, C. (1999) *Developing Teachers: The Challenges of Lifelong Learning.* London: Falmer Press.

Deal, T.E. (1987) The culture of schools, in L.T. Sheive and M.B. Schoenheit (eds), *Leadership: Examining the Elusive, 1987 Yearbook of the Association for Supervision and Curriculum Development.* Arlington, VA: ASCA.

Deforges, C. (2000) Familiar challenges and new approaches: necessary advances in theory and methods in research on teaching and learning. Unpublished BERA lecture, Cardiff.

Delors, J., Al Mufti, I., Amagi, A., Carneiro, R., Chung, F., Geremek, B., Gorham, W.,

Kornhauser, A., Manley, M., Padron Quero, M., Savane, M.A., Sing, K., Stavenhagen, T., Suhr, M.W. and Nanzhao, Z. (1996) *Learning: The Treasure Within*. Report to UNESCO of the International Commission on Education for the Twenty-first Century.

Department for Education and Employment (DfEE) (2000) *Research into Teacher Effectiveness*. London: Department for Education and Employment.

Department for Education and Skills (DfES) (2001) *Learning and Teaching – A Strategy for Professional Development*. London: Department for Education and Skills.

Department for Education and Skills (DfES) (2002) *14–19: Extending Opportunities, Raising Standards*. London: Department for Education and Skills.

Department for Education and Skills (DfES) (2003) *Excellence and Enjoyment – A Strategy for Primary Schools*. London: Department for Education and Skills.

Diamond, M.C. (1998) *Enriching Heridity*. New York: Free Press.

Dick, F. (1992) *Winning*. Nashville, TN: Abingdon Press.

Dryden, G. and Vos, J. (1994) *The Learning Revolution*. Aylesbury: Accelerated Learning.

Dweck, C. (1999) *Self-theories: Their Role in Motivation, Personality and Development*. Philadelphia, PA: Psychology Press.

Earl, L., Watson, N., Levin, B., Leithwood, K., Fullan, M. and Torrance, N. with Jantzi, D., Mascall, B. and Volante, L. (2003) *Watching and Learning 3*. Final report of the External Evaluation of England's National Literacy and Numeracy Strategies. Ontario: Institute for Studies in Education, University of Toronto.

Edmonds, R.R. (1979) Some schools work and more can. *Social Policy*, vol. 9, pp. 28–32.

Education Counts (1991) Special study panel on education indicators, Washington DC.

Eisner, E. (1985) *The Art of Educational Evaluation*. Lewes: Falmer Press.

Elmore, R.F. (2000) *Building a New Structure for School Leadership*. Washington, DC: Albert Shanker Institute.

Feden, P.D. (1994) About instruction: powerful new strategies worth knowing. *Educational Horizons*, vol. 73, pp. 18–24.

Fidler, B. (2000) *Strategic Management for School Development*. London: Paul Chapman Publishing.

Fielding, M. (1997) Beyond school effectiveness and school improvement: lighting the slow fuse of possibility, in J. White and M. Barber (eds), *Perspectives on School Effectiveness and School Improvement*, pp. 137–60. London: Institute of Education.

Fisher, R. (1999) Philosophy for children: how philosophical enquiry can foster values education in schools, in J. Leach and B. Moon (eds), *Learners and Pedagogy*. Buckingham: Open University Press and London: Paul Chapman Publishing.

Frost, D. and Durrant, J. (2003) Bottom up? Top down? Inside-out? Joined up? Building capacity for school improvement through teacher leadership. Paper presented to the International Congress for School Effectiveness and Improvement, January, Sydney, Australia.

Fullan, M.G. and Hargreaves, A. (1998) *What's Worth Fighting for in Education*.

Buckingham: Open University Press.

Fullan, M.G. (1991) *The New Meaning of Educational Change*. London: Cassell.

Fullan, M.G. (1992) *What's Worth Fighting for in Headship*. Buckingham: Open University Press.

Fullan, M.G. (2001a) *The New Meaning of Educational Change*. London: RoutledgeFalmer.

Fullan, M.G. (2001b) *Leading in a Culture of Change*. San Francisco, CA: Jossey-Bass/Wiley.

Gagnon, G.W. (2001) *Designing for Learning*. London: Paul Chapman Publishing.

Galton, M. (1980) *Progress and Performance in the Primary Classroom*. London: Routledge and Kegan Paul.

Galton, M. (1989) *Teaching in the Primary School*. London: David Fulton.

Gardner, H. (1983) *Frames of Mind: The Theory of Multiple Intelligences*. New York: Basic Books.

Gardner, H. (1993) *The Unschooled Mind*. London: Fontana Press.

Gardner, H. (1999) *Intelligence Reframed: Multiple Intelligences for the 21st Century*. New York: Basic Books.

Garmston, R. and Wellman, B. (1995) Adaptive schools in a quantum universe. *Educational Leadership*, vol. 52, no. 7, pp. 6–12.

Garner, R. (2002) Q: why are we putting pupils under so much pressure from exams? Thursday Review, *Independent*, 24 January, p. 4.

Gillborn, D. (2002) *Education and Institutional Racism*. London: Institute of Education, University of London.

Gillborn, D. and Gipps, C. (1996) *Recent Research on the Achievements of Ethnic Minority Pupils*. London: HMSO.

Gilligan, C. (1982) *In a Different Voice*. Cambridge, MA: Harvard University Press.

Gipps, C. (1992) What we know about effective primary teaching. *The London File*. London: Tufnell Press.

Gipps, C. and MacGilchrist, B. (1999) Primary school learners, in P. Mortimore (ed.), *Understanding Pedagogy and its Impact on Learning*. London: Paul Chapman Publishing.

Gipps, C. and Murphy, P. (1994) *A Fair Test? Assessment, Achievement and Equity*. Buckingham: Open University Press.

Gold, K. (2002) Is this the solution to the teacher shortage? *Times Educational Supplement*, 22 March, p. 14.

Goldstein, H. (1996) Relegate the leagues. *New Economy*, pp. 199–203. The Dryden Press.

Goldstein, H. (2001) Using pupil performance data for judging schools and teachers: scope and limitations. *British Educational Research Journal*, vol. 27, no. 4, pp. 433–42.

Goldstein, H. and Spiegelhalter, D. (1996) League tables and their limitations: statistical issues in comparisons of institutional importance. *Journal of the Royal Statistical Society*, A, 159, pp. 385–443.

Goleman, D. (1996) *Emotional Intelligence: Why it Matters More than IQ*. London: Bloomsbury Paperbacks.

Goleman, D. (1998) What makes a leader. *Harvard Business Review*,

November–December, pp. 93–102.

Goleman, D. (1999) *Working with Emotional Intelligence*. London: Bloomsbury.

Good, T.L. and Brophy, J. (1986) Teacher behaviour and student achievement, in M.C. Wittrock (ed.), *Handbook of Research on Teaching*. London: Collier Macmillan.

Gottfredson, L.S. (1997) Mainstream science on intelligence: an editorial with 53 signatories, history and bibliography, in D.K. Detterman (ed.), *Multidisciplinary Journal*, vol. 24, no. 1, January–February. Greenwich Connecticut: Ablex Publishing Corporation.

Gray, J. (1995) The quality of schooling: frameworks for judgment, in J. Gray and B. Wilcox (eds), *Good School, Bad School*. Buckingham: Open University Press.

Gray, J. (2001) Building for improvement and sustaining change in schools serving disadvantaged communities, in M. Maden (ed.), *Success Against the Odds – Five Years On*. London: RoutledgeFalmer.

Gray, J., Goldstein, H. and Jesson, D. (1996) Changes and improvements in schools' effectiveness: trends over five years. *Research Papers in Education*, vol. 11, no. 1, pp. 35–51.

Gray, J., Goldstein, H. and Thomas, S. (2001) Predicting the future: the role of past performance in determining trends in institutional effectiveness at A level. *British Educational Research Journal*, vol. 27, no. 4, pp. 391–405.

Gray, J., Goldstein, H. and Thomas, S. (2003) Of Trends and Trajectories: searching for patterns in school improvement. *British Educational Research Journal*, vol. 29, no. 1, pp. 83–8.

Gray, J., Hopkins, D., Reynolds, D., Wilcox, B., Farrell, S. and Jesson, D. (1999) *Improving Schools: Performance and Potential*. Buckingham: Open University Press.

Handy, C. (1984) *Taken for Granted? Understanding Schools as Organizations*. York: Schools Council/Longman.

Handy, C. (1997) Schools for life and work, in P. Mortimore and V. Little (eds), *Living Education: Essays in Honour of John Tomlinson*. London: Paul Chapman Publishing.

Hargreaves, A. (1994) *Changing Teachers, Changing Times*. London: Cassell.

Hargreaves, A. (2003) *Teaching in the Knowledge Society: Education in the Age of Insecurity*. Buckingham: Open University Press.

Hargreaves, D. and Hopkins, D. (1991) *The Empowered School: The Management and Practice of Development Planning*. London: Cassell.

Hargreaves, D.H. (2001a) Exams head backs calls to halt 'over-testing' of pupils. *Independent*, 17 September, p. 14.

Hargreaves, D.H. (2001b) A capital theory of school effectiveness and improvement. *British Educational Research Journal*, vol. 27, no. 4, pp. 487–503.

Hargreaves, D.H. (2002) We must not botch the job. *Times Educational Supplement*, 15 February, p. 19.

Harris, A. (2002) *School Improvement: Whats in it for Schools?* London: RoutledgeFalmer.

Harris, A., Jamieson, I. and Russ, J. (1995) A study of 'effective' departments in secondary schools. *School Organization*, vol. 15, no. 3, pp. 283–99.

Harris, J.R. (1998) *The Nurture Assumption*. London: Bloomsbury.

Hay, D. and Nye, R. (1998) *The Spirit of the Child*. London: HarperCollins Religious.

Haynes, F. (1998) *The Ethical School*. London: Routledge.

Head, J. (1996) Gender identity and cognitive style, in P. Murphy, and C. Gipps (eds), *Equity in the Classroom: Towards an Effective Pedagogy for Girls and Boys*. Falmer/Unesco Publishing.

Hill, P.N. (2001) *What Principals Need to Know About Teaching and Learning*. Victoria, Australia: The Incorporated Association of Registered Teachers of Victoria.

Hirst, P. (1974) *Knowledge and the Curriculum: A Collection of Philosophical Papers*. London: Routledge and Kegan Paul.

Hopkins, D. (1996) Towards a theory of school improvement, in J. Gay, D. Reynolds and C. Fitz-Gibbon (eds), *Merging Traditions: The Future of Research on School Effectiveness and School Improvement*. London: Cassell.

Hopkins, D. and MacGilchrist, B. (1998) Development planning for pupil achievement. *School Leadership and Management*, vol. 18, no. 3, pp. 409–24.

Hopkins, D., Ainscow, M. and West, M. (1994) *School Improvement in an Era of Change*. London: Cassell.

Huberman, M. (1988) Teachers' careers and school improvement. *Journal of Curriculum Studies 20*, vol. 2, pp. 119–32.

Inner London Education Authority (ILEA) (1984) *Improving Secondary Schools*. London: ILEA.

Ireson, J., Mortimore, P. and Hallam, S. (1999) The common strands of pedagogy and their implications, in P. Mortimore (ed.), *Understanding Pedagogy and its Impact on Learning*. London: Paul Chapman Publishing.

Jencks, C., Smith, M., Ackland, H., Bane, M., Cohen, D., Gintis, H., Heyns, B. and Micholson, S. (1972) *Inequality: A Reassessment of the Effect of Family and Schooling in America*. New York: Basic Books.

Jensen, A.R. (1969) How much can we boost IQ and scholastic achievement? *Harvard Educational Review*, vol. 39, pp. 1–123.

Joyce, B. (1991) The doors to school improvement. *Educational Leadership*, vol. 48, no. 8, pp. 59–62.

Joyce, B. and Showers, B. (1988) *Student Achievement through Staff Development*. New York: Longman.

Kellaway, K. (2001) Back to the bad old days. *Observer*, 2 December, p. 29.

Kreitzman, L. (1999) *The 24 Hour Society*. London: Profile Books.

Kress, G. (2001) *Futures of Schooling*. London: Foresight Group, Institute of Education.

Leadbeater, C. (1999) *Living on Thin Air – The New Economy*. London: Viking.

Leeuw, F. (2001) *Reciprocity and the Evaluation of Educational Quality: Assumptions and Reality Checks*. EU Congress, The Meaning of Quality in Education.

Lightfoot, S.L. (1983) *The Good High School: Portraits of Character and Culture*. New York: Basic Books.

Louis, K.S. and Miles, M.B. (1992) *Improving the Urban High School: What Works and Why*. London: Cassell.

Louis, K.S. (1998) Reconnecting knowledge utilization and school improvement, in A. Hargreaves, A. Lieberman, M. Fullan and D. Hopkins (eds), *International*

Handbook of Educational Change, Part 2. Dordrecht: Kluwer.

Luyten, H. (1994) *School Effects: Stability and Malleability*. Enschede, the Netherlands: University of Twente.

MacBeath, J. (1997) *Learning to Achieve: Evaluatng Study Support*. London: The Prince's Trust.

MacBeath, J. (ed.) (1998) *Effective School Leadership: Responding to Change*. London: Paul Chapman Publishing.

MacBeath, J. (1999) *Schools Must Speak for Themselves: The Case for School Self-evaluation*. London: Routledge.

MacBeath, J. and Mortimore, P. (eds) (2001) *Improving School Effectiveness*. Buckingham: Open University Press.

MacBeath, J., Thomson, B., Arrowsmith, J. and Forbes, D. (1992) *Using Ethos Indicators in Secondary School Self-Evaluation: Taking Account of the Views of Pupils, Parents and Teachers*. Edinburgh: HM Inspectors of Schools, Scottish Office Education Department.

MacGilchrist, B. (1992) *Managing Access and Entitlement in Primary Education*. Stoke-on-Trent: Trentham Books.

MacGilchrist, B. (1996) Linking staff development with children's learning. *Educational Leadership*, vol. 53, no. 6. pp. 72–5.

MacGilchrist, B. (2000) Improving self-improvement? *Research Papers in Education*, vol. 15. no. 3, pp. 325–38.

MacGilchrist, B., Mortimore, P., Savage, J. and Beresford, C. (1995) *Planning Matters*. London: Paul Chapman Publishing.

Maden, M. (ed.) (2201) *Success Against the Odds – Five Years On*. London: RoutledgeFalmer.

Mansell, W. (2003) Former chief inspector lambasts system. *Times Educational Supplement*, 28 March, p. 18.

March, J.G. (1999) *The Pursuit of Organizational Intelligence*. London: Blackwell.

Marzano, R.J. (1998) *A Theory-based Meta-analysis of Research on Instruction*. Aurora, CO: Mid-Continent Regional Educational Laboratory.

Mayo, E. (1930) Changing methods in industry. *Personnel Journal*, no. 8.

McMaster, M. (1995) *The Intelligent Advantage: Organising for Complexity*. Virginia: Knowledge Based Development Co.

Middlewood, D. and Lumby, J. (eds) (1999) *Strategic Management in Schools and Colleges*. London: Paul Chapman Publishing.

Miller, R. and Bentley, T. (2003) *Possible Futures: Four Scenarios for Schooling in 2030*. Nottingham: National College for School Leadership.

Mintzberg, H. (2002) *The Strategy Process: Concepts, Contexts, Cases*. Harlow: Pearson Education.

Mortimore, P. (1991) The nature and findings of research on school effectiveness in the primary sector, in S. Riddell and S. Brown (eds), *School Effectiveness Research: Its Messages for School Improvement*. Edinburgh: HMSO.

Mortimore, P. (ed.) (1999) *Understanding Pedagogy and Its Impact on Learning*. London: Paul Chapman Publishing.

Mortimore, P. and Mortimore, J. (eds) (1991) *The Primary Head: Roles, Responsibilities and Reflections*. London: Paul Chapman Publishing.

171

Mortimore, P. and Whitty, G. (1997) *Can School Improvement Overcome the Effects of Disadvantage?* London: Institute of Education.

Mortimore, P., Sammons, P. and Thomas, S. (1994) School effectiveness and value added measures. *Assessment in Education: Principles, Policy and Practice*, vol. 1, no. 3, pp. 315–22.

Mortimore, P., Sammons, P., Stoll, L., Lewis, D. and Ecob, R. (1988) *School Matters: The Junior Years*. London: Paul Chapman Publishing.

Mott-Thornton, K. (1998) *Common Faith: Education, Spirituality and the State*. Aldershot: Ashgate.

Murphy, P. (1988) Gender and assessment. *Curriculum*, vol. 9, no. 3, Winter, pp. 152–8.

Myers, B.K. (1997) *Young Children and Spirituality*. London: Routledge.

Myers, K. (1980) Sex stereotyping at option choice. MA dissertation. London: Institute of Education.

Myers, K. (1992) *Genderwatch! After the Education Reform Act*. Cambridge: Cambridge University Press.

Myers, K. (1995) School improvement in action: a critical history of a school improvement project. EdD dissertation. University of Bristol.

Myers, K. (1996a) Private report.

Myers, K. (ed.)(1996b) *School Improvement in Practice: Schools Make a Difference Project*. London: Falmer Press.

Myers, K. (2001) Field notes from visit, 31 January 2001, ESRC Project: Consulting Pupils About their Learning. Director, Professor Jean Rudduck.

Myers, K. and Goldstein, H. (1998) Who's failing?, in L. Stoll and K. Myers (eds), *No Quick Fixes: Perspectives on Schools in Difficulty*. London: Falmer Press.

Newman, D., Griffin, P. and Cole, M. (1989) *The Construction Zone: Working for Cognitive Change in School*. Cambridge: Cambridge University Press.

Nias, J., Southworth, G. and Campbell, P. (1992) *Whole School Curriculum Development in the Primary School*. London: Falmer Press.

Nias, J., Southworth, G. and Yeomans, R. (1989) *Staff Relationships in the Primary School: A Study of Organizational Cultures*. London: Cassell.

Noss, R. and Pachler, N. (1999) The challenge of new technologies: doing old things in a new way, in P. Mortimore (ed.), *Understanding Pedagogy and its Impact on Learning*. London: Paul Chapman Publishing.

Nuttall, D.L. Goldstein, H., Prosser, R. and Rasbash, J. (1989) Differential school effectiveness. *International Journal of Education Research*, Special Issue: *Developments in School Effectiveness Research*, vol. 13, no. 7, pp. 767–76.

O'Connor, J. and McDermott, I. (1997) *The Art of Systems Thinking*. London: Thorsons.

O'Donaghue, C., Thomas, S., Goldstein, H. and Knight, T. (1997) *DfEE Study of Value Added to 16–18 Year Olds in England*. London: Department of Education and Employment.

O'Neill, O. (2002) *A Question of Trust*. Cambridge: Cambridge University Press.

Office for Standards in Education (OFSTED) (1994) *Spiritual, Moral, Social and Cultural Development*. An OFSTED discussion paper. London: OFSTED.

Office for Standards in Education (OFSTED) (1995) *Annual Report of Her Majesty's*

Chief Inspector 1993–1994. London: HMSO.

Office for Standards in Education (OFSTED) (2002) *Annual Report of Her Majesty's Chief Inspector 2000–2001*. London: The Stationery Office.

Organization for Economic Co-operation and Development (OECD) (2001) *Educational Policy Analysis*. Paris: Organization for Co-operation and Economic Development.

Organization for Economic Co-operation and Development (OECD) (2002) *The PISA 2000 Technical Report*. Paris: Organization for Co-operation and Economic Development.

Osterman, K. (2000) Students' need for belonging in the school community. *Review of Educational Research*, vol. 70, no. 3, Fall, pp. 323–67.

Pascall, D.L. (1993) *Spiritual and Moral Development*. A discussion paper. York: National Curriculum Council.

Peters, T. and Waterman, R. (1982) *In Search of Excellence*. London: Harper & Row.

Petrides, K.V. and Furnham, A. (2001) Trait emotional intelligence: psychometric investigation with reference to the establishment of trait taxonomies. *European Journal of Personality*, vol. 15, pp. 425–48.

Pollard, A. and Triggs, P. with Broadfoot, P., McNess, E. and Osborn, M. (2000) *What Pupils Say: Changing Policy and Practice in Primary Education*. London: Continuum.

Powell, M. (1980) The beginning teacher evaluation study: a brief history of a major research project, in C. Denham and A. Lieberman (eds), *Time to Learn*. Washington, DC: National Institute of Education.

Prentice, R. (1996) The spirit of education: a mode for the twenty-first century, in R. Best (ed.), *Education, Spirituality and the Whole Child*. London Cassell.

Priestley, J.G. (1996) *Spirituality in the Curriculum*. Essex: Hockerell Educational Foundation.

Putnam, R.D. (2000) *Bowling Alone: The Collapse and Revival of American Community*. New York: Simon & Schuster.

Qualifications and Curriculum Authority (QCA) (1999) *Flexibility in the Secondary Curriculum*. London: Qualifications and Curriculum Authority.

Reed, J. and Learmonth, J. (2001) Revitalising teachers' accountability: learning about learning as a renewed focus for school improvement. *Journal of In-Service Education*, vol. 27, no. 1, pp.11–27.

Reed, J. and Stoll, L. (2000) Promoting organisational learning in schools – the role of feedback, in Askew (ed.), *Feedback for Learning*. London: RoutledgeFalmer.

Reed, J. and Street, H. (2002) School self evaluation: a process to support pupil and teacher learning. *Research Matters*, Autumn, no. 18. London: NSIN, Institute of Education.

Resnick, L.B. (1987) Learning in school and out. *Educational Researcher*, vol. 16, no. 9, pp. 13–40.

Reynolds, D. (2001) Beyond school effectiveness and school improvement, in A Harris and N. Bennett (eds), *School Effectiveness and School Improvement: Alternative Perspectives*. London: Continuum.

Reynolds, D. and Teddlie, C. (2001) Reflections on the critics, and beyond them. *School Effectiveness and School Improvement*, vol. 12, no. 1, pp. 99–113.

Reynolds, D., Bollen, R., Creemers, B., Hopkins, D., Stoll, L. and Lagerweij, N. (1996) *Making Good Schools: Linking School Effectiveness and School Improvement*. London: Routledge.

Roberts, R.D., Zeidner, M. and Matthews, G. (2001) Does emotional intelligence meet traditional standards for an intelligence? Some new data and conclusions. *Emotion*, vol. 1, no. 3, pp. 196–231.

Rogers, C. (1982) *Education – a Personal Activity*. Sheffield: Pavic Publications, Sheffield Polytechnic.

Rosenholtz, S. (1989) *Teachers' Workplace: The Social Organization of Schools*. New York: Longman.

Rudduck, J. (2001) Students and school improvement: transcending the cramped conditions of time. *Improving Schools*, vol. 4, no. 2, pp. 7–15.

Rudduck J. and Flutter, J. (2002) *Consulting Young People in Schools*. ESRC Teaching and Learning Research Programme. Cambridge: Homerton College.

Rudduck, J., Chaplain, R. and Wallace, G. (1996) *School Improvement. What Can Pupils Tell Us?* London: David Fulton.

Rutter, J., Maughan, B., Mortimore, P. and Ouston, J. (1979) *Fifteen Thousand Hours: Secondary Schools and their Effects on Children*. London: Paul Chapman Publishing.

Salovey, P. and Mayer, J.D. (1998) Emotional intelligences. *Imagination, Cognition and Personality*, vol. 9, pp. 185–211.

Sammons, P. (1995) Gender, socio-economic and ethnic differences in attainment and progress: a longitudinal analysis of student achievement over nine years. *British Educational Research Journal*, vol. 4, no. 21, pp. 465–85.

Sammons, P., Hillman, J. and Mortimore, P. (1995) *Key Characteristics of Effective Schools: A Review of School Effectiveness Research*. Report commissioned by the Office for Standards in Education. London: Institute of Education and Office for Standards in Education.

Sammons, P., Thomas, S. and Mortimore, P. (1994) *Value Added Approaches: Ways of Comparing School*. London: Institute of Education.

Sammons, P., Thomas, S. and Mortimore, P. (1997) *Forging Links: Effective Schools and Effective Departments*. London: Paul Chapman Publishing.

Saunders, L. (1999) Who or what is school 'self'-evaluation for? *School Effectiveness and School Improvement*, vol. 10, no. 4, pp. 414–29.

Scheerens, J. (1997) Theories on effective schooling. *School Effectiveness and School Improvement*, vol. 8, no. 3, pp. 220–42.

Schein, E.H. (1985) *Organizational Culture and Leadership*. San Francisco, CA: Jossey-Bass.

Schulman, L. (1987) Knowledge and teaching foundations of the new reform. *Harvard Educational Review*, vol. 57, no. 1, pp. 1–22.

Senge, P.M. (1993) *The Fifth Discipline: The Art and Practice of the Learning Organisation*. London: Century Business.

Senge, P.M. (1995) Leading learning organisations. MIT Centre for Organizational Learning Research. Monograph. Cambridge, MA: MIT.

Senge, P.M. (1999) Leadership in living organisations, in F. Hesselbein, M. Goldsmith and I. Somerville (eds), *Leading Beyond the Walls*. San Francisco, CA: Jossey-Bass.

Senge, P.M. (2000a) *Schools that Learn*. London: Nicholas Brealey.

Senge, P.M. (2000b) Systems change in education. *Reflections*, vol. 1, no. 3, p. 58.

Senge, P.M. (2002) Leadership in living organisations. Paper presented to Leadership for Learning Conference, University of Cambridge, 11 September, from F. Hesselbein, M. Goldsmith and I. Somerville (eds) (1999) *Leading Beyond the Walls*. San Francisco, CA: Jossey-Bass.

Sergiovanni, T.J. (2000) *The Lifeworld of Leadership: Creating Culture, Community and Personal Meaning in Our Schools*. San Francisco, CA: Jossey-Bass.

Shaw, G.B. (1921) The serpent, in D.H. Lawrence (ed.) (1972) *Back to Methuselah*, act 1, '*In the Beginning*'. London: The Bodley Head Bernard Shaw: Collected Plays with their Prefaces, Vol. 5.

Sikes, P.J. (1992) Imposed change and the experienced teacher, in M. Fullan and A. Hargreaves (eds), *Teacher Development and Educational Change*. London: Falmer Press.

Smith, D. and Tomlinson, S. (1989) *The School Effect: A Study of Multi-racial Comprehensives*. London: Policy Studies Institute.

Soar, R.S. and Soar, R.M. (1979) Emotional climate and management, in P. Peterson and H. Walberg (eds), *Research on Teaching: Concepts, Findings and Implications*. Berkeley, CA: McCutchan.

Soo Hoo, S. (1993) Students as partners in research and restructuring schools. *Educational Forum*, vol, 57, Summer, pp. 386–93.

Southworth, G. (1995) *Looking into Primary Headship: A Research Based Interpretation*. London: Falmer Press.

Starratt, R.J. (1991) Building an ethical school: a theory for practice. *Educational Administration Quarterly*, vol. 27, no. 2, pp. 185–202.

Sternberg, R., Conway, B., Ketron, J. and Bernstein, M. (1981) People's conceptions of intelligence. *Journal of Personality and Social Psychology*, vol. 4, no. 1, pp. 37–55.

Stoll, L. and Fink, D. (1996) *Changing our Schools*. Buckingham: Open University Press.

Stoll, L. and Myers, K. (1998) *No Quick Fixes: Perspectives on Schools in Difficulty*. London: Falmer Press.

Stoll, L., Fink, D. and Earl, L. (2002) *Its about Learning (and It's about Time). What's in It for Schools?* London: FalmerRoutledge.

Stoll, L., MacBeath, J. and Mortimore, P. (2001) Beyond 2000, in J. MacBeath and P. Mortimore (eds), *Improving School Effectiveness*. Buckingham: Open University Press.

Sutcliffe, J. (1997) Enter the feel bad factor. *Times Educational Supplement*, 10 January, p. 1.

Task Group on Assessment and Testing (1988). Report. London: DES.

Teacher Training Agency (TTA) (1995) *Survey of Continuing Professional Development*. Research conducted for the TTA by MORI, June. London: TTA.

Teddlie, C. and Reynolds, D. (2000) *The International Handbook of School Effectiveness Research*. London: Falmer Press.

Teddlie, C. and Stringfield, S. (1993) *Schools Make a Difference: Lessons Learned from a Ten-Year Study of School Effects*. New York: Teachers College Press.

Thatcher, A. (1999) *Spirituality and the Curriculum*. London Cassell.

Thomas, G., Walker, D. and Webb, J. (1998) *The Making of the Inclusive School*. London: Routledge.

Thomas, S. (1995) Differential secondary school effectiveness. Paper presented at the Annual Conference of the British Educational Research Association, September, Bath.

Thomas, S. and Mortimore, P. (1994) *Report on Value Added Analysis of 1993 GCSE Examination Results in Lancashire*. London: Curriculum Studies Department, Institute of Education.

Thrupp, M. (1999) *Schools Making a Difference: Let's Be Realistic!* Buckingham: Open University Press.

Thrupp, M. (2001) Sociological and political concerns about school effectiveness research: time for a new research agenda. *School Effectiveness and School Improvement*, vol, 12, no. 1, pp. 7–40.

Tomlinson, J. (2000) *Ethical Principles for the Teaching Profession*. Report of UCET Working Party. London: UCET.

Vaill, P.B. (1996) *Learning as a Way of Being: Strategies for Survival in a World of Permanent White Water*. San Francisco, CA: Jossey-Bass.

van Velzen, W., Miles, M., Ekholm, M., Hameyer, U. and Robin, D. (1985) *Making School Improvement Work: A Conceptual Guide to Practice*. Leuven: Acco.

Varlaam, A., Nuttall, D.L. and Walker, A. (1992) *What Makes Teachers Tick? A Survey of Teacher Morale and Motivation*. London: Centre for Educational Research, Clare Market Papers No. 4, LSE.

Wallace, M. (1994) Towards a contingency approach to development planning in schools, in D.H. Hargreaves and D. Hopkins (eds), *Development Planning for School Improvement*. London: Cassell.

Watkins, C. (2001) Experiencing learning: strengthening the voices. Unpublished talk to Slough EAZ.

Watkins, C. (2002) Will policy-makers always fail teachers? *Parliamentary Brief*, 8:2, pp. 11–12.

Watkins, C. (2003) *Learning: A Sense-maker's Guide*. London: ATL.

Watkins, C. and Mortimore, P. (1999) Pedagogy: what do we know? in P. Mortimore (ed.), *Understanding Pedagogy and its Impact on Learning*. London: Paul Chapman Publishing.

Watkins, C., Carnell, E., Lodge, C. and Whalley, C. (1996) Effective learning. *Research Matters*, no. 5, Summer, London: NSIN, Institute of Education.

Watkins, C., Carnell, E., Lodge, C., Wagner, P. and Whalley, C. (2001) Learning about learning enhances performance. *Research Matters*, no. 13, Spring. London: NSIN, Institute of Education.

Watkins, C., Carnell, E., Lodge, C., Wagner, P. and Whalley, C. (2002) Effective learning. *Research Matters*, no. 17, Summer, London: NSIN, Institute of Education.

Weindling, D. (1997) Strategic planning in schools: some practical techniques, in M. Preedy, R. Glatter and R. Levačić (eds), *Educational Management: Strategy, Quality and Resources*. Buckingham: Open University Press.

West, M. and Ainscow, M. (1991) *Managing School Development – A Practical Guide*. London: David Fulton.

West-Burnham, J. (2003) *Leadership for Learning*. London: RoutledgeFalmer.

West-Burnham, J., Bush, T., O'Neill, J. and Glover, D. (1995) *Leadership and Strategic Management*. Harlow: Longman.

Wheatley, M.J. (1992) *Leadership and the New Science: Learning about Organizations from an Orderly Universe*. San Francisco, CA: Berrett-Koehler.

Willms, J.D. and Kerr, M. (1987) Changes in sex differences in school examination results since 1975. *Journal of Early Adolescence*, June.

Wright, A. (2000) *Spirituality and Education*. London: RoutledgeFalmer.

Zohar, D. and Marshall, I. (2001) *Spiritual Intelligence – the Ultimate Intelligence*. London: Bloomsbury.

Index

Added to a page number 'f' denotes a figure

learning-centredness 73–4, 80
open to scrutiny 141–2
social learning opportunities
158–9
club culture 42–3
co-construction approach, to
learning 52
co-operative plans 45
cognitive psychology, and learning
52
collaboration
between schools 102, 160–1, 162
professional development 94–5
collaborative collegiality 105
collaborative research, obstacles to
135
collective capacities 110
collegial intelligence (CoQ) 115,
128, 132–6, 148
collegiality 102, 105
commitment to shared purpose
133–4
communication, in classrooms 87
community schools 157
competition
between schools 7
boys' motivated by 64
comprehension 88
conditions of learning 66–7
conditions for learning 117
congeniality 105
constraints, school improvement 37
construction approach, to learning 52
constructive psychology, and
learning 52
contextual factors, school
improvement 37
contextual intelligence (CQ) 117,
122–6, 148
continuing professional development
42, 94–5
contrived collegiality 105
corporate intelligence 111, 147–9

corporate plans 46
creativity 31
critical friends 100
critical periods, brain development
59
culture
gender differences in learning 64
perceptions of intelligence in 55–6
see also dependency culture;
school culture
culture of inquiry 94
curiosity 135–6
curriculum, narrowness of 153
curriculum leaders 135
curriculum planning 76

deep learning 138–9
Department for Education and Skills
(DfES) 101
departmental effects (secondary
schools) 19
dependency culture xvi
development planning 35, 41, 128
development plans 45
dialogue, school learning 52–3
didactic teaching 77–8
differential approach, to
improvement 35
differential rates, of improvement 36
direct instruction 87
distributed leadership 128–9

education
changes in 1–16
negative effect of knowledge
economy 14
Education Action Zones 3, 102
Education Counts 24
Education Reform Act (1988) 6
educational reform 2–11
educational software, growth of 11
effective schools *see* school
effectiveness

180